ILOCANO
RICE
FARMERS

ILOCANO RICE FARMERS

A COMPARATIVE STUDY OF TWO PHILIPPINE BARRIOS

HENRY T. LEWIS

UNIVERSITY OF HAWAII PRESS
HONOLULU 1971

LIBRARY OF CONGRESS CATALOG CARD NUMBER 70-127330
ISBN 0-87022-460-3
COPYRIGHT ©1971 BY UNIVERSITY OF HAWAII PRESS
ALL RIGHTS RESERVED
MANUFACTURED IN THE UNITED STATES OF AMERICA

*This book is dedicated to my wife, Nancy,
and my sons, Robert and Kevin.
In so many ways they helped to make it possible.
Most important, they made it worthwhile.*

CONTENTS

PREFACE

Works of anthropology are properly concerned with a particular people studied and the generalizations developed from such studies—not with the trials and tribulations of becoming an anthropologist or doing an ethnography. With few exceptions we stick to our somewhat deadly anthropological prose and the concepts that enable us to generalize about what people do or at least our interpretations of what they do. Although it is true that our own personal experiences and reminiscences about living in a "primitive community" or a "peasant village" would interest the general reader more, we are, after all, anthropologists writing for readers who are either other anthropologists or else people with related and specialized interests, persons willing to wrestle with anthropological metaphor. The work we do stands or falls as anthropology. If we also are, in some incidental way, reasonably good writers (and there are a few in anthropology), so much the better. But our writings will not necessarily be better anthropology.

It is in the short space set aside for the preface that we can comment on a few of the persons and events that entered into the making of the book and the anthropologist. In a formal sense this work is based upon data gathered during a one-year period of field research work—December 1962 to December 1963—in northern Luzon, Philippine Islands. My own personal experiences leading up to the writing of this book, however, began with a tour of service in the U.S. Army during 1948 and 1949 when I made several trips in and about the Ilocos region of northwest Luzon. Memories of the area raised questions that went into the formulation of a field proposal and study problem more than twelve years later. At the same time, some of the friendships made during the year and a half of military service were most helpful in providing assistance in 1963.

Of special interest to me was the fact that the farmers of the Ilocos coastal region were not engaged in the agrarian revolt, the *Hukbalahap* movement, which then characterized central Luzon. At the time, I was only partly satisfied with the statement that

Ilocanos "just don't become Huks." This was somewhat puzzling because, as a result of my work with Army intelligence, I knew that at least some Ilocanos, many living in central Luzon and even some in Cagayan Valley, did become Huks. All this entered into the formulation of a research proposal and field study problem.

My interest in anthropology developed at Fresno State College where William C. Beatty, Jr., in the short period of one semester, managed to turn my head from the study of history to ethnology. I would like to think today that I could teach as well and get as much out of students as he does, but I know better. As a graduate student at Berkeley I was influenced by a number of individual professors, especially by Robert F. Murphy, who is now at Columbia University. The person who most directly affected the writing of this book by his encouragement and criticism is James N. Anderson, and his mark bears very heavily on the strengths of this study.

Learning at the level and intensity of graduate school very much involves the relationships that one has with student colleagues. As anyone who has suffered graduate training knows, nothing before or after ever quite matches the intellectual give-and-take between students. When this is combined with true friendship it involves a very special quality that makes the worst of it all quite bearable. Octavio Romano, Jim Siegel, and Bill Smith make all of it pleasurable and meaningful to recall now.

Most of all I was helped and influenced by William G. Davis—from classes at Fresno State and seminars at Berkeley, to the several occasions in the Philippines when we got together and agonized over the many and varied problems of our respective field studies. Ron Provencher I knew less well as a fellow graduate student but, more recently, as colleagues at San Diego State College, we influenced one another's lives in a number of important ways.

The number of people in the Philippines who afforded assistance is innumerable. At the Ateneo de Manila, Father Frank Lynch and Mrs. Mary Hollnsteiner provided special assistance and helped me through some very rough spots that seriously threatened to disrupt the research. At the Community Development Research Council, University of the Philippines, I was given valuable assistance by Milton Barnett. Other Americans who aided and added to the research were Dan Scheans, William Scott, and Duane Suter.

The Philippine government representatives and employees are far too numerous to mention, but a very special vote of thanks is due Facustino Macuty, then deputy of the Presidential Assistant on Community Development, as well as many other persons of that organization in Manila and the provinces of Ilocos Norte and Isabela.

Also, I am deeply grateful for the assistance and friendship given me and my family by a friend of many years, Ceferina Yepez. In different circumstances, she would have been a first-rate anthropologist and student of human behavior.

To include all those people in the provinces of Ilocos Norte and Isabela who helped make this study meaningful and possible would be most difficult. Not wishing to omit anyone in particular I can only express my gratitude to everyone who extended the many large and small favors that were given me and my family in the Laoag and Cauayan areas.

The largest debt of all I owe to the people of barrio Buyon and barrio Mambabanga who endured, with friendliness and patience, endless hours of questioning. This study is not a description of the "daily life" of either barrio and undoubtedly lacks a sense of intimacy commonly found in ethnographic studies. I regret that I cannot share the personal and emotional character of barrio life with the reader. I do greatly appreciate the fact that I came to know and, in a small way, to understand many of the people as individuals. Living there has added much to my own life. I would like to think that I have somehow, in some way, added to their lives, too.

ACKNOWLEDGMENT

A three-month study period at the Philippines Studies Center, University of Chicago, twelve months of field research in the Philippines, and a six-month write-up period at the University of California at Berkeley—the total period extending from September 1962 until June 1964—were supported by a predoctoral research grant from the Ford Foundation, now the Foreign Area Fellowship Program. The conclusions, opinions, and other statements in this publication are those of the author and are not necessarily those of the Foreign Area Fellowship Program.

ILOCANO RICE FARMERS

1
INTRODUCTION

This is a comparative study of two Ilocano barrios in separate areas of northern Luzon, Philippine Islands. It focuses upon the relationships which obtain between the economic and noneconomic spheres of behavior in two Ilocano villages: one a homeland community, the other a migrant community. The question asked in the study was, "What socioeconomic variability is exhibited in the differential adaptations of two Ilocano communities?" Given this problem the study includes neither all behavior nor, in fact, all economic behavior; it is concerned specifically with that behavior which is shown to be functionally significant to an explanation of socioeconomic variability. Consequently, though the research began with a concentration on technological and economic arrangements, the actual scope of investigation was determined empirically by discovering those patterns of behavior (political, religious, etc.) which were *in fact* important in explaining variability.

By selecting two barrios having the same general technological and economic patterns (wet-rice production), and the same cultural-linguistic tradition (Ilocano), I expected the study to encompass the same general areas of behavior in each setting. The choice of two villages on these and other criteria was purposefully made to allow for some control over, as well as to place some limit on, the number of cultural and technological variables. At the same time, because the study was a comparison of two barrios, certain patterns of behavior were thrown into perspective which might not have been detected otherwise. Such a comparative study also highlighted relationships that might have been evaluated differently or even overlooked in the absence of contrast, and these contrasts often led to my exploring new avenues of inquiry.[1] Anthropologists have more often stressed the wider theoretical importance of cross-cultural comparisons based on existing ethnographic reports, but comparative field studies involving lower-level generalizations are not commonly undertaken.[2]

Since the limits of study in such an approach are self-delineating, I anticipated that the original research plan might require restructuring as a result of conditions and arrangements discovered in the field. Initially I planned to make extensive, almost exclusive, use of several earlier studies completed on the Ilocano—Christie 1914; Nydegger 1960; Nydegger and Nydegger 1963; Orr 1956; I. H. Reynolds 1959; Scheans 1962; and others—as the base line material, a sort of "composite homeland community," on the northwest coast of Luzon, the Ilocos coast (see map 1, p. 195). The main substantive contribution from the field research was to be obtained in the study of an Ilocano migrant community in Cagayan Valley. One of the primary considerations in the selection of Cagayan Valley was its proximity to the Ilocos coast, and, although I did not originally envision an actual barrio study of a homeland community, I planned to make occasional visits to explore relationships omitted from the earlier studies or inadequately covered, for the purposes of this study. However, two general conditions revealed during the field research on the migrant community necessitated my subsequent move to Ilocos Norte, the northernmost province on the west coast. First, the original migrants had come from a distinctive and somewhat unique region of the Ilocos coast, and, second, it became increasingly evident that the earlier works were not specifically applicable, especially as relating to the emphasis in my own study on subsistence and economic arrangements.[3] Consequently, the period spent in Cagayan Valley was reduced to seven months with an added residence time in Ilocos Norte of just over four months.

Although local conditions and developments in the field influenced the final selection of the two barrios studied, certain general characteristics relating to Ilocano culture and society led to the study of two communities of that particular lowland cultural group. At the same time, there were also considerations which led to my studying a migrant community from, and a homeland community in, Ilocos Norte and not other sections of the Ilocos coast. The reasons for selecting the two Ilocano barrios studied are better understood by considering certain general conditions relating to Ilocano culture and society.

ILOCANOS: MYTH AND REALITY

Ilocanos—This hard-working and industrious race occupies the northern and western shores of Luzon, from Point Lacatacy on the 121st meridian, east from Greenwich, to San Fabian, on the Gulf of Lingayan. This includes the three provinces of Ilocos Norte, Ilocos Sur, and La Union. The Ilocanos have also pushed into the northeastern part of Pangasinan, where they occupy seven towns, and they inhabit the town of Alcala in the province of Cagayan, several villages in Benguet, parts of the towns of Capas and O'Donnel in the provinces of Tarlac, and some towns in Zambalas and Nueva Ecija. They are all civilized and have been Christians for three centuries. . . . the Ilocanos are ever ready to emigrate, and besides the places I have mentioned, there are thousands of them in Manila and other parts of the islands. They easily obtain employment either as servants, cultivators, or labourers, for they are superior in stamina to most of the civilized races, and in industry superior to them all.

I have no doubt that there is a great future before this hardy, enterprising, and industrious people. [Sawyer 1900:249–250, 251–252]

Frederic H. Sawyer characterized the Ilocanos thus in describing *The Inhabitants of the Philippines* in 1900, and similar statements have been made by other writers in distinguishing the Ilocano from other lowland Filipino "types." At the same time, this view very nearly corresponds to the folk image maintained by the Ilocanos themselves. It is a central feature of the Ilocanos' explanation of why they have migrated extensively within and without the islands. The regions noted by Sawyer as having been "pushed into" are today areas in which Ilocanos outnumber the original inhabitants. For instance, in Isabela the Ilocanos now constitute nearly 70 percent of the total population, a population now nearing one-half million persons, while the indigenous lowland cultural group, the Ibanags, accounts for but 20 percent. Over three million in all, Ilocanos are the third largest of ten major ethnolinguistic groups making up the complex of Filipino lowland Christian cultures.

Christian Filipino groups differ, to a greater or lesser degree, with respect to ritual practices, food, art forms, and material culture, but all are strikingly similar with respect to the more general normative cultural and behavioral patterns; what Fay-Cooper Cole has described as part of the "fundamental unity" of the various ethnolinguistic groups in the Philippines (1945:126). Yet, as the popularized view would seem to suggest, Ilocanos are somewhat less representative of this "fundamental unity" in Filipino behavior. And, as the materials presented in this study on Ilocos Norte will demonstrate, the popular view of Ilocanos is, in that area at least, not without foundation. Besides the attributed qualities of hard work and industry, the Ilocano is said to be thrifty, frugal, faithful to his moral (and economic) obligations, and possessed of a virtual reverence for land. On the opposite side of the ledger, however, other Filipinos, especially those in areas subjected to the impact of Ilocano migrations, are likely to argue that the Ilocanos are pushy, aggressive, hot-headed, land hungry, excessively jealous, overly quick to resort to violence, and extremely provincial. Ilocano provincialism is often attributed to the social and physical isolation of the Ilocos provinces, particularly in the northernmost section, Ilocos Norte. And, in fact, except for the recent introduction of Virginia leaf tobacco in La Union and Ilocos Sur, the Ilocano has certainly been much less involved than other Filipino groups in the highly American-influenced commercialism of such large cities as Manila, Cebu, Iloilo, and Quezon City.

One Tagalog writer writing on "levels of living" along the Ilocos coast described, in somewhat obvious tones of ethnic and philosophical bias, the Ilocano and Ilocos provinces as follows: "Here [i.e., the Ilocos coast] the people are still politically illiterate. They are still unaware of the labor struggles which are being waged all over the world; there is yet no feeling of class consciousness or even discontent over the existing economic arrangement."

In the next paragraph the author notes, however, "This region supplies the greatest proportion of Filipino immigrant laborers to Hawaii and the mainland of the United States. It is also the region from which the majority of plantation laborers in other parts of the islands come" (Lava 1938:8).

Of the over two-hundred-thousand Filipinos and Americans of Filipino descent in the United States (most of whom are concentrated in California and Hawaii), two-thirds to three-fourths are Ilocano.[4] Lava might also have added that Ilocanos constitute the vast majority of people in the newly pioneered areas of Luzon and, to a lesser degree, Mindanao. Although there have been no revolts in the Ilocos area in over 150 years, there has been an increasing amount of social, economic, and political discontent. This has been characterized by the emigration of large numbers of people and by political feuding and increasing political violence. Since this situation has had no political philosophical overtones (specifically Marxist), it has not been viewed with alarm (if, in fact, even noticed) outside the Philippines. It is more commonly interpreted by other Filipinos as a characteristic of the Ilocano "race." During the election year of 1963 over one hundred "political" killings were reported for the province of Ilocos Sur and, by rough approximation, a quarter of that number for Ilocos Norte. The number of killings has increased steadily since World War II and Philippine independence.[5] Political violence is not uncommon elsewhere in the Islands but, with the exception of Cavite Province, it does not occur to as great a degree or with such intensity in other areas.

Political behavior is mentioned here and examined subsequently at greater length, both because it is involved in the Ilocano folk view of themselves and, more significantly, because it was determined to be functionally important to the explanation of socio-economic variability. This study is by no means offered as a full explanation of the political situation in Ilocos Norte, much less the whole of the Ilocos coast, although it may contribute to such an explanation. It is, rather, a study of two barrios, each community a part of a larger social setting and both affected by and affecting the larger society.

Essentially two general characteristics of the Ilocanos led to their being the subject of study—the distinctive folk view of the "industrious Ilocano" and the impressive extent of Ilocano migration. Related to this was my specific research interest in examining the variable behaviors which might be found with different technological and economic arrangements. Since the research involved the comparison of a homeland and a migrant barrio, the reader may be led to infer that the study also concerns, in a direct way, historical ties and changes linking the two communities—the implication being that historical processes are perhaps also involved *between* the two barrios. However, while the historical background and setting in each barrio is examined in chapter 3, diachronic analyses concern only the recent local and regional histories relating to and affecting the barrios individually; they are not intended to suggest that the developments in the migrant community necessarily or somehow "naturally" followed from the homeland community. The study is concerned primarily with the consideration of two different villages at the same point in time, employing essentially the same social and cultural variables in their respective adaptations.

COMMUNITIES STUDIED

Several considerations led to the selection of the two barrios in the particular regions examined in this study. Cagayan Valley was chosen for the area of primary study as a result of two general and several lesser, but related, considerations. Of special importance were the proximity of Cagayan Valley to the Ilocos region plus the pronounced dominance in numbers of Ilocanos vis-à-vis indigenous ethnic groups there. A study in the Cotabato region of Mindanao, another resettlement area for Ilocanos, would have presented major problems with respect to planned visits to the Ilocos coast. With regard to the position of indigenous ethnic populations, the overall population density and fewer numbers of Ibanags and Gaddangs in Cagayan, for example, as compared to the numbers of Zambals, Pangasinans, Pampangans, and Tagalogs in parts of central Luzon, suggested that the choice of Cagayan Province, Isabela Province, or even Nueva Vizcaya Province would present fewer problems and complications relating to the acculturative situations.

The ultimate choice of Isabela Province instead of Cagayan or Nueva Vizcaya was influenced by economic-technological considerations. A rice economy was chosen because it is the most characteristic form of agriculture in the two areas, and central Isabela is one of the Philippines' major surplus-rice-producing areas. At the same time, the choice of central Isabela Province was also influenced by special conditions relating directly to the Ilocano situation in Ilocos Norte.

Though there are no specific details available on the places of origin of the Ilocano emigrants to Cagayan Valley, the studies suggest that Ilocos Norte has contributed the bulk of immigrants to Cagayan, Isabela, and, perhaps, even Nueva Vizcaya provinces. (The single comprehensive work on this subject was done by the late Felix M. Keesing.) With respect to Isabela at least, this was borne out in both the pre-study of the problem and through inquiries made later in the field. Responses to numerous interviews in Isabela indicated that the majority of Ilocano barrios were founded by individuals from Ilocos Norte and, within Ilocos Norte itself, from the Laoag and Vintar river valleys. This central area of Ilocos Norte is noted also for a development found only in that particular section of the Ilocos coast. Keesing, in listing certain distinct characteristics of the northern Ilocos area, including certain racial and linguistic features, noted the presence of a "special development" there—the irrigation societies reported by Christie over half a century ago (Keesing 1962:144–145). In the pre–study of the field situation for Isabela Province I learned that some irrigation societies, *zangjeras*, had been established by Ilocano immigrants in that area. Consequently, I decided to select an Ilocano barrio in Isabela which had, or was engaged in, an irrigation society. I felt that the presence of such a society would contribute a broader range of materials which might be used in, and contribute to, the comparison of socioeconomic variability. I also felt that the comparison of irrigation societies might throw light on the reasons for this somewhat unique northern Ilocos development.[6]

The study was also pushed toward considering Ilocanos only from the northern Ilocos area because all the earlier works are concerned with the area from Vigan north, no extensive research having been accomplished in the southern portion of Ilocos Sur or La Union. Since the majority of settlers in central Isabela have come from Ilocos Norte and since there was the previous study on irrigation societies by Christie, my choice of a migrant community with links to Ilocos Norte seemed to follow naturally.

Certain other factors entered into the final selection of a barrio in Isabela. Barrios composed solely or primarily of landless tenants, working for one or more absentee landlords, were purposefully avoided. An attempt was made to locate a community in central Isabela with a sizeable number of independent landowners because it is a characteristic of the homeland area, i.e., Ilocos Norte, that the largest percentage of farm families own at least some land, and there has been no history of absentee holdings along the northwest coast. Also, in order to maintain some control over the number of variables to be considered, I felt it advisable to choose a community of a single religious faith, preferably all Catholic or Aglipayan, the dominant religious groups in Ilocos Norte. Finally, because central Isabela is a surplus-rice-producing area, I chose a community engaged in the commercial production and sale of rice, and not one unduly isolated geographically or economically from market centers. This involved my selecting an older community not now involved in early stages of development or located in a remote pioneering area.

The qualification that the barrio be engaged in an irrigation society imposed the greatest limitation on the possible number of communities from which to choose. Pre-study of the situation in Isabela indicated that only *some* Ilocano irrigation societies had been developed. With what, in fact, were less than a dozen viable irrigation cooperatives in the whole of Cagayan Valley, the possible number of community choices turned out to be about thirty participating barrios. From among eight communities considered, the barrio of Mambabanga in the municipality of Luna seemed best suited (see maps 1, 3, and 6, pp. 195, 196, and 198, respectively.

As indicated earlier, the inclusion of an actual barrio rather than a composite homeland community based on previous studies in Ilocos Norte was unforeseen at the outset of the research. As the study in Mambabanga progressed, however, I came to recognize the need for a brief but intensive study of a barrio in the central area of Ilocos Norte Province. The emphasis in the study upon technological and economic features of barrio life led me to examine patterns of behavior not specifically within the purview of earlier studies. Despite the fact that this change in study plan necessarily reduced to seven months the planned research of the migrant community, the advantages of a comparative analysis were greatly enhanced by incorporating a four- to five-month research period in Ilocos Norte. The selection of the homeland community on the west coast of Luzon was determined by what was first found in Mambabanga and by the nature of the Ilocano migration to Isabela.

As detailed at greater length in chapter 3, the migration of Ilocanos outside the homeland region involved the displacement of individual families; it did not effect a mass movement of barrios, extended kin, or large residence groups. The original settlers of Mambabanga were from various barrios and several different municipalities of Ilocos Norte, though all came from the Laoag and Vintar river valleys. Because of these factors, no specific attempt was made to seek out a homeland barrio with direct familial or historical ties to Mambabanga. Instead, economic and technological considerations were of primary importance. As it turned out, there were no direct kinship or other social ties linking the two barrios.

In contrast to the problems I encountered in central Isabela, I had no difficulty locating a barrio in the central section of Ilocos Norte which was participating in an irrigation society, there being an estimated 185 irrigation societies in the whole of the province with 130 of these located in the Laoag and Vintar river valleys.[7] Coastal villages engaged in full- or part-time fishing activities were, for obvious reasons of comparison, purposefully avoided. The more remote interior villages were also not considered, both because of their economic isolation from market centers and because of the greater amounts of land utilized in patterns of "dry" hill farming. Also, in Ilocos Norte there are a number of barrios which, although composed largely of full-time farmers who are active members of irrigation societies, are in effect sections or residential areas of towns such as Laoag, Bacarra, and Vintar. Because Mambabanga, the migrant community chosen, is a rural barrio, these residential areas, too, were excluded.

Finally, the selection of a barrio was influenced by the earlier work done on irrigation societies by Christie. One of the barrios considered for study was the social and geographical center for the Zangjera de Camungao, one of the two examples described in Christie's study (1914:102–104). Since this particular barrio, Barrio Buyon in the municipality of Bacarra, met all general requirements, it was selected as the homeland community (see maps 1,2,4, and 5, pp. 195, 196, 197, and 197, respectively).

Neither Buyon nor Mambabanga is offered as a "typical" homeland or migrant barrio, but they are representative of certain features of the Ilocano way of life on the northern Ilocos coast and in southern Cagayan Valley. First, each barrio has the same cultural and social traditions that neighboring Ilocano communities have, and each has shared and experienced the same regional history. Second, although they may differ from the non-rice-growing communities in each area, all the barrios in a single region are confronted with similar conditions of the wider social and natural environment and they face that environment with the same cultural and social heritage. Each barrio, in its own specific way, represents some of the more general features of the Ilocano adjustment to two different social and natural settings.

I am well aware of the dangers of extrapolation and have attempted to exercise care in developing generalizations about the Ilocanos of Isabela, the Ilocanos of Ilocos Norte, and, especially, Ilocanos in general. However, some license is necessary if we are to do more than describe the "life ways" of a single village or even two villages. In a comparative analysis the investigator is led to make both inquiry and inference. Whereas contrast suggests an emphasis on difference, comparison implies the demonstration of both relative and absolute qualities; comparison should result in explicating qualities or characteristics which individual study or simple contrast may not reveal. It is the contention of this study that comparisons made here can serve as the basis for understanding both variability and constants in the behavior of a single people, Ilocanos, and that it will suggest the nature and importance of behavior characteristic of Filipinos in general.

NOTES

1. Even though the anthropologist is invariably struck by the marked contrast between his own society and the one he studies, he almost always tends to accept certain practices of the people he studies as their "normal" or "proper" way of doing things. It is natural enough to generalize from our

own field experience, but the result may be that we become somewhat "ethnocentric" about our field sample. Because the observer knows of no other way, say, to grow rice, he takes his example without thoroughly examining or understanding the functional relationships involved.

2. This study is not concerned with the comparative method as conceived by many anthropologists. Obviously such a conception is not involved when considering cross-cultural regularities. This study is closer to being what Eggen has called a comparison of "very small scale" and, specifically, "comparative field research in a controlled situation" (1954:758). Befu (1965) did a similar study of two California Japanese communities.

3. I intend, in no way, to criticize the earlier studies. It would hardly be reasonable to fault these works for not emphasizing what I have stressed here. Only the study by Christie (1914) bears directly on one phase of my research in Ilocos Norte and I comment on his material in chapter 12.

4. This estimate is based upon conversations held with representatives of the Philippine Consulate in San Francisco. The Consulate maintains no exact figures on the subcultural backgrounds of Filipinos and Filipino-Americans in California but casual inquiry among resident Filipinos and Filipino-Americans suggests that the two-thirds to three-fourths estimate is a reasonable one.

5. The number of political killings is difficult to obtain for many reasons, one of the most obvious being the question of when is a murder political and when is it not. Government data are not readily available and pertinent documents of the Philippine Constabulary were destroyed by fire in 1962. Newspapers tend to sensationalize such reports, although they do not learn of every incident. Despite the lack of definitive data the estimate of one hundred killings for 1963 is not an excessive one and the number may have been higher.

6. These irrigation societies (discussed at greater length in chapter 12) are similar to those described by Barton in his brief outline of Kalinga irrigation systems, except that among the Kalingas "there is no name for such an association of owners, as there is among Ilokanos" (1949:103).

7. This estimate is based upon data furnished me by the Bureau of Public Works, Office of the District Engineer in Laoag. Senior Civil Engineer Francisco T. Tamayo and his staff were especially helpful in providing me with information. However, I am entirely responsible for the analysis and interpretation of those data made in chapter 12.

PART 1
GEOGRAPHICAL, HISTORICAL, AND LOCAL SETTINGS

2
PHYSICAL
ENVIRONMENT
AND
POPULATION

Northern Luzon can be divided into four discrete climatic and topographical subregions. They are, from west to east: the Ilocos coast, the Cordillera Central, Cagayan Valley, and the Sierra Madre. While the Ilocos coast and Cagayan Valley are the areas of primary interest to this study, the two mountain ranges are the dominant features establishing climatic conditions throughout the entire region. These mountains have had an important influence on the history of northern Luzon and, of specific importance here, the history of Ilocano migrations.

The Ilocos region emerges from Pangasinan Province at Lingayen Gulf into a narrow coastal strip extending over 160 miles north to Cape Bojeador. It is bordered by the South China Sea on the west and by the 5,000- to 10,000-foot Cordillera Central mountains in the east. A series of short but periodically destructive and turbulent rivers cut the Ilocos coast at irregular intervals. The most important among these are the Naguilian, the Amburayan, the Abra, and the Laoag; they and others are paralleled by small and intensively farmed flood plains. The hills which border these flood plains often extend to the ocean itself. The region thus comprises a series of small, riverine valleys separated from one another by intervening hills and ridges rather than a continuous belt of flat land. Nonetheless, relative to the massiveness of the Cordilleras, the Ilocos coast forms a continuous strip of land and certainly nowhere, except perhaps at Abra Gap, have the intervening hills and ridges been an impediment to communication.

The west coast of Luzon is a monsoonal forest region, an extension of the southeast Asian monsoon belt that extends across Burma, Thailand, and Vietnam. The distinct dry season, characteristic of many mainland monsoon areas, intensifies in a northerly direction. As a consequence, the most typical monsoon forest extends north from Zambales. The large numbers and varieties of bamboo, characteristic of this region, probably account for the long traditional use of this material for Ilocano homes.

Moving north from Lingayen to Cape Bojeador there is a direct relationship between the length and intensity of the dry season and the annual rainfall. Thus, though total rainfall for Ilocos Norte is greater than that for Ilocos Sur or La Union, so, too, is the length and severity of the dry season. This dry season ends in late May with the rains increasing in intensity and frequency during June and most of July; peak rainfall comes in late July and continues through August, declining rapidly in September. A large part of the heaviest precipitation may occur during the two or three days of the season on which typhoons occur, dumping twelve inches or more in a twenty-four-hour period. Thus, neither the seasonal nor the yearly rainfall total gives an accurate picture of differences within the Ilocos region itself or, as will be seen, between it and Cagayan Valley. The dominant climatic feature on the Ilocos coast during the dry season is the "rain shadow" formed by the Cordillera Central. This appears during the northeast monsoons when the west coast becomes the leeward side of the island. The extended dry season is then further intensified for Ilocos Norte by the fact that the Cordillera "rain shadow" creates a vacuum into which the winds coming around Cape Bojeador are drawn, resulting in an increased drying of the northern Ilocos area.

Although the Cordilleras on the west and the Sierras on the east tend to limit the total amounts of rain brought into Cagayan Valley by both the southwest and northeast monsoons, at no time is the valley without considerable precipitation. Thus, though the annual rainfall in Ilagan, Isabela Province, is normally some twenty inches less than it is for Laoag (ninety-three versus seventy-three inches), it is much more evenly distributed. The wettest season begins in October, followed by a short dry season (February–April) during which there is some rain. Rainfall increases again from May until mid-September corresponding to the west coast rainy period. The total amount of rain decreases in a southerly direction, i.e., upriver from Aparri to Nueva Vizcaya Province, just as it does on the west coast. Thus, despite the fact that the two areas are in the same longitude, climatic patterns are quite different.

The Cordilleras slope less abruptly into Cagayan Valley than they do into the Ilocos provinces in the west, and the major rivers emptying out of these mountains—the Magat, the Chico, the Mallig, the Siffu, and others—flow eastward to join the Cagayan River flowing northward from the Carabello Sur range, a small chain of mountains linking the Cordillera Central and the Sierra Madres. Another set of large and impressive rivers—the Ilagan, the

Paret, the Dummun—come down from the Sierra Madres on the eastern side of the valley and, in turn, join the Rio Grande de Cagayan. Altogether, this river complex makes up the largest water system in the Philippines, the Cagayan River itself being over 275 miles in length. The rich, alluvial valley which has been formed from this complex of rivers is, from Aparri on the northern coast to San Augustin in the south, over 150 miles in length. At the mouth of the Cagayan, the coastal area east and west of Aparri is both flat and swampy. Upriver, where the Chico joins the Cagayan below Alcala, rolling hills border the river on each side. The southern half of Cagayan Province and the major part of Isabela form the main agricultural section of the valley.

As a consequence of periodic flooding, soils on the primary flood plains immediately adjoining the rivers are regularly renewed with fresh silts. These primary flood plains constitute the main tobacco-growing areas. Farther removed from the rivers, on the larger secondary flood plains, tobacco production gives way to artificially irrigated rice lands, lands which are commonly second cropped with corn. On slightly higher lands, sometimes flat but often composed of small hills, the more level areas are given over to naturally irrigated wet-rice, and the hilly areas to important commercial crops such as sugarcane, pineapple, or peanuts.

Along the Ilocos coast the topography of the riverine valleys is of a much smaller scale, and the agriculture therein is much more intense. Though rice is the major crop grown, it is of virtually no commercial significance; it is necessary, in fact, to import rice to make up for local deficits—and the rice purchased in the market places of Ilocos Norte is commonly from Isabela. The marginal, subsistence-level farming of the Ilocos coast is nowhere more reflected than in the relative commercial poverty of its towns. In Ilocos Norte only Laoag and, to a lesser extent, Batac are real centers of commercial activity. Towns like Bacarra, Vintar, Sarrat, and Paoay are each little more than a cluster of compact barrios surrounding an old Spanish church, a plaza, and the municipal office buildings. In marked contrast to commercial conditions in Ilocos Norte, all of the towns in Isabela, and even some of the barrios, have rice mills where rice is purchased, milled, and trucked to Manila. Even the smallest towns in Cagayan Valley have numerous stores, daily markets, restaurants, gas stations, and many have hotels and movie theaters.

The overall population densities for the two provinces are not especially significant, particularly since both provinces include

large sections of nonagricultural, mountainous land. According to
the 1960 census, Ilocos Norte has 219 persons per square mile;
Isabela has 107. Even the difference in physiological densities (persons per square mile of arable land) belies the very important
differences of agricultural potential, landscape, soils, climate,
water supply, plant cover, transportation, and communication.
The physiological differences are based on the 1960 census, but do
not include fallow land or permanent pasture as do the figures
reported by Wernstedt and Spencer (1967:633).

Area	Total Population	Persons Per Square Mile of Cultivated Land
Ilocos Norte	287,335	2,072.7
Isabela	442,062	729.0
Philippines	27,087,685	1,257.7

The contrast at the municipal level is most pronounced, but the
fact that a large concentration of people—7,268 out of a total of
18,570—lives within the town of Bacarra itself greatly distorts real
differences:

Area	Total Population	Persons Per Square Mile of Cultivated Land
Bacarra, I.N.	18,570	3,721.4
Luna, Isabela	5,209	606.4

More important in terms of actual rural populations are the comparative physiological densities derived from the field work itself:
Buyon has 2,200 persons per square mile of farmland, and Mambabanga has 590 persons. The only population figures which I can
personally comment upon are those from the two barrios, and
they are based upon a house-to-house survey together with a
survey of lands worked, the latter being backed up by spot checks
and measurements of selected fields.

In any event, the figures generally indicate the relative differences between the two areas, the fundamental demographic
contrast being a valid one. The 1960 census indicates that three
times as many people live on the land in Ilocos Norte as live in
Isabela; on the basis of actual field work, the relative difference
between Buyon and Mambabanga is 3.7 to 1. The importance of
this contrast will be examined in terms of the differential land use
and landownership relationships, as well as for the various social
ties affected by those relationships.

The ethnohistory of northern Luzon has received considerable
attention during the past sixty or more years. The focus of studies

has concentrated upon the various ethnolinguistic groups of the Cordillera Central, particularly the Ifugao, Bontoc, Kalinga, and Tinguian, and upon questions surrounding the history and origin of the rice-terracing complex found there. Consequently, the position of surrounding lowland groups has often been peripheral to the central ethnohistoric interest in northern Luzon. The Ilocanos, however, because of their close linguistic and cultural ties to the Tinguians, have received more attention than has been given other lowland groups such as the Pangasinans or Ibanags. The most recent and comprehensive work, by Keesing, goes the furthest in "unraveling connection and contacts between adjacent lowland and highland group" (1962:1), but the center of ethnohistorical attention and interest for that author still remains the mountain-terrace builders. Keesing's work does provide, however, the only single compilation and interpretation of all source materials on the ethnolinguistic groups of northern Luzon. Unfortunately for my interest here, the period least examined is that of the past sixty years, the time of greatest migration from the Ilocos coast to Cagayan Valley. My own historical "sources" are interviews with individuals of a few barrios and towns who were involved in the events as they occurred. A comprehensive study and historical documentation of this period remains to be accomplished.

From the time of the first Spanish contact in the sixteenth century, the population in the Ilocos region was relatively high, and Keesing noted that in Ilocos Norte ". . . the great inland amphitheater of the Laoag river system [was], by the standards of the time, heavily settled" (1962:149). It has been stated that even at this time the Ilocanos were already expanding and pushing south into what was then Pangasinan territory in the southern part of La Union Province (Sawyer 1900:247). The mountain people, more than the mountains themselves, formed a barrier to Ilocano expansion directly east; consequently, the other direction of movement was north around the coast and up into Cagayan Valley. This movement north and east involved the occupation of several small coastal valley areas—Burgos, Bangui, Claveria, etc.—and the displacement and/or assimilation of the people there. The river areas of Cagayan Valley were already occupied by a lowland Christian group, the Ibanags, who had themselves been moving up the Rio Grande carrying out a similar process of displacement and assimilation with various other Cagayans such as the Gaddang and Yogad.

However, the real opening and development of the valley began after 1850 when Spanish authorities stimulated Ilocano migration through the offers of assistance in establishing tobacco farms. By 1900 there were over 50,000 Ilocanos in the three provinces of Cagayan, Isabela, and Nueva Vizcaya, just over 17 percent of the nearly 290,000 persons there. By 1948 the number of Ilocano "native speakers" had increased to over 435,000 while the number of non–Ilocanos, both "civilized" and "wild," had *decreased* by nearly 87,000, a fact which undoubtedly reflects the acculturation and assimilation of these people by the Ilocanos. Today Ilocanos in Cagayan Valley far outnumber all other groups, accounting for over two–thirds of a total population of 1,025,441.

The place and relative importance of non–Ilocano–speaking peoples along the Ilocos coast has been of much less significance than was the case in Cagayan Valley. In addition to the Christian Pangasinan to the south, the group most seriously affected by Ilocano expansion on the Ilocos coast itself has been the Tinguian, the majority of whom are located in Abra Province. Cole's hypothesis that the Tinguians derived from the coastal Ilocano groups is probably correct (1945:149); many towns today are designated Ilocano which were once Tinguian and many others are known as *Bago,* or "new Ilocano." (*Bago* is the Ilocano word for "new." When mountain people become Christian, they call themselves Ilocanos. Ilocanos call them *Bago.*) Those Isneg (also called Apayao) living on the borders of Ilocos Norte have nearly all been displaced or absorbed, with only a few hundred at most living on the western slopes of the Cordilleras in or around the small settlement of Carasi. A few others live around Dumalneg in the north. The 1960 census lists Ilocos Norte as 98.8 percent Ilocano and Ilocos Sur as 97.5 percent. In terms of the social environment over the last fifty to a hundred years, the place of non-Ilocano groups has been much more important in Isabela than it has been along the Ilocos coast. These non-Christian groups were also an important "environmental" factor in the development of social cohesiveness in pioneer Ilocano communities in Isabela.

3
HISTORY

There are a few documents—land titles, maps, tax records—from which some names, places, and figures can be derived specifically about the barrio of Buyon prior to the twentieth century. For instance, a map of a local communal irrigation system made in 1814 shows the network of primary and secondary canals with their relationships to prominent topographical features of the area. Another document, a sort of written constitution or paper of incorporation, gives the date of 1793 for the origin of the irrigation system and includes a list of member names. There are municipal land and tax records, though they are very often unreliable since several generations may pass before title is formally changed. The history of Buyon is virtually unknown prior to thirty or forty years ago except for the few yellowed documents mentioned above.

The histories of both Buyon and Mambabanga are necessarily understood in terms of regional and national developments. Spanish and American colonial policies and developments since Philippine independence have had historical and cultural consequences at the barrio level. However, partly because developments in Cagayan Valley were very recent and very rapid, it is possible to focus upon specific details and events within Mambabanga. In a sense, the changes in Mambabanga constitute a microcosm of the wider regional changes. This is most pronounced in the various alterations in essentially economic arrangements.

The changes within Buyon are of a somewhat different nature. The wet–rice pattern employed today in Ilocos Norte was without doubt established early in, perhaps even prior to, the long period of Spanish colonial control. Although change has been a constant feature in the history of Buyon, it has involved gradual modifications and adjustments within the existing ecological arrangements. Thus, whereas the wider changes in Isabela were duplicated on a smaller scale in Mambabanga, changes in Buyon have been much more gradual and lacking in specific detail or significant events. History as a narrative of events in Buyon is noticeably absent. Consequently, because of the greater historical depth and because of the lack of specific, local detail, Buyon is best viewed and understood by relating it to the history of Ilocos Norte as a whole. Both the length and nature of history on the Ilocos coast require a broader picture and less immediate concern with the barrio of Buyon itself.

The pronounced population density has already been mentioned; the historical records indicate that the population along the Ilocos coast has been relatively high for almost two hundred years. Keesing noted:

The late eighteenth century was a period of marked population expansion, presaging the virtual explosion of Ilocano numbers that was to mark the nineteenth century. Vintar, inland from Bacarra, became a separate community and district in 1774, and the same happened to Piddig and Pasuquin in 1775 and 1784 respectively. Laoag has become the largest town in Ilocos.

. . . Pizarro [a Spanish authority of the time] . . . wrote early in the nineteenth century of northern Ilocos as one of the zones having notable urban crowding and mass discontent. In a list of fifteen "most notable" Philippine towns marked by such conditions, he cites Laoag with 25,242 people, Pavay (Paoay) with 14,840, and Bacarra with 13,064. This marked urban development helped to meet the problem of population increase in such a zone of limited rural space, and was to continue. Away from the towns, correspondingly, the Ilocanos here tended to spread out in small barrios and rancherias to an unusual degree, in order to utilize the cultivable areas most effectively. [1962:161]

In the seventeenth century the northern Ilocos area was characterized by a number of unsuccessful rebellions which were based upon "major discontent, generated at the top level of local leaderships" (Keesing 1962:152). Rebellion and near rebellion continued and in 1788, in the Laoag area, "major hostilities" were narrowly averted over opposition to the imposition of a tobacco monopoly. In 1807–1808 a revolt occurred as a consequence of the Spanish wine monopoly; in 1811 a "religious conspiracy" broke out; and in 1813–1814 the *"kailianes,* or commoners,"* revolted over Spanish tribute arrangements (Keesing 1962:160).

By the mid–nineteenth century Ilocos Norte was an important commercial area. Keesing described the "economic basis for the unusual degree of urban development":

A network of roads and trails threaded particularly its south and central sections. The rural zones traded rice, maize, sugar cane, tobacco, and other crops into the towns, and sustained large horse and cattle ranches . . . . The town households, too, notably swelled commerce by manufacturing cotton, fiber, and silk goods often of "magnificent quality," which were much in demand through the Philippines and even overseas. The ocean, together with plentiful lakes and waterways, supplied fish foods; salt was extracted along the shores; palm and sugar cane wines were manufactured; and the usually accessible mountains had buffaloes, deer, and other wild game. Some gold and other precious metals were also washed from streams in "those mountains," and they were a source for valuable woods, resins, wax, and honey. Currimao, southwest of Paoay, served as the principal port from which the goods of the areas were traded extensively by sea. Not least among exports . . . were surplus people. [1962:162]

Phelan also noted that the Ilocos coast was an important export area for rice (1959:110). I could find no records to indicate the volume of export trade or to indicate when this export trade stopped. The cessation of commercial exports in Ilocos Norte may be suggested, however, by population figures. Sixteenth-century estimates place the population of Ilocos Norte at 25,600; by 1818 the population had risen to 135,758; and by 1845 to 154,392. These compare with populations of 178,995 in 1903, to 251,455 in 1948, and 287,333 for the most recent census of 1960. The population for the whole of the Philippines was approximately 1,500,000 for the year 1800. Between 1800 and 1948 the Philippine population increased a very substantial 1,186 percent; between 1818 and 1948 the population of Ilocos Norte increased by only 85 percent. The population increase between the earlier sixteenth–century estimate and the 1948 report was approximately 880 percent, still less than the 1,186 percent for the Philippines as a whole between 1800 and 1948. Thus, the Ilocos Norte area filled up relatively early in Philippine history. Though no specific figures or dates are available on the early Ilocano export trade, it probably declined over the second half of the nineteenth century with the major "exodus" of Ilocanos from 1850 on.

After 1800 the population of the urban areas of Laoag, Bacarra, and Paoay increased at an even slower rate than that indicated for the province as a whole. Ilocanos, besides emigrating, were also intensifying their occupation and exploitation of areas close at hand. Municipalities such as Vintar, Pasuquian, Piddig, and Solsona possessed "hinterlands" to which people could move, whereas municipalities such as Laoag, Bacarra, Badoc, and Paoay, hemmed in by the sea or other municipalities, offered no more room for expansion. As a consequence, the populations of

Bacarra, Laoag, Badoc, and Paoay increased relatively little after 1800 while the "interior" municipalities continued to expand and increase for a much longer period.

The decline in population increases and commercial exports from the mid–nineteenth century on is correlated with Ilocano expansions and migrations outside the area. In 1850 the northern portion of Pangasinan and the southern section of Ilocos Sur were made into a separate province, La Union, and the Ilocanos rapidly replaced the Pangasinans as the dominant ethnic group there. In Abra Province, "invaded" earlier by Ilocano colonists, Ilocanos quickly outnumbered the Tinguians, and from 1850 onward, an increasing number of Ilocanos began moving into Cagayan Valley. The Ilocano expansion is seen largely as a fait accompli through the periodic census reports on "native speakers" in a given area. Keesing wrote that "the outstanding demographic fact revealed by modern censuses has been not only the very great increase of population numbers and settlement density in the lowland areas, but also a major outward migration of the Ilocano group" (1962:46).

The migration of Ilocanos was a steady, continuous process though, unfortunately, few details concerning the actual migrations exist. Except for the Spanish efforts in the mid–nineteenth century to induce Ilocanos to emigrate to Cagayan, few organized efforts have been made to resettle Ilocanos; such efforts or inducements have never been especially necessary.[1] The result has been that, of the over two million Ilocano-speaking people in the Philippines today, more than two–thirds live outside the Ilocos coast.

Without knowing specific details, we can assume that Buyon was involved in the process of expansion and emigration during the early period. In recent years families have migrated from the barrio, and it is reasonable to suppose that this was also the case in previous years. A crucial factor about the migrations, as well as the conditions leading to a migration, is that, while they involved large numbers of people, they did not affect groups of people *as such*. Individual families were displaced by the increased population densities, not whole sitio (neighborhood) or barrio populations. This is, in part, reflected in the form of the emigrations. In the early stages, because of the dangers and rigors of a trip to, for example, Cagayan Valley, the emigrants went in groups, either sailing from Currimao around the north coast and up the Cagayan River, or else taking the more rigorous land route south over the Caraballo Sur range into the upper end of the valley. Word was spread from barrio to barrio that a group would be formed to make the trip to Cagayan Valley. The leaders of these groups were normally persons with some knowledge of the area and the route to be taken. In some instances they received direct compensation for their efforts. These people went *in* groups but they did not go *as* groups—in much the same manner that most pioneers crossed the American continent. Nowadays, because there is no longer the need for traveling in groups, emigrants from Ilocos Norte journey individually or as families, still following the northern or southern route, but by one of the half-dozen bus lines that link the Ilocos with Cagayan Valley.

The importance of the American colonial period is best seen in terms of its serious alteration of the existing social and economic environment and in the ways in which the Ilocanos responded to these new conditions. The economic impoverishment deriving from overpopulation had had its effect upon all people in the Ilocos, the upper as well as the lower class. By the end of the Spanish colonial period a holding of over sixty hectares in Ilocos Norte was indeed large. American control brought with it a number of opportunities; most important for the upper class was the appearance of socioeconomic opportunities which were acceptable and profitable alternatives to managing family estates. The "American experiment," emphasizing education and political participation, constituted a major change from the Spanish period. Political position, although important everywhere in the Philippines for the economic advantages adhering to public office, very early assumed a special, even extreme, importance on the Ilocos coast. At the same time, as an effect of the reduced acreage of their landholdings, the upper class found it increasingly difficult to finance an education in Manila (usually in the field of law) or an emerging political career. The upper-class landowner was often forced to sell or mortgage some or all of his land to pay for his or his family's education or political future. Land prices were rising (due to the influx of money—another consequence of the American impact on the Ilocos coast), so the selling or mortgaging of land was further enhanced. This development had special importance to the people of rural villages like Buyon.

In the nineteenth century, pressures on barrio people to obtain land were resolved by moving farther inland or emigrating to more remote areas like Cagayan Valley. In the years after the American annexation, a new and quite different solution to barrio economic problems presented itself as an alternate solution—agricultural employment in Hawaii or on the west coast mainland of the U.S. Because of their reputation for industriousness, Ilocanos were recruited by both government and private agencies under a variety of arrangements. This migration abroad had direct and immediate economic effects on the people of the Ilocos coast. The pioneer-type migration within the island had normally involved the movement of entire families, who, for practical purposes, severed both social and economic ties to the Ilocos. Overseas employment, on the other hand, normally involved only single males, and the individual agricultural worker in Hawaii or California found himself socially, culturally, and even sexually isolated, and subjected to considerable racial prejudice. Thus, with little chance of establishing a family overseas, he was readily persuaded to return to the Ilocos. But besides the emotional, cultural, and sociological factors involved, there were strong economic reasons for returning as well. With his savings from five, ten, or even more years, often amounting to as much as five thousand dollars or more, the *Hawaiiano* became a man of considerable economic means and importance in Ilocos Norte.[2]

In addition to the lump savings brought back by Hawaiianos there was, and continues to be, a constant influx of American dollars from pensions, social security checks, investments, and government retirements amounting today to over twenty million pesos annually—an amount in excess of five million dollars. As discussed at greater length in chapter 13, a large portion of the dollar savings and imports are held in local savings accounts and are eventually used to purchase land. The demand for, and corresponding shortages in, land have greatly inflated land values.[3]

Out of all this developed a rather paradoxical situation—an upper class in need of money and a lower class able to supply it. On occasion land was purchased outright from the upper class but a form of mortgage, the *salda,* was very commonly the means used by the landowning upper class to obtain the money needed for education or political activity. The salda involved the mortgagee's providing a sum of money and taking over the use–right to the mortgaged land until the original sum was returned. The interest involved was the total income derived from the land during the period of time it was held by the mortgagee. The interest rate on this type of loan could vary from 100 percent to 300 percent per year!

Often, either on a first or second mortgage, the salda had a time limit stipulated, at the end of which the mortgagee could acquire legal title to the land. This was known as the *salda gatang.*

In obtaining a salda the upper–class landlord preferred to deal with a lower–class, rural individual rather than with the more traditional sources of loaned money, such as the Chinese merchants. Not uncommonly an upper–class landlord obtained a mortgage from the very tenant working the land. Although no income could be derived from such land, the mortgagor still possessed the legal title and corresponding prestige of being a "landowner." Even if the legal title was eventually transferred, a social tie was often involved which might be of future benefit to both parties.[4]

As is the case in most rural areas of the Philippines, interclass relationships in Ilocos Norte traditionally involve interpersonal, unequal social ties; given the possibility of deriving future benefits from such ties, it was natural that the upper class turned to the lower class for funds rather than to the socially neutral, less easily manipulated, Chinese. At the same time, however, this practice seriously weakened the traditional landlord–tenant relationship because of the change in expectations between the two parties and because of what was essentially a reversal of economic roles. Thus, although the upper–class person was able to take advantage of new developments through the use of a traditional relationship, he seriously undermined that relationship by, in effect, reversing the positions involved in the patron–client tie.

The land was mortgaged a few pieces at a time, though not always to the tenant working the given piece of land. In many instances lower–class tenants found themselves suddenly working for lower–class landlords. In others the original tenants were removed, and the new landowner either worked the land for himself or allowed a friend or relative to work it for him. For many landless tenants the shift from an upper–class to a lower–class landlord meant the possible loss of his traditional tenancy "rights"; at the very least it deprived him of an effective social tie with an upper–class townsman with no corresponding easement in the economic demands of tenancy. All of this added to the ever increasing socioeconomic pressures and insecurities of rural farm life in Ilocos Norte.

Buyon has been both subject to and a part of the somewhat unique demographic and historical developments in Ilocos Norte. In previous years, people left Buyon to settle in other areas. A few men in the barrio now are Hawaiianos with small holdings of land representing their savings from several years work in Hawaii or California. It is rare, therefore, to find an individual without some close relative in distant areas. All of the people of Buyon are individually affected by the wider socioeconomic environment and the particular historical events of the Ilocos coast. Yet, even though Buyon, in effect, testifies to general developments in Ilocos Norte, such developments are not directly reflected by specific events involving or affecting the barrio as a whole. On the other hand the history of Mambabanga displays a series of clearly delineated events which affected and influenced the barrio as a whole and which did, in a microcosmic way, mirror regional developments as well.

MAMBABANGA

The most significant historical development in northeastern Luzon was the spread of the Ibanags and, later, the Ilocanos throughout Cagayan Valley. The "Ibanagization," as it has been referred to, of this area was described by Keesing in *The Ethnohistory of Northern Luzon* along with some mention of the late nineteenth- and early twentieth-century phases of the subsequent "Ilocanization." So few studies are available that the actual processes of acculturation and assimilation can at best only be inferred. Research among the indigenous Cagayan groups—including the Ibanags as well as the Gaddangs, Yogads, and others—might explain the continuing "Ilocanization" being effected by Ilocano immigration and culture contact. Brief reference has already been made to the same sort of development in the assimilation of Tinguians on the Ilocos coast. However, this study was not specifically designed to add directly to the understanding of intercultural relations in either Isabela or Ilocos Norte.

A barrio such as Mambabanga is both directly and indirectly confronted with a multitude of cultural and social influences. The acculturative features are treated here, however, as part of the wider environment which has affected the socioeconomic activity of barrio life. Of direct significance are the adjustments made or being made within two villages, Buyon and Mambabanga, to a dynamic and constantly changing social and natural order. The people of Buyon and Mambabanga both share the same cultural traditions, the same guides for behavior, the same social and moral imperatives; but, as the research revealed, the social and natural environments facing the people of Buyon and Mambabanga are considerably different, and this has resulted in variable behavior.

This study throws little light on ethnohistorical questions regarding either the distribution or customs of non–Ilocano groups in Isabela Province. To the people of Mambabanga any non–Christian of the area was and is a "Kalinga," and "Kalinga" is another word for savage. Ilocanos make the obvious distinction between "Kalingas" and Negritoes, but they make little or no discrimination between pagan Gaddangs, Ifugaos, or Kalingas. They recognize different Christian groups, such as Ibanags, Yogads, Christian Gaddang, when such people constitute all or part of the population of local towns or barrios for the ethnocentric reason that these people do not speak "good" Ilocano. It is the anthropologist who tells them (despite their lack of interest) that there are both Christian and non-Christian Gaddangs, or that the "Kalingas" are not always Kalingas.[5] To the Ilocano settlers of central Isabela the "Kalingas" were one of the dangers to be faced in the environment of a pioneering settlement, although the "Kalingas" were much less a real danger than the malaria–bearing mosquitoes. However, even if the danger of "headhunting savages" was more apparent than real, the Ilocanos' fear of these people was genuine enough to effectuate cooperative settlement efforts involving several families in preference to smaller, scattered, nuclear communities (see chapter 6).

The settlement and establishment of Mambabanga followed a pattern which is perhaps characteristic of Ilocano immigration to Cagayan Valley and one that, with little modification, is still being practiced today. Two distinct stages are involved: first, the movement of individual families from the Ilocos coast to the already settled areas of the Cagayan Valley; and, second, the establishment of true pioneering communities in previously unsettled areas.

The oldest communities in Isabela are those located along the Cagayan and other large rivers—towns such as San Pablo, Cabagan, Tumauini, Ilagan, Naguilian, San Mariano, Cauayan, and Angadanan. The populations of these towns fifty years ago were predominantly Ibanag, the result of the earlier spread and assimilative movement of Ibanags into the upper Cagayan Valley. It is in these towns that the largest percentage of Ibanags is found today, though their displacement and apparent assimilation by Ilocanos continues apace. The first Ilocano immigrants to Cagayan Valley established themselves in and about the older Ibanag communities by working the land as tenants or by setting up some other lease arrangements with the established populations. Still other Ilocano immigrants worked on the large, usually Spanish–owned, tobacco haciendas. Many of these original settlers or their descendants subsequently moved into the inhospitable, malaria–infested areas.

Few of the original pioneers, those who left Ilocos Norte and later established themselves in the Luna area, are alive today. However, one individual, a man now 105 years old and a key figure in the first settlements in the Luna area, recalls both the primary and secondary stages of settlement. At the same time, he is related to and influenced the first settlers of Mambabanga itself. Mr. Francisco Agcaoili first came from Bacarra, Ilocos Norte, in 1905 with a few male companions to sell a small herd of water buffalo. Their original plan was to sell the animals in Cagayan Province, but when informed that prices were better in Isabela they journeyed southward up the Cagayan Valley. Eventually he and his associates reached Echaque, a town about thirty kilometers south of present–day Mambabanga, located in an area where a number of Ilocano communities had already been established. Mr. Agcaoili returned to Bacarra where he made plans to return and settle in Isabela the following year. A group of approximately sixty persons—twelve families, some related, some unrelated—was formed from several different barrios in the Bacarra–Vintar area, news being spread by word of mouth that a group was being formed to go. Because Mr. Agcaoili was an experienced traveler in Cagayan, and because it was under his initiative that the group was being formed, he was "elected" to act as leader for the journey. The twelve families left from what was then the main port of Ilocos Norte, Currimao, sailed around the north coast in a hired vessel to Aparri, and from Aparri they journeyed upriver in small boats purchased near the coast. A few of the families left the main group at different towns along the route, though most came as far south as Cauayan. They traveled together for safety and economy, but, upon arrival at their destination, they ceased to exist as a group.[6] Mr. Agcaoili and two other families ultimately settled in Carabatan Grande, a predominantly Ilocano barrio in Cauayan. They remained there for over ten years working as tenants for the indigenous Ibanags or for established Ilocano immigrants. It was in Carabatan Grande that nearly all of the immigrants were afflicted by malaria, the major hazard to life in Cagayan Valley at that time.

At the turn of the century, the Catholic Church owned more than 400,000 hectares of land in the Philippine Islands (Spencer 1952:143). From 1905 on, the government began purchasing this land and selling it to buyers under a variety of arrangements. In central Isabela a total of 18,823 hectares was eventually disposed of by the Friar Lands Estates Office in Aurora. Either in 1914 or

1915, Mr. Agcaoili and five other men visited the Government Lands Office in Cabatuan to inquire about the purchase of Friar Lands from the government. They were instructed by the Lands Office to assemble a group of approximately sixty family heads who would each be sold an amount of land not to exceed 24 hectares at rates averaging about fifty pesos per hectare. During a preliminary survey of the land, the survey party and six representatives for the group were approached and warned by "Kalingas," probably pagan Gaddang, that they were encroaching upon aboriginal lands. The settlers and survey party departed only to return with thirty Philippine constabulary troopers from Echaque. The survey was then completed without further incident. The "Kalingas" were subsequently told by the government that they could have 300 hectares of land but, like the Ilocano immigrants, they would have to pay for it. The settlement area in which the "Kalingas" were located became known as Barrio Kalinga, but the original inhabitants have long since vanished. Traditionally swidden farmers, they were apparently unable to compete successfully with the Ilocano immigrants or, ultimately, to pay for their own lands which the government had required them to buy. Most of the land these "Kalingas" occupied was eventually sold or taken over by Ilocano settlers and, by World War II, the last "Kalingas" had moved to the Cordillera Central mountains.

Groups of "Kalinga" men may have occasionally engaged in headhunting forays, but the Ilocano settlers encountered no real problem with these original inhabitants; never was there a real question of where effective power lay. However, the threat of headhunting "Kalinga savages" was always there, more imagined than real, but, to the Ilocano settlers, a threat nonetheless.[7]

The original group of sixty pioneering families in the Luna area designated itself the Union Bacarrina after the municipality from which the largest number of them came. These people settled in the area north of Mambabanga and formed the nucleus of what are now the barrios of Concepcion, Puroc, Lalog I, Lalog II, Pulay, Macanao, Luyao, Santo Domingo, San Isidro, and, subsequently, Barrio Kalinga. Starting in the area adjacent to Luna, the original number of families was augmented by more immigrants, some of them kinsmen from Ilocos Norte, some of them Ilocanos living in the older settlements along the Cagayan River. The original land purchase by the sixty families totaled over 1,100 hectares. As discussed at greater length in chapter 12, about 150 hectares of the original land purchase became the basis for the Union Bacarrina Irrigation Society. After the establishment of various barrios, the original settlement group, the Union Bacarrina, ceased to be an effective social entity and the term Union Bacarrina now applies only to the irrigation society.

The settlement of Mambabanga itself followed a few years after that of the barrios mentioned above but, again, dates are not precise. Felix Agcaoili, a nephew of Francisco Agcaoili, came with his parents to Isabela a year or two after his uncle had come. His parents, like Francisco, settled as tenants in Mabanted, a barrio of the municipality of Cauayan. After several years, however, recurring crop losses resulting from floods forced them to move, and they settled in the barrio of Nappaccu Pequeno in the municipality of Reina Mercedes, a few miles north of Cauayan. There they remained until about 1918 when the Agcaoilis and thirteen other families applied for the purchase of Friar Lands just south of the original Union Bacarrina area.

According to the records of the Aurora Subdistrict Office for the Bureau of Lands, a formal application was made in June 1920, for 197 hectares of land by fourteen family heads for lots varying from 5.44 hectares to the largest of 43.89 hectares with a corresponding cost of from 285 to over 1,900 pesos. The group of individuals called themselves the Society Mambabanga.[8] In actuality there were twenty families that established houses on the low ridge overlooking the southwestern margin of the Magat River flood plain. In several cases, fathers and sons shared the ownership and development of these holdings. Felix Agcaoili and his parents shared such a holding.

The original pattern of land use in Mambabanga commonly involved a rotation of fields within the section of lands owned. Seldom were more than three hectares under cultivation in any given year, and the nonfarmed areas lay fallow. Tobacco was the only marketable cash crop grown in the valley. Typically, a hectare of land was given over to tobacco production, and two hectares were set aside for subsistence crops—one for the traditional rice, *pagay iloco,* and an additional hectare for mixed garden crops such as corn or beans. There was no second cropping at this stage of land development; most off-season work was directed at clearing and improving lands, the ultimate aim being to establish permanent rice paddies. In terms of the actual crops grown, the agricultural methods differed little from traditional dry-farming practices in Ilocos Norte. However, the cycle of cropping, the size of fields, the pattern of land use, climatic factors, etc., all differed considerably. Most important, the agricultural pattern required the assistance of neighbors and kinsmen.

With the traditional methods of growing rice, even three hectares were too much for one family to handle alone. Consequently, the demand for labor was so increased at harvest time, that one-half the crop was offered to people who often journeyed from the Ilocos coast just to help with the harvest. This need for additional laborers and the consequent contact with relatives and kinsmen from the Ilocos provinces continued until after World War II, when important changes (discussed later in this chapter) occurred in the economic systems of both Isabela and Ilocos Norte. This seasonal migration of laborers from the Ilocos area also provided a preview of Isabela and Cagayan for many Ilocanos who later settled there permanently.

In the twenty years after the founding of Mambabanga and before World War II, several developments in the pattern of landownership began to emerge which were to become characteristic of most of Cagayan Valley. Discussed below, these developments inevitably led to the emergence of larger and larger landholdings with corresponding increases in tenancy. The largest single holding among the original founders of the Society Mambabanga was that of a man to whom I shall refer as "Mr. Cruz." In the original application Mr. Cruz applied for and received the largest holding of land, an area of over forty-three hectares. As in other pioneering settlements of Isabela, a number of families died out, left, or were unable to maintain payments on their land; through mortgage and direct purchase Mr. Cruz acquired an additional thirty-seven hectares from four of the original settlers in Mambabanga. These lots and other purchases resulted in Mr. Cruz's owning approximately 120 hectares, roughly 60 percent of the original lands obtained by the Society Mambabanga. He developed an irrigation system for the area (apparently intending, through its manipulation, to pressure other society members into selling their lands), and brought in a large number of tenants, predominently Ilocanos, from Pangasinan and Tarlac. Mr. Cruz's tenants settled on the western edge of Mambabanga, establishing at first a separate sitio and later a separate barrio, Harana, now composed primarily of landless tenants. Such enlargements of landholdings by more capable and/or unscrupulous barrio residents is not an uncommon story. With the lack of cash crops and the demands of pioneer farming, many early settlers were hard pressed to meet even the smallest payments periodically required for formal title to their lands.

Another pattern in the development of large landholdings occurred with the purchase of large tracts of land by speculators. Most of the larger holdings were applied for in lots of up to 144 hectares, the maximum size allowed a single purchaser during the later period of land sales. However, many holdings were made much larger by applying in the name of various family members. The commercial development of Isabela ultimately depended on the successful pioneering by the original Ilocano immigrants. Once the problem of pacifying and displacing "Kalingas" had been accomplished, along with concerted government effort to reduce the high incidence of malaria, it was possible to open up and develop the area for commercial agriculture. Tobacco had long been commercially important along the main rivers, but a rice economy did not develop until the forest and savannah lands were opened up by Ilocano settlers. These settlers, unaware of the legal problems involved, often did not obtain formal legal title, only to find that the land they had pioneered was owned by land speculators from central Luzon or Manila—a not unfamiliar story in Philippine resettlement areas.[9]

By the late 1930s the lands remaining to be developed in central Isabela were rapidly disappearing. Thus, while the immigrant Ilocanos developed the land for themselves on small holdings, they also paved the way for the large, usually absentee-owned, commercial holdings which have since come to dominate the agriculture of Isabela. Most of these larger holdings were applied for during the twenty years following World War I. Payments were often deferred, some until as late as 1950, to the time when agricultural potential had ceased to be speculative. Removal of pioneer "squatters" followed, and more and more tenants were brought in from central Luzon.[10] The increase in the size and number of large holdings was exactly the opposite of what has been described for Ilocos Norte. The development in Isabela, however, was much more typical of the general, overall pattern for the Philippines. Barrios such as Mambabanga, those founded by and largely composed of independent landowners, are declining in both absolute and relative number. Further decline has been made almost inevitable by the continual division of holdings to satisfy the requirements of equal inheritance, and the corresponding decrease in the efficiency of small-holder farming, with the resultant inability to compete with the large, commercial estates.[11]

The development of a commercial rice economy in Isabela was somewhat delayed by World War II, and, after World War II, by the Hukbalahap rebellion which spread from central Luzon. The leaders of the Huk guerrillas in Isabela, as well as an unknown number of rank-and-file members, are reported to have come from the main insurgent forces in the central provinces.[12] This shift of forces was, in part, a consequence of increased pressures exerted against the Huks after 1949 by the Secretary of Defense, Ramon Magsaysay. With this movement of Huk forces into the area came an active recruitment campaign in Isabela, and Huk "barrio committees" were established in many barrios of the province for the purposes of control, logistics, taxation, and the recruitment or conscription of new personnel. Apparently most support for the Huks came from the barrios composed of landless tenants, especially tenants recruited and brought up from central Luzon. There is, naturally enough, a general reluctance to talk about the importance or extent of the Huk movement in Isabela. Ilocanos did participate in the movement but to what degree or in what numbers is impossible to determine. Government agencies will admit only that there were "misguided elements" of the local populace involved.

Whatever the participation by, or the amount of support received from, the local populace, the Huks were sufficiently strong at one point to attack openly the town of Santiago with a population of over four thousand which was, at that time, a base of operations for government troops in Isabela. The remnants of a few Huk groups, or groups which call themselves Huks, still operate out of the Sierra Madres, and are said to "tax" some of the more remote and isolated barrios of that area. The point is that conditions were sufficiently suitable for the Huks to mount and maintain a considerable force in Isabela; this was not possible in the Ilocos area. Although there are geographical factors which might make Isabela better suited for guerrilla warfare, there were, and still are, conditions involving absentee landlordism that provided a favorable, or at least not unfavorable, atmosphere for the Huk movement.

Though the Ilocano families opened up the area to agriculture, it was the large agricultural interests which converted the traditional subsistence farming of the Ilocano farmers to commercial agricultural production. This was primarily accomplished with the introduction of mechanical threshers from central Luzon. As examined at greater length in chapters 5 and 6, mechanical threshers could not be worked into or added onto the traditional Ilocano system of growing rice. Mechanical threshers were first used in Isabela in the mid–1930s (shortly after the successful Ilocano immigrations), but it was not until after World War II and the decline of the Huk movement that mechanical threshers became available in great numbers. Because the traditional Ilocano varieties of rice were unsuitable for mechanical threshing, they were replaced by several commercially suitable types of rice commonly grown in central Luzon. The change to commercial rice production was especially significant for the towns of Isabela Province which rather suddenly became the centers for rice purchasing, milling, and export. Barrios such as Mambabanga, however, have been less affected in terms of their internal social arrangements than might at first be imagined.

In terms of the province as a whole, the pioneering efforts of Ilocano immigrants ultimately made the commercial development of agriculture in Isabela feasible. The results of commercialization were that changes of major proportions occurred in the wider technological and economic environments of pioneering communities like Mambabanga. Existing social and economic patterns which have been in effect for less than twenty years are in themselves highly transitory. The patterns associated with the pioneering and development of Mambabanga lasted little more than twenty–five years. Before that was the period of tenancy in the predominantly Ibanag settlements along the major river courses. What the precise characteristics of social life were in early periods can only be ascertained or reconstructed in a general way, as they have been in the example of the recent history of Ilocos Norte. The primary concern here is with the comparison of existing relationships and arrangements which, at the time of this study (1963), obtained in two different barrios in two different areas of northern Luzon. Yet, to understand properly the extant social relationships, it is necessary to consider the historical events and conditions which have impressed themselves on the existing social and natural environment. In the chapters which follow, explanations of existing social and economic relationships will often include statements on and interpretations of conditions which previously existed, and which are considered pertinent to the analysis. Some events mentioned or alluded to in the last two chapters will be examined at greater length in the analysis of specific areas of behavior in each barrio.

NOTES

1. Pelzer does describe some of the resettlement programs attempted during the 1930s and concentrates upon one program in particular, a settlement in southern Mindanao involving very few Ilocanos. He does briefly describe a colonization program of Ilocanos in the northwestern section of Isabela Province (1945:243–248).
2. The term *Hawaiiano* refers to almost any Ilocano who has worked abroad, either in Hawaii or on the Mainland. In some instances, an individual will be referred to as a *landing,* for he has "landed" in port.
3. The ratio of savings-to-loans transactions for a major bank in Ilocos Norte was reported to me as being 15:1. The same savings-loans ratio for a bank in Santiago, Isabela was reported to be 1:8. "First class" irrigated rice lands will sell for twelve- to fifteen-thousand pesos per hectare in Ilocos Norte; the same class of land in Isabela (which produces about twice as much per given measure) sells for twelve- to fifteen-hundred pesos per hectare.
4. An additional requirement is often imposed when formal title to land is actually lost through the *salda gatang.* If the new owner ever needs to sell or mortgage his lands, he must agree to give the former owner first opportunity to repurchase it. Today, with more and more barrio people sending their children to college, such repurchases by the original landowners are occurring and the old landlord-tenant relationships are re-establishing themselves.
5. A few Christian Gaddangs from Luna told me that the "Kalingas" of that area speak Gaddang, but, because a "true" Gaddang must be Christian, they were reluctant to claim these people as Gaddangs.
6. Residents in some other barrios of the area traveled the more arduous overland route south along the Ilocos coast and east into Cagayan Valley over the Caraballo Sur mountain range. These groups were also formed from various villages in the Ilocos area and commonly disbanded upon arrival in Isabela Province.
7. The displacement of pagan (and Christian) Cagayan groups by Ilocano settlers continues in the fringe areas of the valley. One group, which may be that referred to by Keesing as *Iraya* or *Irraya,* lives on three upper tributaries of the Ilagan River above San Mariano (Keesing 1962:238, 239, 262, 337). Gaddangs, or "Kalingas," live west of Aurora. In the south of Isabela near St. Augustin and well into Nueva Vizcaya the Ilongots still carry out occasional head-hunting forays to defend themselves against the continuing encroachment of the Ilocanos.
8. The name "Mambabanga" derives from the name given the barrio site when it was no more than a favored watering and grazing area for stock.

It comes from a folk term applied to a species of wild coconut tree which grew there and translates, in effect, as "the place where the wild coconuts grow."

9. See Karl J. Pelzer, *Pioneer Settlement in the Asiatic Tropics,* for examples of similar problems in Mindanao.

10. Individuals also accrued land through legal channels. Disputes over land-holdings naturally increased as the population grew, and attorneys often took their fees in land from small farmers who could not pay in currency. Much more lucrative for attorneys, however, was the practice of going through the original applications for Friar Lands to learn which claims had become delinquent or had been lost by forfeit. Many financially able farmers lost their lands because of their innocence of the law.

11. The dividing of lands into smaller and smaller units will, of course, depend in part upon whether or not existing land reform laws are effectively implemented and maintained. On the other hand, if the larger estate holdings are broken up, and if the population continues to increase—as it surely will—the trend may well be toward something like the minusculization of the landholdings that do exist in Ilocos Norte. The trends in the socioeconomic environments of the Ilocos coast and central Luzon are hardly encouraging.

12. The limited information provided here on the Huk movement in Isabela was gained from interviews with local residents in the area and from some government informants in Ilagan. The degree of reliability is open to some question.

4
GEOGRAPHY

BUYON

Barrio Buyon is situated just east of National Highway No. 3 between Laoag, the provincial capital, and the town and *poblacion* of Bacarra—about five kilometers from the former and less than two from the latter. (See maps 2, 4, and 5.) Buyon is one of twenty-six barrios making up the municipality of Bacarra. It is bordered on the south by the barrio of Pandan, this boundary also being the municipal line separating Bacarra and Laoag. To the east is the barrio of Libong and to the west that of Curarig. The northern border of Buyon is formed by the Bacarra-Vintar River. Buyon, like other barrios in this area, is hardly distinguishable with houses and house clusters scattered here and there, most of them hidden among the trees which mark the division between wet-rice fields and the less productive hill plots. The total population of 543 persons is unequally divided among three different sitios, or sections—Calutit, Buyon, and Tamucalao—in the following way:

Sitio	Persons	Houses	Households
Calutit	124	26	26
Buyon	342	62	79
Tamucalao	77	15	16
BARRIO TOTAL	543	103	121

The flat, wet-rice-producing sections of land in this region are the flood plains of the streams and rivers that cut the Ilocos coast. The rice fields slope gently up from the low centers of these small flood plains to the higher wooded areas, in some places steepening into fairly well-terraced fields. The greater the distance from the coast, the smaller becomes the area farmed in wet-rice and the higher and wider the intervening hills. Buyon lies about halfway between mountains and sea, about six kilometers inland. Few of the ridges are very high—two- to four-hundred feet—and seldom are they more than a kilometer wide.

39

The southern border of Buyon is on one of the higher ridges—the ridge which constitutes the primary watershed between the Laoag and Bacarra-Vintar rivers. On the northern slope of this hill a small, almost unnoticed, barrio road turns off National Highway No. 3 east into the sitio of Calutit, the second largest and southernmost sitio of Buyon. A few yards up and off the national highway this small road is joined and paralleled by a government irrigation canal on the right and irrigated rice fields several feet below on the left. Canal and road continue along what constitute the margins of the Bacarra-Vintar River flood plain, enter the largest sitio of Buyon, Buyon proper, and, in a very winding and irregular course of about four kilometers, pass over into the barrio of Libong. Constructed for use in maintaining the canal, the road is virtually impassable to wheeled vehicles in several places but, as do trails in other sections of the barrio, does serve the needs of the people.

On the main highway, beyond the first barrio turnoff into the sitio of Calutit, the main government road continues north for a short distance to a junction and then angles right, to the north and east. An old road to Bacarra continues directly northward at this point, touches barrio Curarig, and ends a kilometer beyond at the Bacarra-Vintar River where, years previously, a ferry crossing was maintained. On the main road past this junction the highway passes through part of the rice fields within Buyon and, after a few hundred meters, cuts into a peninsulalike projection of land. Here the main road is again joined by a barrio track linking it to the canal maintenance road. The houses are all east of the road and are all in the southern part of the sitio of Buyon. From this junction the national road crosses another half kilometer of open rice fields and again cuts a narrow neck of land, with houses here on each side of the road. On the south face of this small hill, two trails give access to the northern section of sitio Buyon, while on the north side of the hill, and again to the east of the road, a jeep track extends to the main cluster of houses in Tamucalao, the barrio's smallest sitio. Where the jeep or cart track turns into Tamucalao a large irrigation ditch, part of a network of canals used by several communal irrigation systems, passes under the road. This canal supplies irrigation water for rice fields on both sides of the small ridge, to the east and west of the main road, as well as for fields farther west in the barrios of Curarig, Ganagan, and Dibua. Hidden by the trees and just west of the main road opposite Tamucalao is a small *kamarine,* an open–sided shed used by one of the irrigation cooperatives, the Zangjera de Camungao, as a meeting place and temporary storage shed for newly harvested rice. A narrow strip of rice fields separates Tamucalao from a small stream that provides some of the water for the Zangjera de Camungao. At this point a small detour and ford bypass a new bridge which was undergoing construction over the creek to replace one previously washed out during a flood some years ago. This creek is normally a small stream, easy to ford or wade, but the torrential rains which accompany the not-infrequent typhoons require that it be spanned by a fairly high and substantial structure. Just below the bridge construction lie the remains of a broken concrete irrigation dam and spillway which attest to the severity of flood conditions. Across the stream the highway is joined by the provincial road from the town of Vintar, which is but a few kilometers to the east.

The Bacarra–Vintar River is crossed by a fairly long and substantial bridge, but there, too, flood damage is evident and the earthen approaches and makeshift wooden trestles require regular repairs. Though only a short distance across the river from Buyon, Bacarra is often more difficult to reach than Laoag during the rainy months of June, July, and August. In addition to being a barrier to travel, the river is also a constant threat to agricultural lands. The main block of fields farmed by people in Buyon faces a section of the river that has cut deeply into the south bank. The people of Buyon estimate that over twenty–five hectares (about sixty–two acres) of irrigated rice fields have been lost to the severe erosion and flooding in that area of the village. Much of the lands so lost belonged to the Zangjera de Camungao (see chapter 12).

Like most Ilocos barrios, Buyon is far from being isolated. Several families have transistor radios and they can tune in to any one of three local radio stations in Laoag which broadcast a mixed Ilocano–American fare of soap opera and highly Filipinized pop music. Buses and "jeepnies" (jeep buses) pass regularly between Bacarra and Laoag. Buses of the larger transportation companies go by regularly, some headed north around Cape Bojeador and the very rugged coastal route to Aparri in Cagayan Province, others headed south to the central provinces and Manila. Signifying the links between Ilocos Norte and central Isabela is the daily Bacarra–Ilagan bus run, which seems to exist solely for the purpose of transporting Ilocanos to and from Isabela Province. This is an arduous two–day trip, mostly over rough, rutted, unpaved roads. The route is south along the Ilocos coast, east in central Pangasinan Province to San Jose (Nueva Ecija), and then north over the Caraballo Sur range into Cagayan Valley. A much quicker, more direct, but for most people prohibitively expensive, means is via the twice–a–day flights of the Philippine Airlines.

The people of Buyon know the routes that lead from Ilocos Norte and of the opportunities that might be found elsewhere; they also know that such opportunities are now much more limited than in years past. It is rare to find a person without close relatives in places such as Cagayan Valley, Cotobato, Manila, Davao, Hawaii, or California. Several of the people in Buyon have worked as seasonal laborers in Cagayan, and a few have worked for longer or shorter periods "Stateside"—in the pineapple and sugar-cane fields of Hawaii or as migrant laborers in the Salinas or Imperial valleys of California. Yet, despite these ties and despite the extensive lines of communication and transportation, there is a marked provincialism about the Ilocos coast. Buyon and other barrios like it are much less a consequence of cultural contacts and communication than they are the product of specifically local social and economic arrangements.

MAMBABANGA

There are three towns of immediate importance to barrio Mambabanga: Cauayan, Cabatuan, and Luna. (See map 3.) The first of these, Cauayan, is approximately 5,000 in population, smaller by 3,000 than Bacarra in Ilocos Norte. But, whereas Bacarra is little more than a cluster of barrios, Cauayan is a commercial center with a daily market, three hotels, a movie theater, gas stations, three blocks of retail stores, a number of rice mills, and an assortment of cafes. Cauayan is also an important crossroads where the route south from the provincial capital of Ilagan divides, going to Santiago either via Cabatuan and San Mateo along the western side of the valley, or via Alicia and Echague along the more easterly and direct route. The amount of jeepney, bus, and truck traffic along both routes is considerable. Cauayan is also the single commercial airline stop for Isabela Province, and large numbers of passengers arrive and depart from there on the two northbound and two southbound daily Philippine Airlines' flights—the midway, turnaround stop for these flights being Laoag.

Eleven kilometers west from Cauayan is Cabatuan, the second town of importance to Mambabanga. Cabatuan is about one-third the size of Cauayan, with respect to both total population and the amount of business and commercial activity. Relatively small as it is, however, Cabatuan is of much greater economic and commercial significance than the larger towns of Ilocos Norte, with the exceptions of Laoag and, probably, Batac. Once a barrio of Cauayan, Cabatuan has been a municipality only since late 1949. Its growth has been a natural one, a consequence of increasing population and the corresponding development of commercial agriculture throughout Cagayan Valley. Cabatuan, like Cauayan, is also located at an important road junction—the intersection made by National Highway No. 5 and the southern terminal for the alternate, but less important, provincial road along the western side of Cagayan Valley through the towns of Mallig, Roxas, and Aurora. Both Cabatuan and Cauayan are important to the economic life of Mambabanga; the third town, the *poblacion* of Luna, is the administrative and political center for Mambabanga.

Five kilometers west of Cauayan on the way to Cabatuan, a small road branches north to Luna, the smallest municipality (5,209) and one of the smaller towns (1,325) of Isabela. Too close to Cauayan and Cabatuan and situated at the wrong end of a dead-end road, Luna has only a poorly attended, one-day-a-week market. One drug store, a few *sari-sari* stores (small general stores), and a small cafe constitute the commercial makeup of Luna. Only the two-story town hall, adjacent public health center building, and a prominently positioned statue of José Rizal attest to its being a municipal center. Yet, although the commercial importance of Luna is overshadowed by Cauayan and Cabatuan, the simple fact that Luna is the *poblacion* for surrounding barrios gives it a social-political importance which belies its real size. And, because the histories of immigration and settlement in surrounding barrios are linked to that of Luna, both real and ritual kin ties are found between poblacion and barrio.

Four kilometers east of Cabatuan and seven kilometers west of Cauayan, Mambabanga itself is located but a hundred meters north of National Highway No. 5. (See map 6.) There are sixty houses with sixty-two households and a total population of 383 persons in Mambabanga. Like many another barrio in central Isabela, it is situated amid a wide expanse of rice fields. Adjacent to Mambabanga is the barrio of Harana, with a population of 335. As shall be seen, close historical ties link the two barrios, though sociological bonds are much diminished. A number of barrios like Mambabanga and Harana are situated along the ridges above the main flood plain of the Magat River. Access to Mambabanga is made from the main provincial road onto a smaller barrio road, the former connecting with the main thoroughfare at an angle to the north and west. Just over a hundred meters from the highway, the barrio road turns northeast into the cluster of houses, trees, and bamboo thickets that sets the barrio off from the surrounding rice lands. At that corner there are the three buildings of the combined elementary school for the children of Mambabanga and Harana. Past the school, the main barrio road continues for half a kilometer and is paralleled by a less used and more poorly maintained track a few meters north and west. Three very rough, rutted tracks cross the main road at somewhat regular intervals. The most northern and easterly of these continues down into the main Magat River flood plain and then can be followed in a northerly direction some three kilometers to the barrio of Concepcion. The settling of Mambabanga above the Magat flood plain was a safety precaution employed to protect the houses against some of the greater flooding that occurs in the valley. This location also permitted more economical utilization of land, for the houses were built on the less fertile margins of the ridge.

In the area which extends from the southern boundary of Mambabanga to the Magat River, there are three general soil types and three nearly corresponding agricultural divisions. The most fertile portions of land are found along the natural levees of the Magat River itself. The barrios in the municipality of Luna which most profit from these soils are Lalog I, Lalog II, and San Isidro, a barrio on the opposite, northern bank of the river. The silt-loam soils of the Magat River levees are given over almost exclusively to the growing of native tobacco. Such lands are regularly second cropped, mostly with corn or mongo beans. The levee areas, with their slightly elevated position, are virtually impossible to irrigate under the existing technological complex. These fertile lands, however, do not lie within the boundary of Mambabanga and are not farmed by the people of that barrio.

The second type of soil, farther removed from the river, occurs on the primary flood plain. Though poorer in nitrogen compounds, these lands are more easily irrigated, and water control permits the growing of the more productive, slow-maturing varieties of rice. The level of this area is only a few feet above that of the main rivers and numerous perennial streams emerge or cut across this plain to follow meandering courses before emptying into the main river channels. In some instances, such as at Mambabanga, these streams have been dammed for irrigation purposes. Farther up the Magat River at barrio Dacariz, San Mateo, the government has constructed a large diversion dam across the Magat which irrigates approximately 19,000 hectares of such land. As in the natural levee areas, second cropping is in corn or mongo beans.

The third soil and third agricultural division found in the area is found in the higher and older flood plains, the level on which the barrio houses are located. Farthest removed from the main rivers, these areas have the poorest soils and are least suited to irrigation. Because of the higher elevation and the more intense cutting action by streams, water in these locations is less easily diverted or trapped in reservoirs. With the exception of a very few areas where rich landowners have been able to lift or trap water, there is no artificial irrigation. The main crop grown there is almost exclusively the less productive, fast-maturing varieties of rice. Because there is no irrigation, there is virtually no second cropping in this area.

Some barrios, such as Dapdap to the east of Mambabanga, are exclusively involved in farming the less productive, nonirrigated soils which produce but a single crop of rice. Others, such as Puroc to the north, are located on the primary flood plain and are completely involved in the irrigated, double-crop economy. Still others, like Mambabanga and Harana, are situated along the margins between the irrigated and nonirrigated areas and manage to grow crops in both soil regions. As shall be seen, participation in the irrigated areas is often as landowner and operator; participation in the nonirrigated rice areas is very commonly that of tenant on one of the large and commonly absentee-owned landholdings.

Unlike the situation described for Buyon in Ilocos Norte, there are no residential subdivisions, or sitios, in Mambabanga, though the adjacent barrio of Harana was a sitio of Mambabanga until shortly after World War II. Besides the two barrios having a common elementary school, Mambabanga and Harana also share the use of a large, open-sided shed which becomes the barrio market place two days a week. At the very center of Mambabanga, both physically and socially removed from Harana, is the barrio chapel where mass is held every fourth Sunday by an American missionary priest from Cabatuan. Near the chapel is a twenty-by-twenty-foot shed owned by a Chinese mestizo rice buyer from Cabatuan who, with the help of a few individuals within the barrio, uses it as a collecting station for rice contracted for or bought in the barrio.

Except for Macanao Creek to the north there are no natural

boundaries to Mambabanga. The southern boundary is also the municipal boundary but, because it has never been surveyed for either barrio or municipal purposes, and because barrio and municipal lines are not necessarily related to the people's use or ownership of the land, its exact location is neither the knowledge nor special concern of people in Mambabanga. This is also true of the eastern boundary separating Mambabanga and Dapdap, an undefined border which is regularly crossed and worked by people from both "sides." The one boundary, in addition to that of Macanao Creek, which is readily recognized and acknowledged is that which separates Mambabanga and Harana. Although several houses of Mambabanga appear to be a part of Harana, the residents of both barrios are quick to point out that such is not the case. The boundary separating Mambabanga and Harana follows along the lines of several house lots owned by older residents of Mambabanga, and, for this and related reasons of kinship and association, the people are well aware of the border separating the two communities.

The territorial delineation of Mambabanga is based upon a number of social considerations. Macanao Creek is much more than just a natural geographic feature for it separates the original land grant purchases made by the Union Baccarina and the Society Mambabanga. The line separating Mambabanga and Harana has both historical and sociological bases. Largely because most of these lands are owned by absentee landlords, the undefined eastern and southern boundaries exist only in the vaguest way along the irregular lines of fields worked by tenants from Mambabanga vis-à-vis tenants from other barrios. The roughly defined territorial limits are but the spatial dimensions reflecting various social, political, economic, and technological arrangements which, though not neatly or precisely defined, are of primary importance here.

PART 2
TECHNOLOGICAL
ADAPTATIONS

5
RICE CULTIVATION IN BUYON

THE PATTERN OF RICE PRODUCTION

In general outline and form there seems to be little difference in the agricultural regime of Buyon and that of other barrios in the Philippine lowlands. Like many other rural villages, Buyon's wet-rice economy is never quite sufficient to provide for its own consumption needs. In addition to rice, there are a number of other crops grown either on hill plots or as off-season crops in the rice fields during the dry season. Some crops, like tobacco, are raised for a cash income, but most go for home consumption as supplements or complements to rice. The level of technology is geared to the productivity of a farmer, his water buffalo, a simple complex of tools, and a labor force centered on the nuclear family. The year is organized according to the demands of the agricultural calendar and just as unexpectedly disorganized by the vagaries of nature in the form of too much or too little rain. Equally incomprehensible to the farmer are the forces which control his limited commercial dealings. As a buyer he pays prices set by distributors or producers; as a producer he sells at prices set by the buyer. The things which characterize the agriculture of Buyon from other barrios are reflective of regional and subregional patterns in northwest Luzon.

Even the most casual observer notices certain distinctive features of Ilocano agriculture. The contrast with other areas is most pronounced driving north from Manila to the Ilocos region. A glaring difference, one which at first appears to be of a nonagricultural nature, is the strong commercial influence radiating out from Manila. The agricultural differences are sometimes all but obscured by roadside advertising. This commercialism is, in part, simply a measure of the distance to and the importance of Manila. It also reflects the fact, however, that central Luzon is a busy commercial agricultural area. The history of commercial agriculture in that area has been characterized by agrarian unrest—a condition notably absent farther north on the Ilocos coast.

The individual fields of Pampanga, Bulacan, Tarlac, and Nueve

Ecija provinces are quite large in contrast with fields found farther north. In fact, the whole of central Luzon is itself one vast and extended plain broken only by Mt. Arayat towards the south. A considerable degree of mechanization is also evident, again a feature absent in the agricultural economy of the northwest coast. During harvest time, mechanical threshers are scattered across the fields. Large rice mills and storage buildings are found throughout the area and large diesel trucks haul the surplus to Manila. Narrow-gauge rail lines crisscross the roads from sugarcane fields to the *centrales,* or mills. And towns like Tarlac and Angeles, with modern innovations ranging from up-to-date service stations to suburban developments, reflect all this enterprise.

In approaching Lingayen Gulf there is a gradual change in the agricultural pattern. Though rice fields are still very much in evidence, there is less area given over to the growing of sugarcane and more to coconut trees. The amount of corn grown increases greatly in Pangasinan but decreases farther north in the tobacco-growing areas of La Union and Ilocos Sur. Some of the heavier commercial advertising remains past the Kennon Road turnoff to Baguio and up through the seaside resort area between Bauang and San Fernando. Much of it is undoubtedly a condition of the commercial tourism of this area. Even San Fernando, the provincial capital of La Union Province, has the look of being essentially a center for trade and commerce and not, like Vigan and Laoag, an essentially political and religious center which seems only incidentally a place of business. But by San Fernando the agricultural picture has changed and the transition is almost complete. The groves of coconut trees are fewer and more scattered and, though rice, corn, and tobacco are very much in evidence, individual fields and paddies are smaller—a function of both smaller landholdings and topography. By Darigayos Point the change from a rice-sugar complex to a subsistence rice and market tobacco pattern is complete.

Tobacco has long been an important second crop on the Ilocos coast, but the implementation of a price support program for Virginia leaf in 1954 with concurrent import limitations did much to alter the traditional economic setting. This has been especially true of north-central and eastern Pangasinan, all of La Union and Ilocos Sur, and the southern section of Ilocos Norte. Virginia leaf has not been important in most of Ilocos Norte for reasons that will later be discussed. Farms growing tobacco in La Union and Ilocos Sur are characterized by narrow and relatively tall smoke-drying sheds. From La Union north, mountains, not plains, dominate the landscape, and the abbreviated coastal topography is composed of riverine valleys and intervening ridges extending down to the sea. In Ilocos Norte, only the upper inland section of the Laoag River Valley, specifically the area between Banna and Dingras, has large uninterrupted stretches of paddy fields.

Another characteristic of the region from central Pangasinan north is the more intensive use of house plots for vegetable growing—another indication of Ilocano "industriousness" and the intensity of economic life. Also in evidence are variations in the kinds of vegetables favored and eaten by the Ilocanos, particularly *saloyot (Corchorus olitorius),* a semiwild, leafy vegetable. *Marong-gay (Moringa oleifera)* trees, grown for their leaves, blossoms, and fruit, are found bordering each yard. The farmhouses themselves differ with the substitution of bamboo for the nipa more characteristically used in house construction farther south. But just as it is in most of Southeast Asia so it is along the Ilocos coast that the dominant, central feature of agriculture is rice. The very measure and worth of land is in terms of how much rice it produces; the worth and measure of a man is in terms of how much rice-producing land he owns.

To study communities engaged in rice agriculture, some general knowledge of rice and rice production is obviously necessary. A general knowledge, however, is but the point of departure for approaching and analyzing the functional importance of specific arrangements and conditions in any given location. An inclusive, but hardly exhaustive, list of subjects might include the kind and number of species grown; conditions and types of soils; climatic factors; the techniques and tools employed; the systems of water management and control; the size and distribution of holdings; owning, leasing, tenancy, and mortgaging arrangements; the exchange and contracting of labor; pests and pest control. Such a list is limited and locally defined, and would be among the central features of study in an ecological analysis. In this study are included only those arrangements and activities within the "core" of ecological relationships which are shown to be functionally important to the explanation of variable behavior in Buyon and Mambabanga. Steward describes these as ". . . the constellation of features which are most closely related to subsistence activities and economic arrangements" (1955:37).

Consequently, this does not purport to be an exhaustive study of two Ilocano agricultural systems. A comprehensive ecological study would include much more data on both primary and subsidiary agricultural practices than has been given here. At the outset of the field research it was not, of course, immediately obvious what socioeconomic features would be included in the study, though it seemed reasonable enough to assume that some explanation of behavioral differences would be found in or related to the respective systems of rice production in each area.[1] As demonstrated below, the various aspects of rice production in Buyon and Mambabanga constitute relatively cohesive, interrelated patterns of activity which make up two distinct systems of rice production. The initial impression received by the observer is that the agricultural practices of Buyon and Mambabanga differ in many ways, e.g., varieties grown, harvesting tools used, size of plots, and types of soils. However, the crucial differences in rice production between Buyon and Mambabanga are not to be ascertained by simply listing individual traits and practices; they are, rather, to be discovered by examining the *totality* of the two as productive systems.

The distinction between wet-rice and dry-rice is not one normally employed by, nor especially meaningful to, Ilocanos. The two terms suggest both a *way* of growing rice and a *kind* of rice. In both Buyon and Mambabanga the ways of growing rice are not so neatly or simply distinguished, and the varieties of rice are not classified merely with regard to the medium in which they are grown. Most varieties of rice cultivated in Buyon can be grown in a wet or dry environment, and the Ilocanos do cultivate some varieties in both. The distinction between dry-rice and wet-rice can be applied in only a very rough way to the more involved Ilocano classification of land which is made in terms of field type. We shall see that the Ilocano often uses the same words to classify both field types and varieties of rice, the meaning dependent upon context. The terms "dry-rice" and "wet-rice" are used here in only the most general, descriptive way.

NONIRRIGATED RICE PRODUCTION:
UMA, BENGKAG, AND *BANTAY*

Under the classification which we would describe as "dry," the people of Buyon distinguish three different systems. The first of these—and the only one not represented in Buyon—is a swidden or shifting type of agriculture called *uma.* The typical clearing, burning, planting, harvesting, fallow-field pattern of swidden agriculture is not followed at all in Buyon, though it is fairly common in the hilly country just to the east and even in some of the sandy-loam hillocks and ridges south of Laoag. Though uma farming was not practiced in Buyon, people there claimed at least some familiarity with it.

A second method of dry farming, or (better) type of dry-farmed field, is that of *bengkag*.[2] Unlike the uma, bengkag fields are not shifted nor are they intercropped (i.e., corn and rice, tree crops and rice). Bengkag fields are located on the less fertile, though not overly steep, slopes separating the rice-paddy areas from the steeper ridges. Neither uma nor bengkag are necessarily rice or nonrice fields; the classification refers only to a type of field, not the crop or crops which may, or may not, be grown there. In fact, a rather wide variety of crops are grown in bengkag fields, the two most important in Buyon being rice and sugar. The fields are generally plowed and, because they are "dry," do not hold or retain surface water. The rice is planted in rows and is never transplanted. Where topography and soil conditions permit, a bengkag field may be converted to a wet-rice paddy field. Although topography is important, the crucial consideration in conversion to an irrigated field is the condition of soils in the bengkag field and/or the possibility of improving existing soils.[3]

Finally, there are a few fields in Buyon called *bantay*, literally, "hill" or "mountain." Except for the fact that only one variety of rice is ever planted in the bantay fields, (whereas three and even four varieties may be grown in one of the bengkag fields), essentially the same crops are grown there that are grown in bengkag fields. The essential differences between the bengkag and bantay are (1) bantay fields are steeper than bengkag fields and (2) bantay fields are normally less fertile than bengkag fields (though this may be a function of slope and drainage rather than soils). Uma, bengkag, and bantay fields are not especially important to the economy of Buyon and, as shall be seen, have no importance at all in Mambabanga.[4]

SECONDARY WET-RICE SYSTEMS:
DANAO AND *LUBO*

Wet-rice is irrigated rice, whether watered by natural or artificial means. Not one of the four irrigated types of fields is specifically designated as a rice field, but rice is, almost without exception, the primary crop grown therein. The general term for a field of irrigated rice is *talon* but when, for any reason, other crops are grown (as in the off-season growing of garlic, onions, or tobacco), the term no longer applies. Talon is a field in which rice is actually growing, but the land itself is classified on a different basis. Two of the four irrigated types of fields, called *danao* and *lubo,* share the same source and means of water supply; both are watered from beneath—from the seasonal rise and fall of local water tables. Such fields occur in the very lowest areas of water drainage forming gently terraced amphitheaters of land. They are inundated with water throughout the year, seldom if ever draining.

The distinction between danao and lubo depends on the feasibility of working the land with plow and water buffalo. Danao (the word is derived from and also means "lake" or "pond") fields can be worked with the buffalo-drawn plow; lubo (literally, "mudhole") fields can be worked only by hand with a hoe, the buffalo floundering and unable to move in such fields. The practicality of using animals is, in part at least, dictated by local soil characteristics (such as sticky clays), but the distinction between lubo and danao remains one of utility—whether, in fact, a water buffalo can be used. Utility is the underlying factor in all systems of land classification. Both danao and lubo fields are characterized by various swampy varieties of weeds and, because of this, they can be easily distinguished from the surrounding lands. Because they are constantly under water, these fields can support only rice, and this necessarily precludes the second cropping of less water-tolerant crops like garlic or tobacco. However, the water also makes it possible to grow the late-ripening and more productive varieties of rice—the *bayag* varieties mentioned below.

PRIMARY WET-RICE SYSTEMS:
MASAYOD AND *BAYAG*

Masayod fields are those naturally irrigated by the heavy rains from July through September. Before the introduction of a government irrigation system, the Laoag-Vintar Irrigation Canal, most fields were naturally irrigated. Masayod fields now constitute less than 5 percent of the total rice lands. Water in such fields is "trapped," but arrangements must be made for the movement and draining of water during the rainy season. The word *masayod* also refers to the varieties of rice which one would normally plant in masayod fields: the early or short-term varieties which ripen in about 120 days. This necessarily approximates the three- or four-month rainy season.[5]

In volume and in value, the most important lands are those irrigated by man-made irrigation systems; such fields are called *bayag*. Bayag also refers to the varieties of rice grown in bayag fields. These are the late-maturing or long-term varieties which normally require 150–180 days for maturation.[6] With the rainy season limited to three or four months, artificial irrigation is obviously necessary to maintain a crop beyond that time limitation.

As Geertz has noted, the key factor in wet-rice agriculture is the supply and control of water (1964:31). Much more is involved than just being able to depend on a regular supply of water. The greater the number of tillers, or shoots, that a seedling will produce, the greater the productivity; and tillering is considerably higher among the later ripening varieties of rice. Controlled irrigation also results in improved fertility as a result of the nutrient-carrying role of water (Grist 1959:12, 28–49). Besides increasing the productivity of rice, it practically assures a second crop. Although second crops are normally grown on masayod fields in Ilocos Norte, their success is much less reliable, and the reliability of a second crop decreases gradually as one moves north along the Ilocos coast. It is in the dry, northern Ilocos region that communal irrigation systems developed.

The area of artificially irrigated fields stands in inverse relationship to the amount of Virginia leaf tobacco which can be grown. Although "native" tobacco has been grown along the whole of the Ilocos coast, the introduction of Virginia leaf did not affect those areas with man-made irrigation systems. This is because Virginia leaf, which must be transplanted from one to two months earlier than native tobacco, conflicts with bayag production. There are no more than a half-dozen small fields of Virginia leaf grown in Buyon, and all are masayod fields. We shall see that the presence of cooperative irrigation societies and the absence of Virginia leaf tobacco has had political consequences for Ilocos Norte as well.

THE AGRICULTURAL CYCLE

The agricultural year begins with the first rains of late May, before the onset of the actual wet season. Because of the uncertainty of either the volume or duration of rains, the first fields to be prepared and planted are the masayod, or naturally irrigated, paddies. Because only 33 of 653 separate paddy fields (5 percent of the total) in Buyon are naturally irrigated, there is not the intense activity with this crop that there is in some other villages of Ilocos Norte or in the vast majority of barrios further south along the Ilocos coast. The fields themselves are small, from 100 to 1,000 square meters, and the eight, nine, ten, or more different fields of a single farmer are often located in different sections of the barrio. Such minuscule plots seldom require, or for that matter permit, the use of more than one animal or of a work force larger than that of the nuclear family. Where fields are large or where, because of a technological problem, the planting cannot be staggered over time, extra labor will be contracted (if possible, from among one's friends and neighbors). Weeds and stubble from the previous season are plowed under, and the fields are then harrowed. At the same time dikes are repaired and reinforced. A small section of a plot or the whole of a single plot (if several are to be planted in the same area) will be set aside as the seedbed. The seeds are germinated at home for a day, after which they are planted in the seedbeds. The seedlings are allowed to grow from three to four weeks at which time they are transplanted to the remainder of the area.

Both glutinous *(diket)* and nonglutinous *(maguprak)* masayod varieties are planted, but the glutinous rice, used primarily for making sweet cakes and cookies, accounts for a very small amount of the total rice grown. The nonglutinous varieties of masayod are planted slightly before the glutinous ones. While seedlings of the masayod are still developing but before they have been transplanted, work is begun on the bayag paddies, the first efforts again being the preparation of seedbeds. Plowing and harrowing for all fields lasts through the first three weeks of June and, in some instances, even as late as mid-July. The exact time at which all of this begins depends, as it does with the masayod varieties, upon the beginning of the rainy season.

The same plowing-harrowing procedure is followed on the bayag fields, and the germinated rice is subsequently planted in the seedbeds. During the three to four weeks in which the seedlings develop, the other terraces are prepared for transplanting. Much of July will be devoted to pulling, bundling, and transporting the seedlings to the various fields, and to the laborious, time-consuming work of resetting the plants in clusters of two to three each. The seedlings are set eight to ten inches apart (though seldom in any organized row or line) to allow tillers to develop. The tillers eventually fill in to form the seemingly solid green cover. Including the masayod types already mentioned, a total of eight different varieties of rice is commonly grown in Buyon. A cross section of types is selected on the basis of maturation periods, in order to stagger both planting and harvesting, as well as to accommodate personal preference and relative plant productivity. The four varieties of bayag rice grown, both glutinous and nonglutinous types, have maturation periods from 150 to 180 days.

A single, one-acre plot of but one variety would require contract or reciprocal labor arrangements. On the other hand, several separate fields, totaling an acre and planted with types having different maturation periods, can be handled by a single family. The size of family holdings in Buyon has been reduced to the point where exchange or contract labor is no longer needed or desired. Very little weeding is done during the period of growth. Weeds are controlled by the natural (though not always efficient) constraints of the aquatic environment of the paddy field and by the planting of the weed-resistant varieties of rice favored by the Ilocanos.

Around the third week of October, the first rice, the early-ripening masayod varieties, is harvested. Though little land is planted with these varieties in Buyon, other villages just south and towards Laoag have a predominance of such fields. This harvest is one of intense activity in these barrios because this rice crop, unlike that of the bayag, is selected to ripen quickly and at about the same time. This is done to harvest the crop at the earliest possible date and then to plant a rapidly maturing second crop such as garlic, eggplant, or tomatoes. These crops must be planted while some rains are left and before the soils dry out. Because the masayod all ripens at about the same time, a larger combined labor force is needed. This labor force comes from villages (such as Buyon) which do not have large amounts of masayod lands and from the unemployed and underemployed population of Laoag. In the absence of controlled irrigation the economy of staggering production is very nearly absent in masayod fields. When second crops are grown in these fields, every effort must be made to take maximum advantage of soil moisture; thus, time becomes the most important variable.

The main harvest for villages like Buyon, those that have large areas of artificially irrigated rice, begins in late December with the ripening of the glutinous varieties. This is immediately followed in January by the harvest of the nonglutinous varieties. During this period, but arranged to fit the staggered schedule, the bayag varieties which have been growing in the danao and lubo fields ripen and are harvested. The whole harvest period of bayag fields covers from five to six weeks. Persons with larger farms or smaller families, and those individuals who have more than a few danao or lubo fields, must make arrangements for obtaining extra labor. Because the number of these persons is small and because work exchanges demand equal time, it is often impossible to arrange for exchange labor. Consequently, villagers will be contracted to harvest some of the crop, the "wage" amounting to 5 percent of what each harvester cuts.

The method of harvesting in Ilocos Norte differs considerably from that in Isabela Province and much of the rest of the Philippines. A hand knife, called a *rakem,* is the harvesting tool used. This implement consists of a small, three- to five-inch blade set crosswise on a wooden handle which is held in the palm of the hand. With the same hand the harvester grasps a single stalk of rice and pulls it across the blade, the blade passing between the second and third fingers. Each stalk is then taken in the other hand and when enough has been gathered to make up a *bettek,* a bundle about the size of one's wrist or forearm, it is tied. Six bettek are tied together to form a *pungo,* and two pungo make up another measure, the *baar.* The largest measure of unthreshed rice is an *uyon,* which is composed of ten baar, and which is equal to just under eleven fifty-pound sacks of *pagay,* or unthreshed rice. The number of pounds per uyon, and the smaller units therein, varies from one area to another. These sheaf or shock-like bundles are allowed to mature in the sun for a few days and are then stored in the granaries until threshed and winnowed by hand as the need arises. A great deal of pride is taken not only in the volume of rice but also in the neatness with which it is cut and bundled.

The most important second crops planted in bayag fields are mongo beans, tobacco, corn, and string beans. These crops are planted so as to mature during the month of May. Consequently, tobacco, the crop requiring the longest period of growth, is planted in late January to be followed in late February by corn and in early March by mongo beans and string beans. The off-season crops are either grown for home consumption or for marketing in Bacarra or Laoag, though the amounts produced may be pitifully small. In some of the sloping areas, especially in two little vales in the southern part of Buyon, within the sitio of Calutit, certain bengkag and bantay fields are given over to a single crop of sugarcane. Most of this sugarcane goes into the production of *basi,* a wine made from the fermentation of the sugarcane juice which is either sold or exchanged for rice. Besides the house gardens, which run to a wide range of garden "crops," the only other plant of importance is the camote or sweet potato *(kamotit).* This is grown in the bantay fields, and both greens and roots are consumed.

RICE PRODUCTION AS A SYSTEM

Rice production in Ilocos Norte and Isabela follows a similar, basic pattern. In fact, throughout the whole of Southeast Asia, there is a marked likeness in wet-rice agriculture: the terracing and diking of fields; the water buffalo and moldboard plow; the process of transplanting from prepared seedbeds; the flooding and draining of fields; the often stalk-by-stalk method of harvesting. Yet this basic sameness and uniformity belies important technological, economical, and social arrangements which may suggest keys to understanding many regional and local differences in behavior and custom. Buyon and Mambabanga are generally the same, but, on a finer level of comparison, there are specific and important differences.

A distinctive technological feature of harvesting rice along most of the Ilocos coast is the continual and almost exclusive use of the rakem, or rice knife. The tool itself, having a wide distribution and a history of traditional usage in Southeast Asia (particularly within Malaysia), is not uniquely Ilocano. Grist noted:

> This implement is well known in Malaya as *pisau penuai,* in the Philippines as *yatab,* Sarawak as *ketap,* Java as *aniani* . . . Where the *yatab* is not used—and this includes all India, Burma, Indo-China and Japan—the sickle is employed, and this implement appears to be gradually replacing the *yatab* in Malaya and Java. [1959:129–130]

The sickle, or *kompay,* has also replaced the hand knife in most of the Philippines, nonetheless, the rakem continues to be employed almost exclusively along the Ilocos coast and in Mountain Province. It continues to be used, under certain circumstances, in Cagayan, Isabela, Nueva Vizcaya, Zambales, and many other provinces. Its continued use is not based simply on its relative efficiency or inefficiency. Nor can its persistence be accounted for under the rubrical reasoning of "traditional practices and beliefs." In almost every case—and in each one examined in Ilocos Norte and Isabela—the rakem is associated with the growing of awned or "bearded" varieties of rice, the "beard" or hair extending beyond the individual spikelet from one-half to as much as one and one-half inches. The awned varieties of rice are known collectively as *pagay iloko*.

South of Laoag, in the area between San Nicolas and the coast (see map 2), many fields (bengkag) are dry-farmed to awnless varieties of rice, and, in that area, for awnless varieties only, the sickle is used to harvest the ripened crop. In Buyon, all but one of the nine commonly grown varieties are awned, and these eight types are all harvested with the rakem; the single awnless variety is harvested with the sickle. Although both methods are laborious and demand intensive labor, the rakem requires almost five times as many man hours as does the sickle. However, savings in man hours are not the most important consideration. The rakem does have certain technological advantages: because each pannicle is harvested individually, a minimal amount of grain is lost or overlooked; the shattering of individual grains is greatly reduced; and fewer extraneous weeds are collected.

Obviously, something more than a few technological advantages is involved in the use of the rakem, because the awnless types grown nearby are always harvested with the sickle. If wastage were the only or primary consideration, the rice knife could be employed for awnless varieties as well. The answer is to be found not by comparing the rakem to the sickle but, rather, by examining the rakem as a part of the prevalent system of rice production in Ilocos Norte, a system in which the rakem is but one interrelated element in the cultivation of pagay iloko.

When an individual is asked why he uses the rakem instead of the kompay, he will normally reply, "It is because of the way rice is tied and bundled, and the way it is stored in the granaries." If the investigator is asking the informant this question in terms of comparing the rakem and the kompay the answer seems evasive, a sort of circular reasoning—which, in effect, it is. The Ilocano simply does not consider the rakem as something distinct or apart from the total process of growing pagay iloko; the question posed to him is a false one. His "circular reasoning" reflects the fact that the rakem, like the tying, bundling, and storing, is but a part of a series, or set, of activities which he sees as logically related. Thusly considered, the rakem is but a single element in a complex system of rice production which, *as a system,* has technological functions of a wider scope which relate to matters of rice physiology, religion, esthetics, taste, social organization, work arrangements, and plant adaptation. The rakem must be viewed as something more than just an interesting cultural artifact.

In each case, the rakem is used in the harvest of awned varieties of rice, the pagay iloko, which are considered unsuitable for threshing by mechanical means. Also, awned varieties store best when left unthreshed, whereas the opposite condition is found with the highly polished varieties grown for commercial purposes. With neither mechanization nor commercialization being features of rice agriculture in Ilocos Norte, the growing of awned varieties does not present a problem. Rather than being unsuitable, there are certain physiological characteristics of pagay iloko which account for its persistence in the Ilocos situation. First, the total water requirements for these types are generally lower than for awnless varieties; and the Ilocos coast, as noted earlier, is the only major water-deficient area in the Philippines. Second, these varieties can be grown on soils of low fertility, and the soils of this area are relatively poor and impoverished through overwork.[7] Third, the awned varieties of rice are more resistant to the infestations of birds and insects and, possibly, to rice blast. Fourth, because of thick stems and foliage plus a rapid initial growth, they tend to shade out weeds more effectively than other varieties. Fifth, they resist lodging, or falling over, making them more resistant to wind damage and easier to harvest with a rice knife. Finally, they shatter less than most other types do, resulting in less wastage. The varieties of pagay iloko are well suited to the technology and environment of the Ilocos coast. But, again, the physiological characteristics, as well as the technological factors, are but a part of the total process of rice production in the Ilocos.[8]

Matters of taste are important, and all types of pagay iloko, like most bearded varieties, are relatively aromatic, a quality which Ilocanos maintain is important. Ilocanos also complain that the tasteless, "imported" varieties do not fill the stomach or give sufficient energy to do a day's work. Since pagay iloko is not machine milled and polished, most of the more nutritious, vitamin-rich endosperms are not lost. Thus the Ilocano's preference in taste is nutritionally sound. Esthetic values too are involved, and the Ilocano appreciates not only the volume of rice he produces but the neatness with which it is cut, tied, bundled, trimmed, and stored. The Ilocano farmer takes great pride in the quality and quantity of the maturing sheaves of rice which he sets in front of his house.

Religious elements are also involved and are especially important in terms of the "conservative" character of spirit beliefs. Religious group ceremonialism is not specifically associated with rice production in either Buyon or Mambabanga. Only the irrigation societies have a ceremonial-religious importance with respect to agricultural activities, and the activity there, as we shall see, is not involved with the planting or harvesting of rice. The primary importance of religion in the total system of rice production is tied up in a highly personalized set of spirit beliefs. In dealing with pagay iloko, or any other rice varieties, the individual farmer is not concerned with upsetting a "rice god"; his concern is with the local spirits *(anitos)* who have traditionally been associated with him at this particular place and with the growing of this particular variety of pagay iloko (or whatever). Spirits come in all shapes and sizes, and they are often classified on the basis of their appearance (e.g., *kibaan,* the "little people") and generalized kinds of behavior. However, it is their specific character more than their general nature which is important. Spirits are like people in that each has a personality and must be dealt with accordingly. Lynch noted that "spirits . . . are normally neither for nor against one, but [are] dangerously able to do no end of harm if aroused [and] it seems eminently logical to take all means possible to discover what these spirits want one to do" (1961:106). Pagay iloko has only specifically local religious importance. Like the characteristics of a particular kind of soil or local problems of water management, the specific conditions involving the spirit world are necessarily understood and dealt with if one is to be a successful farmer.

Whereas the farmer in Buyon may work alone, not engaging in reciprocal forms of labor exchange, he is hardly free of social constraints or coercion. The restrictions placed upon him are not developed and nurtured in the give-and-take of routine agricultural activity; instead, he is constrained and coerced by the totality of what others are doing individually, each on his own. The relationship of field neighbors, unlike the relationship which will be demonstrated for house neighbors, does not serve as the basis for regular patterns of social interaction in Buyon. In fact, when tenants have changed or when individuals have come from different barrios, field neighbors may be, and may remain, virtual strangers. The need to coordinate activities results from the essentially technical demands of the local agricultural system; the technology of Buyon does not include regular patterns of social interaction.

When a water supply is involved, and especially when that water is supplied from a man-made irrigation system, the work in a given area must generally coincide. One farmer cannot be tracking through the fields of others to plow his own lands while his neighbors' crops are ripening. One individual cannot flood his own land when his neighbors wish to keep their lands dry nor, conversely, can he grow a dry crop when others around his are irrigating. Coordination, not cooperation, "organizes" the activities of individual farmers, and the coordination derives from the demands of the rice technology employed, the complex of fields involved, the subsistence needs of any individual family, and the implied threat of coercion.

In the case of the irrigation societies, examined at length in chapter 12, specific activities regarding the maintenance and repair of the system are based upon both the need for cooperation and the fear of coercion—specifically the loss of irrigation water. The cooperation and exchange of labor involved in these cases, however, concerns work and activities associated only with the irrigation system; there is no direct relationship involved in farming the fields so irrigated. With respect to the actual growing of crops, individuals and individual families work alone, the coordination of their activities being based upon the mechanical and technical demands of the irrigation system.

The growing of late-maturing, bayag varieties of rice involves a primary and, for all practical purposes, unalterable commitment in the agricultural pattern of central Ilocos Norte. As a consequence of this the growth of off-season crops, for example, "native" tobacco, onions, garlic, in the same wet-rice fields must be made to conform and complement the growth of pagay iloko, specifically, the bayag varieties. A very pronounced example of the need to conform to existing agricultural commitments can be seen in the successful introduction of Virginia tobacco in the southern Ilocos region during the 1950s. Virginia tobacco was accepted as an off-season crop only in those areas which produced the early-maturing, masayod, varieties of rice; it was not accepted in areas having extensive man-made irrigation systems—the areas which have traditionally produced late-maturing varieties of rice. The off-season following the growth of bayag is insufficiently long to permit the growth of Virginia leaf, and this automatically precludes the cultivation of Virginia tobacco in most of central Ilocos Norte.

The relationship between first and second cropping, as well as the primacy of bayag production, is well understood by the farmers in Buyon. The commitment to rice grown on lands irrigated by man-made systems prohibits growing any crop which would interfere or conflict with the established commitment to bayag rice. To date, changes and additions have been worked out within the limits of the existing system, either as modifications in the pattern of second cropping or in increased intensification of bayag production. Intensification and specialization also result in greater rigidity of the established pattern. This, in essence, is what Geertz has called "agricultural involution": ". . . the overdriving of an established form in such a way that it becomes rigid through an inward overelaboration of detail" (1963:82). The situation which Geertz has so effectively demonstrated for Java and that which has been described here differ in a number of ways, not the least of which would be the "degree" of intensity (however one might attempt to measure it). However, both involve specific adaptations to a highly labor-intensive, wet-rice agricultural pattern.[9] We shall see, when we examine rice production in Mambabanga, that a similar commitment has been made to bayag rice there, but that commitment is neither so intense nor of exactly the same type.

NOTES

1. To explain differences, it is necessary to collect and analyze data which do not explain, or are only incidental to the explanation of, variable behavior. Obviously the pertinent relationships are not "self-evident."

2. Vanoverbergh's *Iloko-English Dictionary* (1956:48) defines bengkag [his spelling: *bangkag*, a phonetic rendering of the word as spoken in the southern Ilocos area] as: "field . . . not a rice field."

3. I observed two such conversions—one in Buyon itself and a second in a barrio south of Laoag. Although a small amount of clay soil was introduced in the field in Buyon, it would be presumptious to state that this was the only, or most important, factor involved. The dynamics of soils, water, varieties of rice, and so forth are too little understood even by authorities on rice production (see Grist 1959:11–15), much less comprehended with the more-or-less-limited knowledge an anthropologist brings to the subject.

4. Uma farming has been important in the pioneering of Cagayan Valley. As mentioned in chapter 3, early agriculture in Mambabanga was based upon a fallow-field (uma) pattern. Ilocanos in both Buyon and Mambabanga see uma as a means by which uncultivated lands are transformed into permanent fields, though they do not see all uma farming this way as it often is itself an end to agricultural development. Uma farming was carried on in

Isabela, even in the flattest areas, for some years after the initial settling, and still is the main means by which the Ilocanos open up lands to fixed forms of agriculture. In fact, *aguma* (ag + uma) means to clear land for cultivation. The Ilocano "pioneer" does not shift settlements; he simply follows a fallow-field system until conditions of the land are suitable for adapting to nonfallowing systems.

5. There are several factors which distinguish one variety from another and which crosscut the four basic subspecies of *Orysa sativa: indica, japonica, brevindica,* and *brevis.* Whether the rice is glutinous or nonglutinous, awned or awnless, short grained or long grained, aromatic or nonaromatic determines the subspecies into which it is classified. Masayod varieties have one or more of these characteristics but all masayod varieties are short-term maturing types. Long-term varieties require 150–180 days for maturation.

6. The fact that masayod and bayag are the rice varieties grown on lands which are called by the same names does not confuse the fact (for the Ilocano) that the words have different references. In Isabela, for instance, one landowner was growing three masayod crops of rice a year in his bayag fields. Though some people felt this was bad farming, they were not confused semantically.

7. Reed states that overworking the land reduces the nitrogen content of the soil. This, together with the pronounced monsoonal climate of the Ilocos coast, has created ideal conditions for growing Virginia leaf tobacco (1963:356–359). Again, however, the complex relationships between soils, water, rice varieties, etc., make any statement on the merits of soil fertility most tenuous.

8. I am especially indebted to Dr. Akira Tanaka, plant physiologist, International Rice Research Institute, Los Baños, Laguna Province, for information on the general place, importance, and particular characteristics of awned varieties of rice. His information (which is in the form of personal correspondence as well as conversations with members of his staff) on the adaptive features of these varieties is important for understanding rice agriculture in Ilocos Norte. Dr. Tanaka has informed me that these varieties are classified as *Orysa sativa subjaponica,* a more or less intermediate group between *O. s. indica* and *O. s. japonica.* These varieties, he states, are traditional and are, by and large, limited to insular Southeast Asia—those areas in which the rice knife has been commonly used.

9. Although my study is not concerned with the theoretical implications of the concept of "agricultural involution," the similarities are worth mentioning here.

6

RICE CULTIVATION IN MAMBABANGA

THE PATTERN OF RICE PRODUCTION

Mambabanga is both like and unlike Buyon in its pattern of rice cultivation. Even the most cursory observation will reveal some differences, but the more apparent contrasts are only suggestive of the underlying social character and differentiation. Although rice also constitutes the basis of Mambabanga's economy, over 50 percent of all rice produced is sold through commercial outlets, some of it perhaps eventually finding its way to the marketplace in Bacarra or Laoag. Corn, rather than onions, garlic, or native tobacco, dominates the off-season production in irrigated fields, although quantities of these crops are also sold. The essentially mechanical techniques of the wider technological system are structured around the use of the water buffalo and moldboard plow. Yet, both in terms of tools and techniques, there are differences: the kompay is used in place of the rakem and the exchange of labor, *ammuyo,* is extensively employed. Both masayod and bayag varieties are grown in Mambabanga but, with few exceptions, these different early- and late-maturing varieties of rice are all awnless types introduced well over a decade ago from central Luzon; they are not the traditional "bearded" Ilocano subspecies of pagay iloko. To understand the differences which obtain between Buyon and Mambabanga, it is necessary to examine closely the wider regional situation confronting and involving Mambabanga.

The most striking geographical feature of Isabela is the flat, almost unbroken expanse of plains in the southern part of the province, from slightly north of Cauayan south to the mountains of the Caraballo Sur in Nueva Vizcaya. Coming from the Ilocos between the months of January and May, when the fields of the west coast are dry and brown, the visitor to Cagayan Valley is struck by the vast green extension of paddies and grasslands. This is the result of the less variable rainfall conditions of northern Luzon's central valley. With rice growing in the fields, the southern valley is a checkerboard of green, broken only by the occasional road or waterway, with most villages strung out along throughfares, ridges, and streams. Some barrios, situated on small hillocks that only slightly rise above the nearby rice lands, form compact and distinct, island-like communities. Much less commonly do the barrios of Isabela blend one into another as they do in Ilocos Norte.

The commercial character of rice-growing in Isabela is visible everywhere. Large diesel trucks, either arriving empty from, or departing loaded with rice for, Manila, are more numerous than are private autos. Though more commonly found in towns, rice mills and storehouses are even located in some of the rural barrios. The mills vary in size from the smallest operation working with a four-horsepower disc-huller—milling what the average family wants to keep for home consumption—to the large, diesel-powered band-huskers that are capable of turning out several tons of rice per day. At harvest time, further mechanization and commercialism is evident with the movement into Isabela of tractor-powered threshers from central Luzon. Mostly American-made McCormick threshers are used and a few are to be found year round on the larger, absentee-owned estates of Isabela. Most, however, come into Isabela from the south for the harvest only.[1] At places in the fields selected for the actual threshing will be a score or more of *mandala,* or stacks—ten to fifteen feet in height and eight to ten feet in diameter. The pannicles of rice are all faced inward and the stack capped with straw for protection against the rain during the two weeks or more of drying and maturing which follows the harvest and precedes the actual threshing operation. One or more mandala will represent the rice production of a single family in a given area of fields, the total number of stacks representing the number of field owners and/or tenants for a particular block or section of land. These displays are impressive when compared to the rows of small bundles drying before the homes of Ilocos Norte.

The mills, the trucking, and the mechanical threshing are all made possible by the fact that the average Ilocano farmer in Cagayan Valley produces a marketable surplus of rice. The typical family in Mambabanga is able to grow three to four times the amount of rice it needs for home consumption and, because more rice is grown, the home consumption "needs" are greater in Mambabanga than in Buyon.[2] All this is, of course, a part of the greater economic and social differences which separate Isabela and Ilocos Norte. The importance of these differences can be understood by comparing the agricultural patterns of the two areas.

It was mentioned in chapter 4 that the small ridge on which the houses of Mambabanga are located acts as an effective protection against the infrequent, but very serious, floods of the Magat River. In 1936, one of the worst floods in the history of Isabela forced a prolonged evacuation of the people from the barrios between this ridge and the river. A number of families from the barrio of Concepcion (see chapters 12 and 14) received permission from the established residents of Mambabanga to remain permanently, and, though their lands are several kilometers away, they are able to commute to their fields, all of which lie beyond Macanao Creek. This ridge also represents the boundary dividing the naturally irrigated and artificially irrigated fields. Below the ridge, to the north and west and extending for three to four miles to the nonirrigated levee-lands bordering the Magat, are the artificially irrigated, bayag fields; above the ridge, to the south and east of Mambabanga, are the naturally irrigated masayod fields.

The people of Mambabanga farm both areas. Most of the land which they themselves own is on the lower, richer, alluvial flood plain—the area of bayag fields. These are the lands which were originally pioneered by the Society Mambabanga. On the other hand, the less rich, less productive masayod fields are owned almost exclusively by one of three absentee landlords, and are worked on tenancy arrangements by the people of Mambabanga and people from the nearby barrio of Harana. Thus, Mambabanga is directly involved in the provincial economy of Isabela in the form of small, owner-operator, commercial farming and as a supplier of tenants for the large, highly commercial absentee-landlord estates.

NONIRRIGATED RICE PRODUCTION

Unlike the situation in Buyon, no dry-rice is grown in Mambabanga although, as we shall see, dry-rice systems were extensively employed in the process of developing wet-rice fields during the formative years. Only the smallest amount of land is available or used for permanent bengkag fields, and none of these are used for the cultivation of rice. Instead, these small areas are commonly planted to single crops of mongo beans, corn, or sweet potatoes with an occasional intercropping of bananas. In Mambabanga these lands are located on the less steeply sloped areas of the ridge itself, and they are few and scattered. The major area of lands which are classified bengkag, none of which are to be found within the limits of Mambabanga, are the very rich and almost annually inundated levee-lands which parallel the major rivers of the valley. These are, and have traditionally been, the prime tobacco-growing areas. It is these areas which were being farmed by the indigenous lowland Christian group, the Ibanags, when the first Ilocano settlers began arriving over one hundred years ago.

SECONDARY WET-RICE SYSTEMS:
DANAO AND *LUBO*

There are a few swampy, boggy places which might be converted to danao or lubo plots but, in fact, have not been so developed. One such area borders the small reservoir behind the dam of a local irrigation cooperative, the Union Bacarrina. The owner of this land claims that the periodic—weekly and even daily—variability of the water table makes the risk of growing crops there excessively high.[3] Population pressures have not made the farming of such marginally productive lands necessary in Isabela, though undoubtedly the time is not far off when this will no longer hold true.

PRIMARY WET-RICE SYSTEMS:
MASAYOD AND *BAYAG*

The development of masayod and bayag fields in Mambabanga followed a pattern of farming which may still be found along the western slopes of the Sierra Madres where the pioneering of new lands continues.[4] Interestingly enough, the varieties of rice being grown in the new farm areas of the Sierra Madres are all reported to be the traditional pagay iloko. Inasmuch as these areas are seldom accessible by road, the people there are largely restricted to an essentially subsistence economy and consume most of whatever they grow. As mentioned in the previous chapter, pagay iloko has characteristics which make it suitable for conditions faced in the isolated pioneering settlements. It is resistant to bird and insect pests, weed resistant, and has favorable storage properties.

Varieties of pagay iloko were grown in Mambabanga from the time the land was opened to agriculture until the introduction of commercially suitable varieties from central Luzon. Like many people in the foothills of the Sierra Madres today, the original settlers had no market outlets for rice. They were, at the same time, faced with similar environmental problems which they more or less successfully met by cultivating pagay iloko. Family size by and large set the limits for family lands cultivated; a man could acquire no more labor than he actually could return in exchange. The reciprocal exchange of work assured a man that he had enough labor at a given moment and could thus complete a task (e.g., clearing, burning, or planting) more efficiently—efficient in the sense that any single task could be completed in a relatively short period of time without prolonging the completion of an agricultural phase in a single field. The limit of lands which any one family could farm was generally about three hectares, or seven and one-half acres. Expansion beyond this was impossible because there is an obvious physical limit to the number of hours a single individual could exchange. To expand beyond this required the hiring of extra labor, and extra labor did not become available until transportation facilities permitted the influx of seasonal workers from Ilocos Norte and elsewhere. Despite the fact that some families owned fifteen or twenty hectares while others owned fewer than five, the original settlers actually farmed no more than three hectares of land.

Uma farming was less a system of using land than it was of clearing land for more fixed forms of cultivation. The length of the fallow period for any one field depended upon the size of the family holding, and so a family which owned twelve hectares would have a fallow period three times as long as would a family with a total holding of six hectares. The Ilocano farmer did not, however, see his future in swidden farming; use of the water buffalo quickly converted uma fields into settled, bengkag fields and these, after being worked a number of years, were subsequently leveled to catch and hold water as masayod fields. The final stage, bayag, came with the completion of a local irrigation system in 1939. In the initial stages of converting the lands to wet-rice paddies, before contracted labor became available or while it remained in short supply, the three hectares being farmed were commonly divided into three different crops: one hectare of rice, one of garden crops (corn, beans, bananas, etc.), and one hectare of tobacco—the "cash crop." The best areas for growing tobacco were (and still are) along banks of the major rivers. Tobacco grown away from the river areas is of poorer quality. Furthermore, in the absence of roads, transportation from the place of cultivation to towns along the river was difficult and costly. As a consequence, little cash could be earned from a hectare of tobacco in locations removed from the river—little more than enough to buy the tools and household items that a family would need to last the year.

CHANGE AND MAINTENANCE OF THE
TECHNOLOGICAL SYSTEMS

The traditional cottage industries for which Ilocos Norte is noted persisted in Isabela only as long as agriculture remained an isolated, essentially subsistence-based economy with limited opportunities for individuals to sell or buy in a market system. With the opening of Cagayan Valley to commercial trade, with the involvement of Mambabanga in that trade, and with money available to purchase manufactured goods, the requirements for cloth, hats, pottery, bolos, etc., were more quickly and economically satisfied by buying cheaply made factory items, usually Japanese or American in origin. The traditional Ilocano crafts declined and, with money available from the sale of rice, it was no longer necessary to maintain these time-consuming, burdensome tasks.[5]

The key to the commercial development of rice agriculture came with the opening of the area to roads. The main link for Cagayan Valley with the rest of Luzon is southwest across the Caraballo Sur Mountains; through the upper Magat River Valley; past Bayombong, the provincial capital of Nueva Vizcaya; and finally south over the eastern side of the central plain to Manila. This road, National Highway No. 5, is the main commercial artery for the whole of Cagayan Valley.

The shortest route from Ilocos Norte into Cagayan Valley is around the northern tip of Luzon on National Highway No. 3 which connects with National Highway No. 5, the main north-south road for the valley, just south of Aparri in Cagayan Province. This northern, coastal link from Bacarra and Laoag is less commonly used than the indirect but more reliable route south along the Ilocos coast and back over the Caraballo Sur range. Though the journey from Bacarra to Ilagan is well over 150 kilometers longer along this southern route, the road is both better surfaced and less often closed due to flooding or landslides. Some buses do ply the rugged northern route but they always terminate at Aparri, on the northern coast, and transfers are made from there. On the other hand, the traveler can take one of several Bacarra-Ilagan buses which go via the longer southern route.

Because of the staggered agricultural seasons between the Ilocos coast and Cagayan Valley, Ilocanos from the west coast came in large numbers following their own annual harvest to work the rice crop of central Isabela. In the early years of these seasonal migrations, laborers were paid as much as 50 percent of all they harvested—ten times what is now the normal pay for contracted labor. The attraction of high-paying work, better tenancy arrangements, and new lands still to be settled induced many Ilocano laborers to remain or to return later and establish their own farms. This seasonal "preview" was undoubtedly instrumental in the decisions of many individuals to take up permanent settlement in Isabela. The influx of labor began to increase in size in the late 1920s and did not decline until several years after World War II, by which time the domestic labor supply was more adequate and wage inducements (down to 5 percent of the harvest) were no longer sufficient to offset the cost and expense of making the trip. It was at this time, too, that Virginia tobacco was becoming important as a second, off-season crop on the west coast.

The opening of roads and the availability of surplus labor set the stage and made it possible to bring in mechanical threshers from central Luzon. Threshers began to appear in the late 1930s but they nearly disappeared during the war years. In the late 1940s with the importation of new machines and with the availability of parts, threshers began to return to Cagayan Valley in increasing numbers. The introduction of threshers was necessarily contingent on the changeover to more productive, more commercially suitable varieties of rice. It naturally followed that *pagay tagalog,* the nonbearded, awnless types found in the important rice-growing areas of south and central Luzon, would accompany the introduction of threshing machines from the same region. The special adaptive features which pagay iloko had in Ilocos Norte and in the pioneering areas of Isabela were no longer so important. In effect, a new environment developed with a new set of demands, limitations, and opportunities—the demands, limitations, and opportunities which stem from a commercial rice economy.

The first to accept and adopt the new system were the large landholders, either those who had filed for title to land on speculation or those among the original settlers who, through enterprise, circumstance, or guile, had expanded their original holdings. The successful growing of the new varieties by the owners of the large farms was followed by the raising of these new varieties by owners of small farms and by tenant farmers, those persons less willing or less able to change. Besides the fact that change to commercial rice was now possible and that the Ilocano farmers were motivated towards that change, there were sound technological and economic reasons for following the lead of the large landholders. For instance, no contract laborer was willing to work for the 5 percent that he could harvest with the rakem as against the 5 percent that he could harvest with a sickle—a tool five times more "efficient" than the hand-knife. In addition, almost all villages like Mambabanga had some full-time and many part-time tenants who worked on the large estates, and these workers could hardly afford to exchange labor with the large landholders at such an unequal rate as five-to-one. To this could be added the hours which would be lost in threshing and milling. The acceptance of the new system by a large number of people would have made it increasingly difficult, if not impossible, especially with labor still in relatively short supply, to continue with the more labor-demanding needs of the pagay iloko system. The "logic" of growing pagay tagalog was emphasized even more by the fact that, in good soils, it easily outproduced pagay iloko, and the soils of Isabela are among the best in the Philippines. However, the fact is that Ilocanos were motivated and did make the change. It should be noted, though, that they really had little choice. Once the change was made by the large landholders, the small farmers were virtually required to follow suit; the change was only facilitated by the fact that they did consider it desirable.

The innovative pattern of the very large farm operations still holds true—and necessarily so. As discussed in the previous chapter, the dependence and interdependence of the patterns of work and cooperation, together with the particular technological demands of the rice system used, requires a high degree of conformity among small farm operators in a given area; it is highly unlikely that single cultivators would or could make innovations or adopt new techniques which conflict with existing practices. Owners of large farm operations, with their control over a large number of tenants and with the actual capital to invest, can afford to risk (socially as well as financially) adopting a system recommended by the government agricultural offices or one with which they have had experience in central Luzon. The large farm operator, controlling as much as three hundred hectares, is able to change and direct what amounts to an ecological community of his own—a complex social and technological system of interdependent parts. The small farmer, on the other hand, constitutes but a single part of such a system. The small farm owner-operator, no less than the landless tenant, is affected by conditions and changes in such an ecological or agricultural community. Only the large estates are in any sense "independent" (granted it is only relative); the small farms are highly "interdependent."

By the late 1940s the changeover to commercial rice production was complete. The environment, in the widest sense of the word, had changed; the pioneering of central Isabela was complete. The important thing about this change was that it did not simply involve the substitution of pagay tagalog for pagay iloko, or the sickle for the rakem. Rather, it involved the substitution of one *system* of growing rice for another *system* of growing rice. The "problem" of substituting one element for another, e.g., the sickle for the rakem, was abrogated by changing the whole system.

Though of minor economic importance, one variety of pagay iloko, diket, is still grown in Mambabanga. This continued production of diket points up the significance of rice production as a system. In both Isabela and Ilocos Norte, diket is cultivated in small amounts for pastries and cakes, items of special importance on festive occasions.[6] Every family grows its own small field of diket, in an area seldom larger than one hundred square meters. Whereas diket varieties can command a relatively high price, they present a number of problems, characteristic of glutinous types in general, which precludes their becoming an important commercial crop. They are less resistant to plant pests and diseases, have weak stems, and increased lodging, and are less productive than nonglutinous varieties. Unlike the nonglutinous or "hard" varieties of rice, glutinous types are all of poorer milling quality; this apparently is a result of their being soft grained. In addition, glutinous varieties tend to lose flavor and sweetness if stored for any period of time after hulling. These factors, reinforced by the stated preference in taste for glutinous Ilocano types, seem to account for the persistence of these small amounts of awned or bearded rices and the complex of harvesting, storing, pounding, etc. traditionally associated with them. Thus, though the sickle is used to harvest all the commercial varieties of rice in Mambabanga, the rakem persists as the tool used to harvest the small amounts of diket. The rakem is part of one system of rice production; the sickle is part of another.[7]

The more general features of the technology involved in the preparation of seedbeds and fields are not significantly different from what they were under the pioneering conditions in Isabela or from what they were (and are) in Ilocos Norte. The carabao and moldboard plow are used to prepare the land, seeds are germinated, the seedbeds planted, and the seedlings transplanted to the prepared fields. A detailed consideration of the bayag and masayod patterns in Mambabanga, or even the schedule of agricultural activity, is not of special importance here, inasmuch as these subjects do not account for variable behavior. The single, most crucial consideration in the agricultural practices in Mambabanga concerns the need for and use of exchange labor. Yet, although the use of exchange labor has important social consequences, it is not a variable factor dependent upon either the system of growing pagay iloko or the system of growing pagay tagalog. With respect to the actual system employed, or the techniques and methodology involved, the pattern is not altered by the fact that the land may be worked by two men or twenty. Some people in Mambabanga do, in fact, have small enough holdings or individual fields that they can work with only the help of family members. Also, in Ilocos Norte there are occasionally large work groups, e.g., on the communally owned lands of the irrigation societies. An individual farmer works what land he can; he may exchange labor or he may not; this does not affect the methods and techniques which he employs. The agricultural, rice-growing system does not require exchange or contract labor; only individual farmers require, or do not require, extra assistance, depending upon the amount of land and the size of fields which they as individuals must farm.

Nearly all families in Mambabanga, both tenants and owner-operators, work parcels of land sufficiently large to make the exchange of labor necessary. Such has been the situation since the lands were initially opened up by the Society Mambabanga nearly fifty years ago. In the early period, exchange labor facilitated opening and working new lands. Two problems were posed by the local environment then which encouraged interfamily cooperation: the fear of living near pagan, head-hunting "Kalingas," and the very serious threat of endemic malaria. In Buyon, on the other hand, there has been neither the need for nor the desire to exchange labor.

In Mambabanga, the availability of relatively large tracts of land set the basis for a number of economic relationships, essentially in the form of reciprocal work exchanges. These work exchanges encouraged the establishment of a wider set of social relationships, and these social relationships, which stemmed from a need for labor, are still important. Families in Mambabanga work together in their everyday economic pursuits, and these ties are carried over and extended into other spheres of social activity. In contrast, individual families in Buyon work as individual economic units, and this is reflected by the relative social isolation of families there (see chapter 14).

NOTES

1. Because the agricultural season in Cagayan Valley is one to three months later than in western and southern Luzon, the mechanical threshers from central Luzon are available. A few of the thresher operators are private entrepreneurs making their living from the normal 5½ percent commission charged for threshing. Most, however, are owned by large, absentee-land-holding operations in central Luzon, which may or may not have holdings in Cagayan Valley.

2. No actual tabulation of rice consumed per year was made, and it is doubtful if any good statistics could have been compiled without devoting more time and energy than the subject warranted. Because rice is a very high prestige food, people in both barrios were reluctant to admit that they did not eat rice three times a day. It was obvious from a few casual observations, however, that the people of Mambabanga had more rice; therefore, their "needs" were higher. I judged that the people of Mambabanga consumed about twice the amount of rice that the people in Buyon did.

3. The suggested comparison with danao and lubo fields in Buyon may not be fair, because the water level in those fields is, in a sense, guaranteed by the controlled water of the irrigation systems. The water behind the dam in Mambabanga fluctuates according to the rainfall, and this affects the uncontrolled level of the stream bed. However, there are areas in Ilocos Norte, though none in Buyon itself, where such "high risk" lands are farmed even though part of the crop is lost.

4. On the eastern side of the valley, along the slopes and foothills of the Cordillera Central, swidden farming has had a much longer history. Here the land is bare and nearly denuded of even secondary forest cover. A similar condition is certain to develop along the slopes of the Sierra Madres where the degree of slope and the weakly developed soil profiles prevent conversion to fixed field systems like masayod.

5. Cottage industries persist along the Ilocos coast even where Virginia tobacco has become an important commercial crop. *Any* economic activity here, whether it enters into a market complex or not, is a matter of subsistence for those families engaged in it. Thus, given the lower standard of living in Ilocos Norte, it is still possible for labor-intensive cottage industry goods to compete "successfully" with imported industrial goods. Cottage industries in Ilocos Norte are but one more feature of the labor-intensive character of the economy.

6. It would be interesting to speculate about the use of diket varieties in a ritual context, especially during fiestas and on other occasions involving inter- and intra-family relationships. However, the important fact here is that cakes and candies made from the diket are prestige foods. They have no more symbolic, emotional importance than do other prestige items such as Coca-Cola or San Miguel beer.

7. It is worth noting, however, that even the techniques employed to harvest

pagay iloko have "suffered" as a result of the more general change to pagay tagalog. Compared to the same system in Ilocos Norte it is, in a word, "amateurish." There is none of the neat, meticulous cutting and bundling that one finds with stored rice in Buyon; the procedure employed is the same, but the tops of the bundles are neither trimmed nor so neatly tied, and extraneous materials may not be removed. Though I was shown several stores of diket in Mambabanga, they were not of the "quality" one sees in Ilocos Norte. The technique by which rice is cut, bundled, and stored in the Ilocos is too much out of tune with the more general, and ultimately impinging, demands of commercial rice in Isabela.

PART 3
SOCIAL
ADAPTATIONS

7
SOCIAL
ORGANIZATION
AND
CULTURAL THEMES

THE SOCIAL SETTING

The Ilocano communities of Buyon and Mambabanga differ as a result of particular historical developments and local socioeconomic arrangements. On one hand, the common cultural tradition which these two barrios share distinguishes them, along with other Ilocano communities, from Ibanags, Pangasinans, Tagalogs, and others. On the other hand, Buyon and Mambabanga share characteristics which are more or less common to all Philippine subcultural groups, especially the more general patterns of behavior which characterize lowland societies. Thus, while the focus in this study is upon the local level of difference, both higher levels of contrast are pertinent to the analysis.

What clearly distinguishes Ilocanos from non-Ilocanos is language. Unfortunately, however, interpretations of Philippine languages as indices of real cognitive differences have not been accomplished. The discussion of "linguistic dynamics," Keesing noted, "will have to await the availability of more data from future research" (1962:340). Granting the lack of such substantive data and analyses, one does receive the impression that Philippine languages, although they do differ phonologically, morphologically, and even grammatically, differ little in logic or in the general analyses of experience. There is nothing to suggest that Philippine languages reflect distinct or divergent world views. No one has ever suggested that Philippine cultures are significantly different, either in terms of the more general values and patterns of behavior, or in terms of the Filipinos' perception and interpretation of the world around them. Thus, despite apparent differences in language, disparities in the general configurations of Philippine culture and social organization seem to be absent.

In addition to language, each subcultural group can be characterized by a wide number of distinctive traits such as food preferences, dress, and house styles. Ilocanos are noted for eating

81

boggoong, a kind of preserved fish, and *saluyot,* a leafy spinach-like vegetable. Their headgear is often the traditional *tabungao,* a hat made from a bottle gourd, and the cloth for shirts is made in traditional patterns and on traditional Ilocano looms. The houses, unlike those commonly constructed of nipa in central Luzon, are characteristically made of bamboo. Such a listing of distinctive material features (traits) could be extended considerably. For the purposes of this study such a list is not especially significant.[1] Much more important, and central to the interpretation of this study, are the behavioral patterns and the folk images which have come to characterize Ilocanos.

Of primary significance at this point are the social and cultural features which Ilocanos share with other Philippine groups. Keesing was well aware of these factors when he wrote,

> One of the striking features of the northern Luzon record, of importance not only for comparative study in other areas but also for cultural theory generally, is the repetitive nature of certain phenomena of persistence and change. Most obvious, in zone after zone, are patterns of response to Spanish penetration and pressures . . . .
>
> For both lowlander and mountaineer, a selective merging of old and new elements occurred to make up a reformulated way of life. Although the lowland groups leaned much more to new things, partly because of great accessibility and ecological flexibility, and partly by force of the alien control, economic, familial, religious, festive, and other usages continued to give an indigenous stamp to their cultural milieu . . . . [P. 343]

This "indigenous stamp" to which Keesing referred is characteristic of perhaps all Philippine cultures. The "repetitive nature of certain phenomena" is crucial to an understanding of what occurred in the change from Ilocos Norte to Isabela and to an understanding of the behavior of Ilocanos relative to other Philippine groups. In the material which follows, we will examine the respective behavior of Ilocanos in Ilocos Norte and in Isabela and relate this behavior to a generalized, essentially normative, structure of Filipino social relations and to the general pattern of Filipino culture.

NORMATIVE SOCIAL SYSTEMS AND CULTURAL THEMES

The basic social organization and the fundamental cultural themes of the Ilocano have wide application throughout the Philippines. The structural principle of social organization, in its most reduced form, is one of bilateral kin groupings separated into generations with the fundamental unit being the nuclear family. This is supplemented by a well-established system of ritual coparenthood with both symmetrical (intraclass) and asymmetrical (interclass) components. The culture stresses values which support the bilateral kin group and nuclear family along with a wider set of beliefs common to much of the rest of Malaysia: a well-integrated, highly personalized pattern of spirit beliefs; the importance of smooth interpersonal relationships; a concentration on and devotion to the achievement and maintenance of status and prestige; a wide system of cultural proscriptions on behavior leading to individual shame, or *bain* (Tagalog, *hiya*); and the maintenance of self-esteem. This abbreviated statement of Ilocano cultural themes probably has application to the majority of Philippine subcultures: it is the basic warp of all values; it is that which ultimately flavors all social relationships. What Ilocanos do with these social systems and cultural themes in the two different economic and environmental settings of Buyon and Mambabanga will be elaborated in sections to follow, but it is necessary to have this basic outline in mind.

Ilocano social structure is based upon a combination of several ego-centered systems: the bilateral kin group, affines, age-mates and friends, neighbors, work-mates, and ritual or fictive kinsmen. This "bundle" of social relationships is both something more and something less than simply the total number of those people potentially or actually involved. It is not a formal, corporate system, nor is it even stable or fixed in membership. Except for the nuclear family, a great deal of flexibility exists in terms of individual selectivity, which alters the range and intensity of social relationships. Even the nuclear family does not include an unalterable set of social obligations. The establishment of new families, new circumstances, age of members, residence patterns, relative wealth, etc., can result in variant degrees of sibling and filial loyalty. The total network of interdependent, ego-centered systems is similar to that found throughout the Philippines and has been designated an "alliance system." The term "alliance system" was first used in Philippine studies by Lynch (1959:49–55). This principle has been cited more recently by Hollnsteiner (1963) who related it to political power:

Where power is concerned, a network of supporters is crucial to the person interested in gaining and maintaining power. These followers are provided through the alliance system, a network of reciprocal relationships whose members extend to one another and expect mutual assistance and loyalty.

One is expected to go all out for an ally. He may be a kinsman, a compadre, a neighbor, or friend. These relationships in themselves do not guarantee membership in one's alliance. It is when a kinsman, compadre, neighbor, or friend is emotionally close, and therefore tagged as an ally, that he can really be counted on. [P. 63]

The emphasis in Philippine culture is on social acceptance and the maintenance of congenial, or at least smooth, interpersonal relationships, on the maintenance of self-esteem, and on the avoidance of situations which may bring shame upon oneself or someone else. This theme in Philippine culture is not based on conformity to a set of rules or ideals, or to an ethical system; rather it involves adjustment and flexibility in relating to other people in specific situations. Prescriptions for behavior in Filipino culture are negative rather than positive: one should normally avoid conduct which will generate conflict, not simply do what is "right." At the same time, the prescriptions stress social pragmatism with relation to the individuals concerned at this particular time; a concern with both the immediate and wider social setting of which this relationship is but a part; the utility which this relationship holds in terms of future expectations. This stress upon social pragmatism and other-directedness is reflected in the pattern of spirit beliefs. Lynch has noted that the spirit world is inhabited by supernatural beings who must be handled or placated in the the same way that humans are maneuvered or manipulated (1961:106). The principle of smooth interpersonal relationships is equally applicable to the spirit world since the "other-world-view" is very much an extension or image of the "this-world-view."

The social systems and cultural patterns which affect life in Buyon and Mambabanga have been briefly outlined and distinguished here; at the same time the flexibility of their form and organization has been stressed. The remaining chapters of this book are devoted to demonstrating the application and adaptation of such social and cultural features in the respective economic and environmental circumstance of a "homeland" and a "migrant" community. In so doing, this study may shed light upon, and lead to further questions about, the nature of social and cultural patterns as they are found in other subcultural situations of the Philippines.

NOTE

1. Even at the level of contrast presented here, however, there are differences between Buyon and Mambabanga. Although bamboo is characteristically used in Mambabanga, and although the Ilocano taste for boggoong and saluyot is still maintained, the traditional Ilocano cloth and the tabungao are not produced in Isabela. The economic variables related to the existence of cottage industries on the Ilocos coast and their absence in Cagayan Valley is considered in chapter 15.

8
KINSHIP, INHERITANCE, AND LANDHOLDING

In both Buyon and Mambabanga kinship is bilateral and ego-centered. The terminology used (see appendix 1) is essentially the same as that reported in other Ilocano studies (Nydegger 1960; Nydegger and Nydegger 1963; Scheans 1962, 1963). In addition to the consanguineal and affinal systems of kinship, Ilocanos have a set of fictive, ritual kinsmen, their compadres. Reference terms applying to consanguines and affines can only apply, of course, to certain classes of "biological" and marital kin. However, terms of address for consanguines are also used for affines, a number of emotionally close compadres, and an even wider number of non-kinsmen. The terms of address used for "first degree" consanguineal kinsmen are extended, at one time or another, to most people with whom an individual has continued social contacts. For instance, women of an older generation will be addressed as *nana,* or "mother," whether they are consanguines, affines, or of no formal relationship whatsoever. The same applies to sibling terminology: *manong,* or "older brother," may also be used in addressing slightly older males whether cousins, in-laws, friends, neighbors, work-mates, or even a resident anthropologist.

Yet, persons so addressed do not necessarily have emotional significance. Just as all consanguines are not equally important, neither are all persons addressed by close kinship terms equally important. Terms such as *nana* or *manong* are often extended to all persons whom one knows (or wishes to know) of a particular age and sex, and the use of these terms is very often only a social gambit for a particular matter at hand. At best, kinship terms, whether of reference or address, only suggest a relationship; the give-and-take of social life among Ilocanos is much too loose and too flexible for the observer to assume automatically that such terms define a relationship. Reference terms of the consanguineal and affinal kin systems designate a formal and specific set of biological and marital ties. The terms of address for consanguineal, affinal, *and* ritual kinsmen designate a much wider range of people and include persons of widely varying emotional significance. Whatever Ilocano kinship "lacks" in terms of neatness and definition is more than made up for in its ability to make adjustments to a wide range of social and environmental situations.

As mentioned earlier, the effective dimension of social relationships is what Lynch defined as an alliance system, ". . . a network of reciprocal relationships constituting firm claims on the favor or assistance of those who are joined by them. It is not an aggregate of the relationships found in the locality system, the consanguineal, friendship or economic partnership" (1959:49). He notes further that it is "how close" a person is which determines membership in this or that alliance system. Consanguineal and affinal kinship are important in deciding membership but they do not a priori determine position or importance.

To be close is to be on intimate terms, friendly, affectionate, attentive, sympathetic, and actively interested in each other. It is the quality of a good friend. Its opposite is to be distant, which suggests a coolness of feeling between the two, or unfriendliness, uneasiness, disinterest, and perhaps even complete estrangement, whether the persons be blood relatives or not. [Lynch 1959:55]

Thus, consanguineal and affinal kinship ties are the starting points for developing and elaborating an alliance system. The fact that the membership in an individual's alliance may be largely composed of kinsmen in no way alters the fact that it is the alliance system, and not the formal kinship system, which is the social and dynamic factor of Philippine social organization. Ilocano kinship ties, like friendship ties, are forged out of common interests and extended associations; such interests and associations are often linked to landownership.

THE DIVISION OF LANDS

In both Buyon and Mambabanga the inheritance of land is central to the importance of both the family ties and the wider alliance systems. Work and residence on traditional family lands results in continued intrafamilial and interfamily relationships with corresponding shared interests. Landowning families are important to the makeup of alliance systems since they do have emotionally effective ties. In principle, land is equally divided among all children regardless of sex or age differences; in practice, this is seldom the case. No single family in Mambabanga, even the wealthiest, has lands which can or (more importantly) would be divided exactly equally. Ilocanos in Isabela will not and cannot reduce fields to the minuscule, tenth-of-an-acre plots found in Ilocos Norte. The smallest fields in Isabela are ten times larger than the smallest in Ilocos Norte: one acre versus one-tenth acre. Based on the simplest logic of growing rice, individual fields around Mambabanga could be cut into much smaller sections (as conditions on the Ilocos coast attest), but the regional conditions of farming in Isabela mitigate against making a field significantly smaller than the surrounding fields. Field size, as mentioned earlier, is geared to the total commercial complex of growing rice, and field size in Isabela is no less important than field size in Ilocos Norte to the pattern or system of rice production. Reduction in individual field size will probably take place eventually, but the availability of other lands to be worked (even if only as tenant lands), or new ones to be pioneered, makes intensive parcelization unnecessary—at least for the present. Yet, because there is more land in Mambabanga, the idea of equal inheritance is more nearly approached there than in Buyon.

When lands cannot be divided equally, informal (and sometimes formal) agreements may be arranged among siblings. In Mambabanga a married brother who formally takes possession of a piece of land may provide one or more siblings with part of the owner's share after deducting his part of that share plus what he earns as the "tenant," i.e., 70 percent. (The tenant's share is regularly 70 percent.) Sometimes a cash settlement, often based on the promise of future or extended payments, will be arranged.

Of primary importance in deciding which offspring will inherit the land are the needs of the parents in their old age. Besides status and prestige factors, or even specific seasonal agricultural returns, a consideration in landownership is the acute awareness by parents that their "old age security" can depend upon their considered and wise allotment of lands to their children. "A man with no lands," it is said, "cannot count upon his children." "Count upon" in this sense means being able to *depend economically* upon children during old age. Old people spend their last years with or near one or more of their children and their children's families. If they have had no land to pass on to their children, they only add to an already difficult burden. They may then be shuttled from the house of one child to the house of another. The care of parents and grandparents is in the first order of moral obligations, and people do care for the old. However, the absence of family lands does impoverish and reduce the social, economic, and emotional security of older people. If, however, they do own land, and if they do not break it into too many and too small units, they can "count upon" one or, perhaps, more offspring. They insure their future by giving the land to a son or sons in the form of a male dowry, the *sabong.*

A MALE LAND DOWRY: THE *SABONG*

Ilocano custom ideally prescribes equal inheritance of property, and national Philippine law upholds this custom; the *sabong* abrogates custom and law by the act (or promise) of giving land to one male heir or more. The sabong is considered necessary for a "proper" marriage. Apparently widespread among Ilocanos, the sabong is essentially the same in Buyon and Mambabanga. Among landowning families the marital agreements and arrangements include an amount of land to be provided by the groom's family to the soon-to-be-married couple. Very often this is formally made in the form of a written contract (see appendix 2), though this is less common in Isabela. The arrangement involves the transfer of lands, normally rice land and preferably artificially irrigated rice fields, though it may involve a cash settlement in lieu of land. This land then becomes the property of the new family.

The sabong provides parents with a means for giving family lands to one or more of only the male offspring so that family resources are not spread economically too thin. It also gives parents considerable control and influence in the selection of proper marriages for their children. This in turn adds socioeconomic "insurance" to the already existing emotional tie between parents and the heir apparent, assuring the parents that they will be able to "count upon" someone in their old age. A desirable marriage provides a reason for parents to divide their land inequitably through the sabong. This custom, although it does not eliminate familial conflict, is generally recognized as being necessary. Although unequal inheritance of land may well result in rivalry between siblings, the same unequal distribution of land by means of the sabong less commonly results in conflict. First, the sabong is necessary for the marriage of a brother and the formal linking or reinforcing of ties between two kin groups. From the marital ties families and individuals will be in a position to draw upon a wide number of new social resources that go into the composition of their alliance systems. To oppose the sabong, therefore, is to oppose much more than just the unequal inheritance of property. Second, a sabong can be the basis for more than one marital link between families. This is related to the importance which the sabong has for maintaining existing status lines; those parents who have lands to offer at the marriage of one or more sons are also those who can demand a sabong in the marriage of their daughters. Those families without lands can neither offer a sabong for their sons nor expect one for their daughters. Status lines, consequently, tend to remain relatively fixed. A third consequence is that marriage ties sometimes develop between sets of siblings in the same two families with the result that land resources are kept within the family.[1] Also, among the higher-status landowning families, first-cousin marriages are not uncommon, resulting in further conservation of the family resources.

There are essentially two different and opposed considerations in marriage: the desire to extend family ties and to extend existing alliance systems; and the desire to conserve family resources (i.e., land). The result is that those families with little or no land seek to extend social ties, but, because they lack wealth and position, their own alliance systems are seldom strengthened. Those families with land follow a more centripetal pattern with paired-sibling and close-cousin marriages which can maintain, and even increase, family resources. At the same time the alliance systems can be maintained, reinforced, and, in some cases, improved upon.

Where status differences exist, it is much more commonly the bride who marries above her socioeconomic position rather than the reverse. A young man from a poorer family has little or nothing to offer and, since marriage to him would, in effect, deprive a girl of her "rightful inheritance," he is all but precluded from marrying above his family's status. Parents, too, would be against such a marriage: the sabong is a measure of the social worth of a girl and her family, as well as being a socioeconomic bond between families. Though it is the groom and his family who are contributing property to the new family, it is the bride who stands to lose or gain the most in an unequal marriage. A girl seeks to arrange a marriage which will equal or better the sabong provided her own brother. The man, though his family might object to a serious difference in the socioeconomic position of his choice for a bride, will not lose by marrying slightly below his status. Consequently, girls, more often than boys, marry above their position: young men marry girls of the same or of a lower status while girls marry men of the same or of a higher status. Statistically, at least, this results in a tendency towards hypergamous marriages.

By giving or withholding the sabong, parents exert considerable control over the marriages of their children. In terms of their own future security, the sabong provides them with the means for manipulating property inheritance and favoring one or more children. It is a socially prescribed means of selecting an heir apparent in a society which, in both custom and law, stresses that all offspring are equal heirs-at-law.

The form and function of the sabong are essentially the same in Buyon and Mambabanga except that in Buyon it is both subject to and cause for greater social pressures. The intense need for parents in Buyon to administer wisely the distribution of lands is exceeded only by the need of the various children to inherit those lands. Consequently, out of both need and circumstance arises the increased potential for conflict, both among siblings and between children and parents. Conflict over inheritance is not uncommon in Mambabanga but the situation differs greatly in degree from that in Buyon. The loss of any land is more significant in Ilocos Norte because it is in shorter supply and because it is so expensive to replace. Another significant difference in Isabela is the fact that there are lands—to be either leased or pioneered—which can be worked; in Ilocos Norte such alternatives are all but nonexistent. The loss of land in Isabela can result in relative deprivation; in Ilocos Norte the loss can be absolute.

All the problems surrounding the giving of a sabong are intensified in Ilocos Norte. The parents themselves have less to give and, correspondingly, less to depend upon as security in their old age. Because there is less to give and because the need of any single child to receive is that much greater, the parents in Buyon tend to absolutely favor one son. Intrafamily tensions are, therefore, that much greater. Further, parents cannot afford to give the sabong too early in life with the result that the older son or sons must marry or seek other alternatives. (Favored alternatives have been migration to the United States for agricultural work or emigration to Cagayan Valley or other parts of the Islands for permanent settlement.) In some instances, parents have been able to make double use of the family lands: as a sabong for one son and as a mortgage for financing the overseas travel expenses of another.

Following the American take-over of the Philippines, Filipinos (especially Ilocanos, with their reputation for being "hardworking," "thrifty," "industrious") were recruited to do agricultural work in Hawaii and on the Mainland. In some instances transportation was paid, but it was often required that the individual pay his own travel expenses. The standard method for obtaining cash, then as now, was to arrange for a salda (see page 26). A piece of land was mortgaged to finance the travel expenses of an older son to work in the sugar or pineapple plantations of Hawaii. Later, having earned very high wages by Philippine standards, the son would send his parents enough money to pay off the salda. When the salda was paid, the land could be used to provide a younger son with a sabong. After several years the older son might return to Ilocos Norte, a rich Hawaiiano, with his savings from several years' work to offer as his own sabong in cash or in lands purchased from his savings.

The need for parents in Ilocos Norte to hold off giving the sabong and to use land to finance an older son abroad has resulted in a somewhat different pattern there than has been the case in Isabela. As mentioned earlier, inheritance is not always equal in Mambabanga. Although all children ususally receive some lands or a cash settlement in lieu of lands, often the oldest son receives the largest share of the inheritance, thus displaying at least a tendency towards primogeniture. In Buyon, because of the pattern mentioned above, there is a slight tendency toward ultimogeniture. The dispossessed in Mambabanga have other alternatives, particularly that of working as tenants, and can consequently afford to wait for some future settlement; such alternatives are seldom found within Ilocos Norte. As mentioned above, the sabong is less crucial in Mambabanga. The whole pattern of inheritance in Isabela is less fraught with critical social and emotional factors. Cash settlements between siblings are both more easily made and paid; the Ilocano penchant for land is not so pronounced in Isabela.[2]

In Buyon those who have no land have little choice but to find work as landless tenants, which is seldom easy to do. They may join the underemployed and the unemployed in Laoag or Vigan, or the thousands of Ilocanos in Manila. Others may try to migrate to Isabela or Cagayan provinces. Most have relatives there and many have visited the area in years past as seasonal farm laborers. Without farm animals or tools, the life of a landless tenant in Isabela is not easy, but it is often a far more attractive alternative than being a landless tenant in Ilocos Norte.

As mentioned in chapter 3, a consequence of this has been that most emigrants to Cagayan Valley have come from the landless families of Ilocos Norte. Not having family land to "finance" them abroad, the children of landless tenants often do not have the choice of working in Hawaii or California. On the other side of it, those families with land in the Ilocos often feel that they have too much invested in land to give it up for the uncertainties of pioneering. It is not surprising, then, that there are more individuals who own land in Buyon than in Mambabanga; nor, on the other hand, is it surprising to learn that one family in Mambabanga owns more land than all the families in Buyon put together.

THE RELATIVE SIGNIFICANCE OF LANDOWNERSHIP IN BUYON AND MAMBABANGA

It is necessary to examine the local significance of landownership and its relative importance in Buyon and Mambabanga to appreciate fully some of the behavioral differences in the two barrios. Data on land use and ownership are not especially difficult to obtain; Ilocanos are quite proud of how much land they own and work. There is a problem of reliability, of course. A government census taker, for instance, is very likely to obtain figures considerably less than exact because of the landowner's concern over taxation. An anthropologist, on the other hand, will probably obtain data in excess of real land areas because of the people's wish to make a "proper impression."[3] Just as importantly, or perhaps even more importantly, the anthropologist is *relatively* neutral with respect to landownership. Fortunately, there are means of checking and confirming the general reliability of data so obtained and it is the relative difference and the related attitudes which are most important here.

Many of the lands in Buyon and Mambabanga are worked for local, barrio-resident landlords, and the information from both tenant and landlord concerning a single field can be compared. Official land and tax records are not very reliable. In Mambabanga, at least, there are the original government land surveys of less than fifty years ago, the time at which the Friar Lands Estates were subdivided and sold to the immigrant Ilocano families. These lands have since been divided and inherited by the second generation and the original survey reports, assuming them to be fairly reliable, can be compared against the totals which these people now claim to own. In addition, spot checks and measurements of selected individual fields can be made. The figures obtained in a house-to-house census in Mambabanga tended to be greater than the figures derived from either the original Friar Lands survey or from spot checking individual fields. Furthermore, there was often a lack of correspondence between statements made by Mambabanga's landlords and tenants with estimates erring by as much as 10 percent, sometimes in favor of the tenant, sometimes the landlord. In Buyon, on the other hand, there was an almost exact comparison between the reports of landlord and tenant, and this reliability held up even further in the spot checking of fields. The relative reliability of census data for the two barrios relates directly to the shortage of land in Ilocos Norte and its abundance in Isabela. It is not that Ilocanos in Isabela are less honest about giving such information; it is simply that a few square meters do not have the cardinal importance that they do in Ilocos Norte.

Another factor involved is the different way in which land is measured in the two areas. In Mambabanga, land is described in terms of type (bayag, masayod, etc.) and size (hectares), secondarily in terms of production (cavans). In Buyon, on the other hand, fields are always described by type (bayag, masayod, etc.) and production (uyons), but not on the basis of hectares or square meters. In Buyon size is important only where land may have additional value for business or residence purposes, such as where farm lands border a town like Bacarra or Laoag. The uyon, the local measure of harvested rice in the Ilocos, is also the measure of land. This system of measurement, based upon and still an integral component in the traditional Ilocano system of growing rice, reflects the dominant importance of production and the irreducible relation of production to the measure and worth of land. The amount of rice produced is the true measure of land and, in turn, the amount of rice produced determines the realty value of land. Together the real measure and realty value very nearly determine the subsistence and prestige levels of any given family.

The amount a given field will produce in Mambabanga is significant, too, but it does not have the paramount, virtual survival-subsistence importance which it does in Buyon. For instance, in Isabela the production from any given bayag field may vary from sixty to eighty cavans per hectare. Thus, two bayag fields, equally fertile and farmed in the same way, will vary according to the motivation and ability of the individual farmer, the amount of effort he is willing to make in terms of weeding, and the money he can expend for fertilizers.[4] In Buyon, the facts of economic life mitigate against such variations in individual inclination and motivation. Given the local system and conditions under which rice is grown in Ilocos Norte, each individual will derive all that a given piece of land will produce simply because he must. There is no alternative to hard work, and the necessities of life on the Ilocos coast become virtues in Ilocano culture and behavior. Needs of the individual and his immediate family are invariably sufficient to insure maximum use of the land. If for some reason, however, a person is not individually motivated, social pressures are brought to bear upon the situation. Because landlords know what a given field will produce, tenants must produce that amount or soon forfeit their use-right to others. Even the independent farmer is not free from pressures to work his land "properly," inasmuch as his ownership of that land often means that one or another sibling did not inherit it. Traditional family rights to that land can be exerted against the deviant family member to allow another relative to work the land. In extreme cases departures from the norm can result in the actual loss of the land to other relatives.[5] Also, if the land is a part of a cooperative irrigation society, the combined membership may withdraw the individual's use-right to irrigation water, especially where deviant behavior might be disruptive to irrigation schedules and activities. The single most important fact remains, however, the basic, irreducible subsistence needs of the individual family. The fields, already reduced to a minimum size and few in number, are worked for as much as they will produce within the limits of the given agricultural arrangements. Differences which do exist from year to year are a consequence of the vagaries of nature and affect everyone; such differences are seldom (or long) a result of individual predilection.[6] Thus, while what a field in Mambabanga will produce is generally known by a number of people, production on any given field in Buyon is specifically known by any and all interested persons.

No single scale exists for comparing the socioeconomic worth of lands in Buyon and Mambabanga. The amount of rice which a field will produce is basic to establishing the cost of land in either area but such production-price ratios are relative to wider socioecological conditions. In Mambabanga a hectare of artificially irrigated rice land (bayag) can command a price of 1,200 to 1,500 pesos; in Buyon comparable land, much poorer in nutriments, will bring 12,000 to 15,000 pesos. In Ilocos Norte the returns from a 13,500-peso investment (given forty cavans at 10 pesos per cavan) amount to little more than 1.5 percent per annum; in Isabela (given sixty cavans at 10 pesos per cavan) the returns from a 1,350-peso investment would be over 13 percent.[7] Although supply and demand are certainly factors in establishing land prices, they are obviously not the only ones. Rice is hardly a worthwhile or profitable commercial undertaking in Ilocos Norte whereas rice accounts for over 70 percent of all commercial food crops grown in Isabela. Yet, land, essentially rice land, is the economic base of Ilocos Norte, too; it simply has a different economic importance and social significance.

In addition to the small returns in subsistence, whether it be to landlord, tenant, or owner-operator, land is economically important in Buyon as the most desirable form of savings. Besides the relatively small income in rice and the security of savings in land, land is the basis for status and prestige and the possible development of political importance and power. In Buyon and other barrios of Ilocos Norte, a landowner with three hectares of land is in a position to influence as many as sixty tenant families; a counterpart in Isabela will have perhaps three tenants. Thus, in Mambabanga, with much more land available, that much more is required for both prestige and political importance; though land is commercially important it does not have the intense and wider social worth and the kind of significance which it holds in Buyon. The particular relationships involved in landownership and political position are discussed in chapters 12 and 14.

There is still another factor involved in the high price of land in Buyon. This occurs as a result of the continual flow of money into Ilocos Norte from outside the Islands—from overseas Ilocanos in Hawaii, California, and elsewhere. Like the stay-at-home Ilocanos, many expatriates wish to acquire land, and this can be arranged by having a relative purchase it for them or else they do it themselves upon their return to the Ilocos coast. A few overseas Ilocanos will acquire more commercially profitable lands in places like Isabela but most prefer the overpriced and overworked fields in the Ilocos as a social investment on their return home. The socioeconomic condition of the older generation of overseas Ilocanos does much to enhance their ideas of eventually returning. Often socially unacceptable and culturally isolated, occupying lower-prestige, lower-paying jobs, living in agricultural labor camps in California or Hawaii, often single and all but deprived of female companionship, the older expatriate Ilocano finds little inducement to remain permanently in the United States. In Ilocos Norte the returnee with a few thousand dollars or more is an important person, perhaps a *baknang*—a member of the elite—sought after in marriage, flattered and entreated by family and kinsmen, often solicited by persons of political importance—a marked contrast to the social and relative economic poverty he faced in the United

States. Despite the fact that many fall prey to scores of confidence schemes designed for the unwary Hawaiiano, enough are able to realize their original goal to make such returns known and attractive to those still abroad. The two-story, concrete-block houses—the Ilocano version of a home in California or Hawaii—that one finds here and there in almost every barrio testify to the realization of a large number of such dreams.[8]

The urge to acquire land is not based upon the Ilocano's "love of the land"; he does not obtain a rice plot because he enjoys tilling the soil. His land hunger stems from his need to meet minimum subsistence requirements on the one hand, to his search for social worth and political power on the other. In Isabela the subsistence needs are higher, simply because they can be more easily fulfilled. In terms of relative social worth, however, the minuscle, productively poor rice plots of Ilocos Norte are worth much more than the commercially rich, alluvial rice lands of Isabela. "A man without land is nothing," the Ilocanos will claim, but it is the complex of socioeconomic factors which give value to both man and land.

NOTES

1. The Ilocanos' special term of reference for the sister or brother of one's spouse who is, in turn, married to one's own brother or sister, is *abirat*, though as a term of address it is applied to many more affinal kin. Scheans (1963:226–227) has discussed the abirat tie in terms of its formal, organizational principles; the interpretation here suggests a possible correlate of the relationship. The term is distinct from the normal word for "brother-in-law," *kayong*, or "sister-in-law," *ipag*. Such affinal relationships, or paired sibling marriages, seem to be most common among those families with land. Being a sexually neutral term it is applicable in either sister-brother brother-sister marriages, or in brother-brother sister-sister marriages, and both types exist in Buyon and Mambabanga. Land is status and, in these paired sibling marriages, status positions can be maintained through the reciprocal, affinal tie expressed in the *abirat* relationship and the use of the sabong.

2. As an example of how the ethnographer perhaps accepts the maxims and adages of a people more seriously than they, I was quite taken aback when my landlord in Mambabanga asked about buying a jeep I had purchased locally. Since I had already learned, alas, that Ilocanos in Isabela were not thrifty, I asked him how he could obtain the more than three thousand pesos to buy my somewhat old, but not inexpensive, vehicle. Even though

he was one of the wealthier men in the barrio and had tenant-farmed lands which he could economically "spare," I was quite shocked when he said he would sell some of his land to raise the money. The fact that most people in Mambabanga did not sell land to buy something like a jeep was an indication of what they could not, rather than what they would not, do. The "love of the land" is more a popular myth of the upper class and, I suspect, of some anthropologists than it is a fact of village life.

3. One field assistant in Mambabanga had taken the government census within the barrio and he noted the disparity between the land figures given during that census and those gathered with me in a house-to-house survey. He also noted that the government census figures were somewhat less than the actual amount and the figures given me were sometimes excessive.

4. The average production for a hectare of bayag in Mambabanga is between 60 and 80 cavans. Some of the larger operations in which mechanical equipment is used will produce 70 to 90 cavans. One individual in Mamba-banga produced 185 cavans on a single hectare when competing in a national and provincial rice-growing contest. He did this by exerting considerable effort in weeding, using selected seed and fertilizers, maintaining constant water control, etc. After the contest, however, he discontinued the extra work, and the production on that particular piece of land reverted to 60 to 70 cavans. This incident reflects two interesting features of Ilocano custom and practice: first, the importance of the contest was the contest, not (as the agricultural agent might have hoped) to learn by example and experience; and, second, the practices of a single farmer must be geared to the practices of other farmers (e.g., to labor exchanges) and to the technological and (even) political milieu of the given agricultural system. After a special event, such as a government rice-production contest, farmers will revert to the "traditional" practices, that is, the technological patterns practiced with and by their field neighbors.

5. Such a case occurred in Buyon where a middle-aged man and his sister were deprived of their land because they did not properly farm it. This departure from the accepted standards in farming had been part of a general pattern of deviant behavior. Though they lived next to siblings on traditional family house plots, they did not enter into extended family activities nor were they considered to be neighbors by any of the families, relatives, and nonrelatives living nearby. For all practical purposes they were completely asocial, living only on a small amount of food given them by brothers and sisters.

6. The different units of measurement (battek, pungo, uyon) will vary much less than the actual number of rice granules since these units refer to sheaves or shocks of grain. Thus, the actual amount of rice can vary from one battek to another and from one year to another without formally changing the production figure. This is not the case with cavens which is simply a bulk measurement of rice grains.

7. These percentages are based upon the shares received by landlords in each of the two areas: in Ilocos Norte this is 50 percent of the crop; in Isabela it is 30 percent of the crop.
8. Recent changes in American immigration laws now permit greater numbers of Filipinos into the U.S.—20,000 in 1969. This influx of new immigrants seems to have had an impact on the pattern of Ilocanos returning to Ilocos Norte.

9
INTERACTIONS
AMONG NEIGHBORS
AND
KINSMEN

Ilocanos express the tie with neighbors as: *Kaaroba isu ti kabsatmo wenno kabagiam,* "A neighbor is the same as your relative or sibling." As it is with other systems of social interaction, the relationship between one neighbor, or *kaaroba,* and another is both ego-centered and highly flexible, based largely on pragmatic and utilitarian considerations. What constitutes utility or pragmatism is of course based upon Ilocano values of material and social worth. Such variables as ownership of a house lot, proximity to fields, suitability and nearness of water, nearness to friends or relatives, restrictions in topography, and beliefs regarding specific local spirits control the selection of a residence site. Among the many possible considerations in selecting a house site, not the least of them will be the desirability or undesirability of potential neighbors. Why and whatever the choice, physical propinquity then becomes the primary factor in establishing the neighbor tie. However, just as some cousins and siblings are more important than others, so it is that certain neighbors are more important than others. We shall see that the means by which Ilocanos begin, make use of, and end the kaaroba bond reflect, in no small way, the situation and contextual importance of social ties and obligations.

Close relatives are often neighbors with the residence "pattern" being ambilocal, though a tendency toward virilocality exists, especially where a sabong has been involved in the marriage contract. Often neighbors will be distant cousins or affines, and kaaroba ties may be the basis for, or even the result of, compadre relationships. Not uncommonly, however, some neighbors are neither formally nor fictionally related and they may or may not have economic ties, of either a reciprocal or commercial nature. Yet, related or unrelated, neighbors are addressed by the closest kinship terms: *manang* (older sister), *manong* (older brother), *ading* (younger sibling), *nana* (mother), *tata* (father), etc.

Kaaroba is a term of reference, not of address; the importance of the neighbor relationship is in terms of the individual, not a group of individuals. It is *ti kaaroba* (the neighbor), not *dagiti kaaroba* (the neighbors), which is important; the kaaroba tie is a dyadic relationship established by an individual with several other individuals, but, together, they do not constitute a closed primary group. Regardless of the location or spatial arrangement of houses, ego-centeredness is the organizational principle of all kaaroba ties. In both Buyon and Mambabanga, however, isolated clusters of houses give the suggestion of discrete, closed units. In some such instances three, four, or even more houses constitute a "neighborhood" with what seems to be "exclusive" membership. This does not alter the fact that the kaaroba relationship must be defined in terms of a given family in that "neighborhood." In fact, there is no Ilocano word which corresponds to "neighborhood"; there are only neighbors. Where houses are lineally arranged or where there are a number of houses in a cluster, the designation of neighbors is limited to those houses (usually three or four in number) near at hand. Buyon and Mambabanga are the same in this respect; in terms of values and formal organization, the kaaroba tie does not differ. Differences exist because of the wide social functions involved in being a neighbor and the inextricability of the kaaroba tie from other social relationships.

SETTLEMENT PATTERN

The most apparent difference between Buyon and Mambabanga in the overall settlement pattern is the general arrangement of houses. In both barrios, houses are situated on high ground unsuited for rice farming. In Buyon (see maps 4 and 5) the houses border the rice lands. They follow the contours of the higher grounds which once formed the banks of the Baccara-Vintar River; in Mambabanga (see map 6) the houses are almost all clustered along two main "streets" and three crosscutting "streets" located at the apex of the ridge dividing the bayag and masayod fields. The patterning of houses in Mambabanga, however, is neither typical nor atypical of barrios in Cagayan Valley. Though many barrios are so arranged, particularly in central Isabela where almost all land is good for farming, many others follow a lineal arrangement with clusters of houses here and there along a ridge, stream, or road—the pattern common throughout most of Southeast Asia. However, the general settlement pattern is not a valid index of social cohesion. In Buyon houses are much more scattered, but the character of the kaaroba relationship there is not a function of the general settlement pattern. Correspondingly, the general settlement pattern has no specific importance for the dynamics of the relationship between neighbors in either Buyon or Mambabanga.

The settlement pattern does, however, relate to the average number of kaaroba ties in each barrio. The usual number of neighbors for a family in Mambabanga is three to four; in Buyon it varies from one to three. In both barrios there are families whose houses are located some distance from other houses and, consequently, these people have no neighbors; still others will have only one neighbor. Such families are well aware of the social gap involved by this spatial isolation, but they do not live isolated from others simply because they wish to be alone or because others wish them isolated (though these can be factors). They live where they do for various reasons which prevent their having neighbors, not the least of which is the ownership of a house lot. In Mambabanga this is especially true of the poorer families who must take what they can afford; in Buyon, with the extremely high cost of land, this problem affects everyone. The single most important reason for the people in Mambabanga averaging more neighbors than families in Buyon is simply propinquity: there are more houses close to each other in Mambabanga than there are in Buyon, a result of the settlement pattern. Proximity in Mambabanga invariably involves someone living across the "street" and, in some cases, persons living behind a house facing on another "street." In Buyon only a very few houses face each other (and the occupants are always neighbors); most houses face onto open rice fields and are backed by a steep hill. Thus, there is little to distinguish Buyon from Mambabanga with respect to kaaroba ties: where houses are close, persons are neighbors; where houses are separated, people are not neighbors; and in Buyon economy and topography produce fewer neighbors.[1] The fact that clusters of houses are widely separated in Buyon, houses in the northern section of the barrio being more than two kilometers away from those in the southern portion, has significance for the social cohesion of the barrio as a whole. It does not reflect on the importance of social bonds within a group of houses, or, more to the point, the actual relationship existing between any two neighbors.

In both areas physical propinquity is the most important consideration in selecting and being selected a kaaroba, but it is incorrect to assume that it is the only factor of importance. Neighbors are defined both socially and spatially. Social and emotional propinquity are important, too, and in this way many other aspects of barrio life come into play. Kinsmen, compadres, or age-mates may take advantage of nearness to establish the kaaroba tie whereas, with persons less emotionally important, there might be neither need nor desire to include them as neighbors. On very rare occasions, on the other hand, it may be that a next-door resident will not be considered a neighbor because of some serious breach in either the kaaroba tie or another social relationship.[2] Disharmonious relations between two families are a strain on all other social ties and, over a period of time, such problems must either run their course or an individual family will, if possible, move to another area of the village.

Being "neighborly" involves a wide number of social and economic obligations, most of them in the form of reciprocal services. An individual may use a neighbor's draft animal when his own is sick or lame, borrow his cart or use his tools, baby-sit or watch over his house during an absence from the barrio, bed down his extra guests or help out during an illness, obtain a loan from him, or give him advice. The number of things which neighbors may do for each other is limited only by the number of different problems which can arise for which a neighbor can help. Thus, this reciprocal system of exchange provides each family with an economic and social "reserve" which they can call upon (and help often comes without asking) in times of need. Though less "economically" important than the ammuyo exchange of labor and less permanently "fixed" than the formal kinship ties, the kaaroba ties are emotionally able to thrive and persist out of the day-to-day, person-to-person contacts. Although it is often the case that one or more neighbors are siblings or close relatives, the fact that they relate to each other *as neighbors* in a highly interpersonal relationship makes the kinship tie even more emotionally meaningful. There are other factors, the most important being the ownership of land, which make kinship important, but it is in the context of interpersonal relationships, particularly in being a neighbor, that the moral obligations and gratitudes are consistently maintained and reinforced.

THE EXCHANGE OF FOOD: *PADIGO*

A ritual dimension of being a kaaroba is found in the custom of *padigo*, the taking of "extra" foodstuffs to one's neighbor or neighbors. Any such "surpluses" of food will be distributed to one, more than one, or all neighbors, and such occasions provide opportunities for visiting and gossiping. In fact, it is the visiting which is claimed to be of importance and the gift of food is treated as only incidental. Such exchanges take place at least once a week and may involve the giving of a vegetable just picked, fruits, cakes, meat (which otherwise might spoil), or any specially prepared dish. The actual giving of the item takes place in a very casual way. Often little is said about the item unless it is something out of the ordinary (e.g., cakes, cookies, meat), which perhaps requires both explanation by the giver and comment by the receiver. The actual exchange does not take place simultaneously because in essence it is a spontaneous gift, not a commercial transaction. At the same time, there is no overt concern about equivalency though a sort of "running account" is generally kept by both parties. Rice, cooked or uncooked (except glutinous varieties used in cakes and candies), is never involved for it would never be considered "extra"—to either giver or receiver. Rice would only be given as an act of charity and this, as shall be seen, alters the kaaroba relationship.

Kaaroba ties are initiated at the time a house is built or when a house is moved into a new area. It is always the place of the new neighbor to initiate the ties. When constructing or moving a house, food is always provided the friends and kinsmen (and, if being moved, between neighbors) helping with the task at hand (a relationship known as *tagnawa* which is discussed below). Besides the food provided for the working group, extra plates will be taken to the nearby houses, to one's prospective neighbors. The kaaroba tie is not formally established by this act, but the first step has been taken. The tie is established when the gift is reciprocated, but, as propriety dictates, at a later time. Once established, the relationship continues with neither party attempting or wishing to arrive at a balance.

There are occasions which require very specific and exact distributions of food. These may result from a strictly family gathering, or from a visit by a landlord or friends from another barrio; that is, those social events at which a meal was prepared but to which some or even all neighbors were not invited. At these times, plates of food will be taken around to each neighbor. These occasions seldom involve a stop or excuse for visiting, and the giving and receiving takes place in a furtive, almost embarrassed, manner. However, to omit taking food to a neighbor at such a time would be most imprudent. In a sense the padigo at this time constitutes an apology for not having been "able" to invite them to the affair. Such occasions are normally few unless pronounced status differences exist between neighbors, and this relates to another characteristic of the tie between neighbors: the competition for status and prestige.

The number and social importance of people who visit a family from outside the barrio are normally in direct proportion to the relative status of that family in the barrio ranking system. In Mambabanga, visitations by "important people" from outside the barrio are more common than is the case in Buyon. There is also a wider range of socioeconomic differences, especially in terms of "real" income and land owned, between the families of highest and lowest status. These measurable differences are relatively less important in Mambabanga; in Mambabanga where the average person has more income and where there is more to "spend" (in every sense of the word), economic distinctions are correspondingly less important. Status differences in both Buyon and Mambabanga are relative to the respective areas (just as is the price of land); they are not comparable in any exact way. Thus, the people of high status in Mambabanga have more to compete with and must, therefore, compete that much harder; in Buyon, with less to spend, spending is valued that much more. The townsmen who visit the barrios are invariably those of influence and position: upper-class, politically active people. When they do come, they visit the influential persons in the barrio—those people who can influence others within the barrio, and, accordingly, can materially afford and socially prosper from such visits. Some or all neighbors of such people may be excluded from these events. Instead, special dishes of food which they can seldom afford or hope to "repay" are distributed to them. They can neither afford nor merit the luxury of important contacts in town. The gift of special foods has the effect of reminding them of the status differentiation between themselves and their more affluent neighbor. On many occasions lower-status neighbors will be invited, but they are expected to participate only in a very marginal way. They watch but they do not actively take part in the conversation and activities, again admitting or recognizing their subordinate status ranking. Usually status positions do not change quickly; essentially deriving from the ownership of land, such distinctions in Buyon and Mambabanga remain relatively stable. Yet, on occasion, statuses are altered and in such situations those individuals improving their social standing must be especially solicitous in their competition with others lest they create jealousy and antipathy. Thus, the kaaroba tie is both a system of considerable social security and a vehicle for expressing and/or establishing status and prestige.

The "residual" benefits of being a neighbor differ in Buyon and Mambabanga. These derivative activities are essentially of a commercial, economic nature. For instance, if a neighbor needs to employ people, and if, for some reason, it is either impossible or undesirable to use exchange labor, he will normally give the first choice of such employment to a neighbor. In Mambabanga this can involve extra work, outside the normal ammuyo work exchange arrangements, e.g., harvesting a field some distance away; a piece of land being converted to wet-rice production; the building of a shed, or any one of a hundred reasons which may require hired labor, or *pakiawen.* Such jobs are extra to the regular field work and are requested by persons of some means who do not wish to use or involve themselves in cooperative work arrangements such as tagnawa. As mentioned earlier, most families in Buyon are able to work all of their own land and they have no need of ammuyo exchange. However, some families do require work, either regularly or because of some emergency which requires extra work in the fields. It is customary to hire laborers who are usually paid with rice, and it is in these instances that neighbors are given the first opportunity to accept work. The identical pattern of hiring neighbors for field work is reported by Nydegger and Nydegger for Ilocos Sur (1963:720). Thus, in both barrios, being a neighbor can result in the occasional opportunity of working for one of several neighbors on tasks, some scheduled, some unscheduled, which fall outside the normal assistance expected from the kaaroba tie. Though the actual work itself is, by definition, noncooperative and commercial, the participants are linked to the employer by close social ties and these ties provide the opportunity to gain employment.

COMMUNAL ASSISTANCE: *TAGNAWA*

On certain occasions neighbors are called upon for special work, well over and above the regular favors and padigo exchange, which involves the cooperative effort of several individuals working together. Such cooperative assistance is called *tagnawa.* The most common use made of tagnawa is in the construction or moving of a house. The individual may be called upon on the basis of his obligation as a neighbor, but the tagnawa work group is by no means composed only of neighbors. The obligation to assist in such a work project may derive from any close social bonds which an individual may have and can involve consanguineal kin, in-laws, friends, barrio compadres, work-mates, and neighbors. The "host" provides food and drink for such occasions, and there is a great stress upon sociability.[3] All people generally agree that in most instances it is more "economical" to hire labor than to make use of the tagnawa exchange. This is especially true if the house is of a "modern" style rather than the traditional bamboo structure. The persons who can afford "modern" houses, of course, are also the ones who can afford to hire labor and, under the pretext of needing professional carpenters, they will explain their need to hire individuals. The poorer families often have no other alternative than to seek tagnawa assistance. Besides the fact that this arrangement further illustrates the social and moral obligations involved in being a neighbor, it also stresses the dyadic importance of the kaaroba tie since tagnawa exchange is by no means restricted to the "neighborhood." Tagnawa derives from the moral obligations which the individual has accumulated in the real emotional context of various sets of social relationships. As mentioned, such obligations are found between kinsmen, work-mates, friends, compadres, and neighbors.

As suggested above, the important difference between the neighbor relationship in Buyon and Mambabanga is the way in which it relates to other social ties. In Mambabanga the ammuyo work groups, the consanguineal and affinal kinships systems, and the compadre ties are all much more significant than is the case in Buyon. Consequently, the kaaroba relationship, because it is but one of several important sets of relationships, is relatively less important in Mambabanga than it is in Buyon. It can be argued, by a sort of "social vacuum" analogy, that the kaaroba relationship is, in fact, more important in Buyon. This is true in the sense that the people of Buyon relate more *as* and *to* neighbors than they relate in other social contexts. Yet, because of this, the kaaroba tie is different in Buyon and Mambabanga. This can be viewed in the following way.

In Buyon, the kinsman-neighbor situation is often the source of considerable conflict, invariably as a consequence of property inheritance. At the same time, the set of neighbor ties accounts for most social interaction. Also, with land expensively priced, the individual in Buyon is restricted in his ability to move and thus to alleviate any conflict which he may have with his neighbors. It is the shortage of land, therefore, which both generates family strife and maintains it.

In Mambabanga, on the other hand, the individual relates to many people in a number of different roles and such roles are not usually at variance with each other. Though a neighbor in Mambabanga may be a sibling or close relative, such kinship ties are not especially laden with real or potential discord. There is invariably some degree of conflict but it is seldom excessive. House lots in Mambabanga are relatively cheap and such land can be purchased or rented at nominal costs so that kaaroba ties can be broken and new ones established should immediate or potential conflict necessitate. Finally, the exchanges between neighbors, though about the same in number and frequency in each barrio, are more free and easy, involve more things, and are less contrived and calculated. Ties between neighbors in Buyon are still important, but the wider social system creates tensions and problems, which make the functioning of ties tenuous.

NOTES

1. The reader may be interested to know that it was the fact that families in Buyon have fewer neighbors (coupled with the lack of ammuyo, or work-partnerships) which first led me to suspect that barrios in Ilocos Norte were not as cohesive as those in Isabela. My suspicions were correct but not for the reason first imagined. Only after unraveling the settlement pattern, the way the houses were clustered, and the operating principle of the kaaroba tie did I realize that the "number" of neighbors was not especially significant and could not be used to illustrate the lack of social cohesion in Buyon.

2. One such example in Buyon involved a break in relations between one man and five adjacent residents, the nearest two of whom were his own siblings. He was not included as a neighbor because he did not "act like a neighbor"—he took things that did not belong to him and behaved in a generally "unsociable" way. Though everyone recognized that the man suffered from a mental disorder, his actions were not excused by the fact that he was a sibling to the two closest residents. This, however, did not absolve the siblings of their familial responsibilities though, as one might expect, it did place a considerable strain upon the family relationship.

    Another incident was reported to me in Mambabanga. This breach developed out of a dispute over water rights which, naturally enough, affected the tie of kaaroba. In that instance some (but not all) neighbors broke the kaaroba tie. Both examples point up the interrelatedness of the kaaroba tie with other systems of social relationship.

3. In some instances, however, such work groups are contracted partly on a pakiawen arrangement and partly on a tagnawa basis. The needs and

demands of a particular individual for a particular job require flexibility in such arrangements. Such "mixed" arrangements can involve using the meal provided tagnawa help as a small part of the pay for pakiawen. These various possibilities present no real social problem, but they do involve making proper arrangements.

10
LABOR
EXCHANGE
AND
WAGE LABOR

An understanding of the technological systems employed in Ilocos Norte and Isabela is crucial to a study of the wider ecological adjustments made in these two areas. For all practical purposes, the tool inventories are the same, the characteristic features being the use of the moldboard plow and the water buffalo. The technologies of the two provinces do differ significantly in the system of rice production itself and in the complex of socioeconomic relations involved in this production, specifically those arrangements made for the contracting and exchanging of labor. The interpersonal relationships derived from working the land can constitute a large and very active set of social ties and obligations. Such ties, however, are the ones most subject to direct influence by local economic, geographic, and demographic conditions. The kinds and degrees of differences in economics, geography, and demography have already been discussed. The amount of arable land, the population density on that land, and the kinds of agricultural systems employed have, of course, direct consequences on the socioeconomic relationships associated with agriculture and on social relationships as a whole. However, the most important and immediate condition affecting the contracting and sharing of labor is the actual size of individual fields worked by each family and not the total number of fields or the total amount of land.

Families in Buyon farm, as tenants or owner-operators, an average of .62 hectare, or 1.53 acres, of land. Due to parceling out of land through inheritance, total lands held are usually broken into six or more separate, often widely scattered, paddies. The size of individual fields will normally range from a maximum of one-half to a minimum of one-tenth of an acre. With the tools being used, it is technologically unfeasible to reduce the land area of a field to less than one-tenth of an acre. In addition, fields are often scattered requiring, in some cases, that some plots be farmed by tenants. The result is that such "landlords" must often become tenants to compensate for the 50 percent loss of income from the tenant-farmed fields. As will be noted in chapter 11, being a part-time tenant is as often a consequence of geography as it is a matter of economics or status position. The important point is that, in Buyon, fields are usually so small that individual families do most or all of the work required, regardless of the owner-use relationship involved. Because the size of the work force is geared to the size of individual paddies, the man with total holdings of one hectare is affected no differently from the man with one-half hectare, or the landless tenant. Individuals work the total number of fields which they and their families are able to work, and any "surplus" lands are leased to tenants. Thus, the social relationships deriving from agricultural work itself are, in Buyon, relatively few.

In Mambabanga, on the other hand, the average area of lands farmed by an individual family exceed those of Buyon both in total amount (3.2 hectares or 8.9 acres) and in the size of individual paddies (about 2–3 acres each). Distant fields may be leased, as they are in Buyon, while the owner works as a tenant on lands nearer the barrio. Consequently, the man who is both landlord and tenant, or even landlord, tenant, and owner-operator, is quite common. The size of total lands held and individual plots farmed requires that people in Mambabanga make use of exchange or contract labor. In Buyon, where a single, one-half hectare field might require the exchanging or contracting of labor, the individual sizes of seven separate paddies makes it unnecessary. For most families in Buyon the "labor force" begins and ends with the family or household unit; in Mambabanga the family is but the focal point of larger work groups. Because the respective practices differ in degree and not in kind, labor exchange and wage labor in Buyon and Mambabanga are considered together in the following sections.

THE RECIPROCAL EXCHANGE OF LABOR: *AMMUYO*

In Mambabanga the extra labor needed to work the two- and three-acre-sized rice paddies is normally obtained through the system of exchange labor called *ammuyo:* essentially a one-for-one, hour-for-hour exchange of work. For example, if an individual asks nine others to help him for a day's work at a given task, such as harvesting, he is then indebted to each of them for a similar day's work. It is, at the same time, a relationship which normally persists from one year to the next involving the same individuals at the same task and in the same field. When, as sometimes happens, an exchange imbalance arises as a result of landholdings of unequal size, the difference will be made up in money or rice, and additional persons will be hired on what is essentially the commercial contractual arrangement called *pakiawen*, which is discussed below. The farmers of Mambabanga also make use of family members in a particular household as the nucleus of their own work group, the larger the family, the fewer people needed from ammuyo exchanges. Although a grown son with a family and lands of his own normally continues to work for his parents on the basis of cooperation, grown siblings usually work for each other through an ammuyo arrangement.

There are several factors affecting the selection of ammuyo exchange partners. The number of people involved in an ammuyo group is related to the size of the field to be worked, with ten to twenty different people being utilized on a hectare-sized field. Adjacent fields are often owned by siblings and cousins who are normally chosen as ammuyo partners. Because neighbors are often close kinsmen, ammuyo partners can be both kinsmen and neighbors. Compadre ties may also be a basis for the selection of ammuyo help. Not the least important, the particular location of fields and the people working neighboring fields may determine work partners, so that an ammuyo partner may not be kinsman, compadre, neighbor, or close friend. In the final analysis, ammuyo partners will be determined by the sociability of the work group as a whole and the ease and facility with which the group can move from the task in one field to the same task in another. Lands belonging to a neighbor or kinsman may be so inconveniently located as to mitigate against neighbors and kinsmen exchanging labor.

The flow and speed of work is facilitated when the laborers need to move only into an adjacent or nearby field. This is especially important where artificial irrigation is involved because a time schedule must be followed in these fields with respect to the allocation of water. Yet, distances are never so great that any individual would be excluded on this basis alone; sociability of the ammuyo group is more important than being able to move quickly to an adjacent field. If the fields are, in fact, too far away to be worked by ammuyo exchange arrangements, they are simply leased to tenants. Where distance is an inconvenience to ammuyo partners, the contractor of the group is expected to provide the midday meal, the food being brought to the fields.

On a number of fields within Barrio Concepcion, on lands owned by the immigrant families who came to Mambabanga in

1937, the ammuyo groups are largely composed of Mambabanga residents and not the people from Concepcion whose lands the fields actually border. Although a few individuals in these ammuyo groups may be from Concepcion, the arrangements point up the problems of contracting and maintaining exchanges with people (related or not) in other barrios. These arrangements are also cause and effect in the assimilation of these families into Mambabanga since 1937.

Given the above considerations, we are not surprised to learn that ammuyo partners on one piece of land are often the same or nearly the same individuals found working on another piece of land belonging to the same individual. Yet, the ammuyo group is seldom exactly the same on all of a person's lands because of the variation in size and scattering of fields.

There are four tasks which regularly require ammuyo exchange on fields of one acre or more: the plowing and harrowing of paddies; pulling and transplanting seedlings; irrigation and water control; and harvesting. Three additional tasks normally involve using ammuyo exchange on fields two acres and larger: hauling the rice from the fields; stacking bundles preparatory to threshing (the actual threshing being done mechanically); and hauling rice to and storing it in or near the homes. Depending on a number of specific conditions (the time available to complete the work; location of fields; artificial or natural irrigation; soils; the varieties of rice grown; estimated crop yield; etc.), the combined tasks will require from ten to twenty different persons on a single-hectare field. The farmer with three to four hectares will have ammuyo arrangements with ten to twelve different families, with one or more members from each. As a result of the overlapping membership, the ammuyo groups are seldom, if ever, mutually exclusive, the web of relationships extending throughout the barrio. In the whole of Mambabanga, the only people who do not participate in ammuyo arrangements are the very old who no longer work, a few wealthier people who are full-time landlords or have other incomes, and two families with very small holdings which do not require exchange labor. As mentioned above, the ammuyo relationships, once established, tend to remain fairly constant. Adjustments will be made as needs arise, but the associations derived from a particular field and from the particular tasks involved tend to persist from one year to the next. Also, although naturally irrigated land (masayod) is not second cropped in Isabela, bayag fields are, and other ammuyo exchanges are used in those instances. Because of the different labor requirements for growing, say, corn and beans, the ammuyo relationships are not necessarily the same as those for rice.

"THE DYADIC CONTRACT": *AMMUYO* AND *BETARIS* HELP

In an ammuyo arrangement the accounting of hours is characteristically informal, though accounting there is, nonetheless. Since the number of hours of work needed changes little from year to year, each person knows what to expect of others and what is expected of him. Although ammuyo can hardly be classified under the rubric of "peasant harmony and cooperativeness," it is not simply a commercial contract. In some instances hired labor, or *pakiawen,* will be used when additional help is required from outside the normal ammuyo exchange. This can occur when an individual has larger fields than those of his neighbors or when he wishes to perform an extra task, such as weeding. The relationship between contracted and contractor in pakiawen ends when the specific task is completed. Though the stated goals (getting a job done) are essentially the same in ammuyo and pakiawen, there are latent consequences which derive from ammuyo which are significantly absent in the pakiawen relationship. Pakiawen labor involves an essentially impersonal, socially nonobligatory economic relationship, although it may be used to meet or reward social obligations; ammuyo is a socially obligatory "dyadic contract." The conceptualization of the dyadic contract by Foster has application for the ammuyo exchange:

> In the absence of corporate units, contracts can occur only between pairs of individuals; they must be dyadic. In the absence of legal or ritual validation, contracts must be considered informal or implicit. Informal or implicit contracts can be validated and maintained only by means of recognized reciprocal obligations, manifest by the continuing exchange of goods and services. [1961:1190]

As mentioned in chapter 7, there are no corporate groupings in either Buyon or Mambabanga except for the nuclear family and the irrigation societies. The principle of ammuyo organization is egocentric, involving individuals in a series of morally obligatory, dyadic relationships which persist over time and which involve continual exchanges of goods and services. However, the comment by Foster that "a functional requirement of the system is that an exactly even balance between partners never be struck"

(1961:1185) would seem to abrogate ammuyo as a dyadic contract since partners do work an hour for an hour, arriving at a general balance or equivalent exchange. There is, however, a derivative relationship of the ammuyo pact, called by the Ilocanos *bataris,* which indicates that a balance is not struck (though there is the assumption of eventual equivalence). *Bataris* is a sort of cumulative, socioeconomic "interest" which builds up between ammuyo partners. An emergency may arise (e.g., a draft animal unable to work, sickness in the family, the need to replant a storm-damaged field) which requires additional help and for which it is impossible to reciprocate directly through the ammuyo tie. In such a circumstance an individual will ask his ammuyo partners for bataris help, and they have the moral obligation to assist. Under similar circumstances they would expect as much. Bataris is not based upon an immediate, equivalent return; it is "extra" to the normal exchange of ammuyo labor, extra in the sense of involving unforeseen circumstances, emergencies which cannot be calculated in the normal hour-for-hour exchange. It is a reciprocal, moral obligation developing out of the ammuyo relationship and based on the continuing exchange of mutual services. The intensity or effectiveness of the obligation is not as great as the socially active and emotionally important ties between close kin, friends, and neighbors. It is the most flexible of social ties since it is necessarily an accommodation to both the wider ecological and the specific economic needs of barrio life. Yet, although highly subject to change by nonsocial factors, ammuyo does receive emotional reinforcement as a consequence of the fact that the contracts are normally arranged with persons who are socially and emotionally important—kinsmen, friends, neighbors, and compadres. Thus, ammuyo relationships are "structured" by the needs of the particular situation and by the particular people involved. A considerable range of emotional intensity is found in the nuclear family; a similar range is found in any given set of ammuyo obligations.

Ammuyo relationships are one of the most direct means of controlling deviant behavior, especially such behavior relating to agriculture. Failure of an individual to meet an ammuyo obligation may result in the stoppage of assistance on any or all phases of agricultural work. The threat is implicit in the relationship and seldom needs to be stated.[1] The essence of the ammuyo relationships also mitigates against innovation since innovation often disrupts established ties and obligations. The individual who wishes to adopt new agricultural practices must alter or do away

with his ammuyo ties since changes or additions are not a part of
the normal exchange, nor would they qualify for bataris help.
Since the obligations contracted in ammuyo are all part of a wider
set of relationships, which themselves collectively tend to reinforce any single obligation, there is considerable pressure to maintain existing patterns.

THE HIRING OF LABOR: *PAKIAWEN*

There are families in Buyon that do make use of additional agricultural labor. Some families, with either "too much" land or with
too few family members, require extra help from year to year.
Still other families must obtain additional labor to meet some
specific exigency. Yet, whether the need is a projected annual
requirement or an unforeseen event, the arrangement used is invariably *pakiawen*, or hired labor.[2] The pakiawen contract does
not in itself result in a continual exchange of goods and services,
nor does it involve a reciprocal or equal obligation on the parties
involved. Other social ties often impinge upon the pakiawen contract, however. As in Mambabanga, the people of Buyon who
require hired labor normally employ a neighbor, close kinsman,
friend, or compadre.[3] The contractor thus recognizes his obligation as kinsman, friend, or neighbor, and the individual contracted
becomes obliged (in a small way) for having been given the opportunity to work. It is one of the economic dividends of social life,
and, in Buyon especially, is an important reward for the socially
and economically insecure. Ammuyo, on the other hand, is both a
system of reciprocal obligations and of economic rewards. Although the choice of ammuyo partners is commonly influenced by
other social obligations, it effects even more social obligations,
such as the bataris aid and an elaborate system of social interdependency. The pakiawen contract does not result in a system of
social relationships; receiving work does place a moral obligation
on the recipient but pakiawen in itself does not constitute a
system of social relations. The contractor for pakiawen labor has
social obligations to kinsmen and neighbors, and, by giving them
the opportunity to earn extra money, he is recognizing and ful-
filling that obligation.

The same type of hiring arrangement of kinsmen and neighbors
has been observed and reported on in Ilocos Sur, though not
specifically designated by the word pakiawen:

> At harvest, the harvest help is . . . paid from the rice. . . . When the rice is ready to harvest, work groups are arranged among kin and neighbors. . . . Payment for harvesters varies between communities, but in Tarong it is approximately one tenth of the rice harvested by the worker. [Nydegger and Nydegger, 1963:717,720]

In Isabela the uniform pattern with respect to both lands worked and lands owned is facilitated by the exchange of labor in the various phases of agricultural work. Because of this pattern, fields are seldom reduced to less than one-half hectare, the size of the fields being an integral part of the total agricultural system. Probably, as population pressures increase, the average size of the fields, as well as the number and sizes of ammuyo work groups, will be reduced. The pattern of fields worked and owned in Ilocos Norte is not suited to ammuyo exchange. Those persons who do require additional labor obtain it through the more expedient arrangement of hired labor. In both Mambabanga and Buyon, shared labor and hired labor involve the use of kinsmen, friends, compadres, and neighbors. In Mambabanga the number of people so "employed" is much larger, and the social relationships are more important; in Buyon such contacts are much more limited and much less important. Even more significant, the ammuyo relationships in Mambabanga constitute part of the total social fabric of the society. In Buyon, with very limited and impoverished social ties, the system of hired labor bestows no more than a small economic reward.

NOTES

1. One such threat was actually made while I was doing field research in Mambabanga. The particular individual involved drank excessively and was considered to be of "bad character." He was advised several times, by an uncle by marriage, that he would lose all help in the future unless he immediately met and maintained his ammuyo obligations. A landless tenant with practically no resources, he further worsened his family's situation by selling his seed rice to buy "gin." His wife's relatives (for her sake and that of her children, it was said) came to his aid and loaned him the rice necessary for the following year's planting. Though he finally met his ammuyo obligations, people doubted that he would continue to do so for any length of time. In this example, the threat of withdrawing ammuyo help was not considered to be without substance but, rather, that the individual was beyond impressing with such threats. "Such things," it was said, "do not need being told [a normal person]."

2. Pakiawen labor is also employed to meet other work requirements which a family cannot or does not wish to do itself. The most common use of contracted labor outside of agricultural labor is in house construction. Here the individuals so employed may be working with persons contracted on a tagnawa arrangement (see chapter 9).

3. In some instances during the harvest of bayag rice, when most people in Buyon are involved in their own work, people from other areas of Ilocos Norte will be hired on a pakiawen basis to work the few fields requiring extra labor. These people will either be from areas where little or no bayag rice is grown (the masayod rice ripening much earlier) or from population "centers" like Laoag. No social considerations are involved in the hiring of strangers.

11
LANDLORD
AND
TENANT

There are four ways of deriving income from land: as landlord, owner-operator, tenant, or laborer. All four commonly involve different kinds and sets of interpersonal relationships and social ties. The most commonly seen relationships are those which take place in the context of field work: the shared exchange and the contracting of labor, ammuyo and pakiawen, discussed in the previous chapter. Ammuyo and pakiawen relate directly to the needs of agricultural work, they are not functions of landownership.

The landlord-tenant relationship is both situationally and structurally different from the exchange of labor. It can be viewed in terms of the second type of dyadic contract proposed by Foster in which "patron-client contracts tie people of significantly different socio-economic status . . . who exchange different kinds of goods and services. Patron-client contracts are phrased vertically, and they can be thought of as asymmetrical since each partner is quite different from the other in position and obligations" (1963:1281).

The asymmetrical dyadic contract is applicable to the landlord-tenant relationship in Ilocos Norte and Isabela in some instances but not in others. The most characteristic form of the landlord-tenant relationship involves people of obviously different socio-economic statuses, usually an upper-class townsman and a rural, lower-class farmer. If the landlord and tenant are not of different status positions, they cannot enter into an asymmetric dyadic contract. There are numerous tenants in Buyon and Mambabanga who work for upper-class landlords; there are also many who work for local, barrio-resident landlords with whom there are little or no social differences. A knowledge of the different forms of landlordism and tenancy is necessary to understand the wider social and economic situation.

The four means for deriving income from land are not simply four separate status groupings: they constitute but four of the fifteen possible ways by which individuals may relate to and derive

income from land. The fifteen ways of classifying people according to land-use relationships are:

1. landlord
2. landlord:owner-operator
3. landlord:tenant
4. landlord:laborer
5. landlord:owner-operator:tenant
6. landlord:owner-operator:laborer
7. landlord:owner-operator:tenant:laborer
8. landlord:tenant:laborer
9. owner-operator
10. owner-operator:tenant
11. owner-operator:laborer
12. owner-operator:tenant:laborer
13. tenant
14. tenant:laborer
15. laborer

Yet, although individuals in both Buyon and Mambabanga can be
so classified, the above classification is not one employed by the
people in Buyon and Mambabanga. The fifteen possible permuta-
tions do not constitute a folk system of classification. To be a
landlord or a working landowner (i.e., owner-operator) is important in terms of the overall status ranking system, but the different
positions and the combination of these positions are far from
being the only variables involved in status ranking. The point being
made is that the landlord-tenant relationship does not necessarily
involve people who are of unequal socioeconomic status. Equality
or inequality is not based simply or exclusively upon the land-use
relationship. The nature of any landlord-tenant tie depends upon
the socioeconomic status of any two individuals who enter into a
particular contract. One factor involved, of course, is the individual's respective position in that contract as either landlord or
tenant. His position can and does influence his place in the status
ranking system, but it alone does not determine his rank. The
various facets of tenancy develop in the following ways.

A family may own land so far from its own barrio that it must
lease that land to an individual living in a barrio nearer the fields.
Then, because they no longer derive the full produce from the
land, the family must often work as tenants on lands nearer at
hand. Persons too old to work or widows without able sons may
derive their subsistence income as landlords. The leasing of land in
these cases is not based upon the owner having too much or even
enough land, nor does it normally improve his social standing. In
Mambabanga there are a few families that own more land than
they can farm and the "surplus" is leased out to tenants. Still
other families have jobs in town, are school teachers in the barrio,
or are overseers and assistants to the large absentee landlords, and
have neither time nor need to work all the lands they may own.
Such people are usually of relatively higher status but rank does
not accrue to them simply because they are landlords. Yet, what-

ever the "real" social position of landlord and tenant may be, the landlord-tenant contract is not an equal or essentially reciprocal relationship. Although the social positions of the two individuals may not be different, the obligations involved in the contract do differ, and the way is open for the development or use of status distinctions. The relationship is unequal if for no other reason than that it involves control of land use and this control ultimately resides with the landlord, whatever his relative status or class position. Thus, although being a landlord does not automatically establish or reflect status differences, it is basic for obtaining and maintaining social position. Landlord-tenant contracts between persons of unequal class or status position differ significantly from those between social equals.

THE EXCHANGE OF "EXTRA" GOODS AND SERVICES

There is always one kind of exchange, and there can be two, involved in the landlord-tenant contract. The first exchange is basic to tenancy and is essentially economic: the tenant pays a percentage of the crop for the right to farm a piece of land. In Mambabanga this exchange involves the division of the rice crop on a 70–30 basis, the tenant receiving the larger share. In Buyon the crop is divided on a 50–50 basis. These arrangements, which are discussed below, apply to the landlord-tenant contract regardless of social differences involved; they concern the minimal, irreducible economic consideration—the division of the crop. The second kind of exchange, which is not always performed, concerns the flow of "extra" goods and services between landlord and tenant. This involves doing favors, some solicited, some unsolicited, but all expected in terms of that particular relationship. This kind of exchange is commonly carried out where a significant status or a real class difference exists, and in this context landlord and tenant are also patron and client. It characteristically involves expected patterns of behavior which reflect and, at the same time, reinforce the status or class difference. For instance, the tenant may take his landlord firewood or a vegetable from his garden when he visits town. He will perhaps help his landlord build a fence or he may come occasionally to clean up around the landlord's home. The tenant's wife may assist the landlord's family during a party or wedding. Of special political importance is the fact that the tenant will often defer to the landlord's choice and recommendation of a candidate for elective office. In return the landlord may assist his tenant in settling a tax problem or in obtaining legal advice. He might assist a near relative of the tenant to obtain a job or an appointment with a municipal official. He may provide medicine during an illness in the tenant's family or even advance him money until after the harvest. He will often act as sponsor at the marriage of a tenant's child.

The goods and services in this type of exchange are unequal and of a quite different kind. It is the most common asymmetrical dyadic relationship found between lower-class, landless tenants and upper-class landlords. The services provided by the tenant are of a type which the landlord, a member of the upper class, would not, and in some cases cannot, do for himself. Conversely, the landlord provides services for his tenant which normally are beyond the reach of lower-class persons. Such vertical exchanges are basic to the maintenance and reinforcement of status and class differences. They are also of primary importance to the operation and composition of politically important alliance systems. In addition to providing the upper-class landlord with goods and services, the relationship necessarily involves interpersonal behavior appropriate to the social distance involved: terms of address employed, speech intonations, physical attitude, a degree of humility, and a submissive, reserved familiarity—all the social ingredients necessary in relating to a member of the elite, a *baknang*. Though the landlord-tenant contract is not the only way in which people gain and maintain social position, it constitutes the single most important relationship influencing and reflecting status and class position.

The immediate and direct economic value of this exchange is normally greater for the tenant than for the landlord, in both relative and absolute terms. For instance, the landlord can hire others to provide the same services given by the tenant, whereas the tenant is seldom in a position to obtain for himself that which the landlord can provide. The landlord has contacts (symmetrical dyadic contracts) with others of the elite and can unlock doors in the social-political setting of the town, especially in the municipal government, where the tenant must occasionally involve himself and where he lacks effective social ties. In addition, the tenant gains the local, barrio prestige of being linked to an important person. Thus, where class and status positions are different, the landlord-tenant contract can provide extra socioeconomic benefits to both patron and client.

Whether or not these additional exchanges are part of the landlord-tenant contract involves more than just the question of whether or not the landlord is a social equal or someone of the upper class. Of primary importance is the relative need of the individual tenant for the kinds and degrees of socioeconomic security which a baknang can provide. In Buyon, the landlord-tenant tie can be an important source, both real and potential, of social and economic security. It often is of more "profit" to the tenant than to the landlord, despite the real disparity in power and position of landlord and tenant.[1] In Mambabanga both real and relative needs are not so great and, consequently, tenants are less willing to enter into the exchange of "extra" goods and services, and, as shall be seen, this feature of the landlord-tenant relationship is less commonly found in Isabela. Under "normal" circumstances the relationship is nurtured by the recognition of social obligations by both landlord and tenant, the recognition that both parties are involved in a "debt of honor," or *utang a naimbag iti nakem.* The social effectiveness of the moral obligation involved is validated and maintained with the continued exchange of goods and services.

THE MORAL IMPOVERISHMENT OF THE PATRON-CLIENT RELATIONSHIP

Ideally, the emphasis of the landlord-tenant relationship is upon a *social* obligation. When the goods and services used assume a real, material importance out of proportion to their symbolic importance, the tie becomes morally impoverished. This condition is especially pronounced in Ilocos Norte where such services from the tenant are expected more and more as part of the basic, economic relationship between landlord and tenant. Ideally, the goods and services are seen as gifts which "simply" accompany an economic relationship; they are prestations which are, as Marcel Mauss notes, "in theory voluntary, disinterested and spontaneous, but are in fact obligatory and interested" (Mauss 1954:1). Very often, however, this exchange is only a means by which the landlord derives more from the leasing of his minuscule fields than the formal 50–50 division of the rice crop. Where land is scarce, the goods and services involved can be used, both by landlord and tenant, in bargaining for the tenancy contract itself. In the municipality of Bacarra, it is less a moral obligation that links the tenant to the landlord than it is the bare economic necessities of life on the Ilocos coast.

In Mambabanga, where the tenant works six or seven times as much land, the arrangements again differ from what would be expected under "usual" or ideal circumstances. Although one sees deference and appropriate behavior being accorded upper-class landlords, much less commonly does one observe tenants actually performing the extra services for landlords. In Isabela it is the upper-class landlords who complain that tenants are "not like they are in other places." Some tenants provide landlords extra services, but most consider this an unnecessary economic burden. If landlords become too demanding, (by standards the tenants consider appropriate in Isabela), there are always other landlords to work for or, as a last resort, new lands to be pioneered in the Sierra Madres. The tenant in Mambabanga is willing to pay due respect and act properly toward persons of social and political importance. He will, if possible and practical, defer to the advice of a landlord on voting. But, beyond the show of deference and proper behavior, the tenant is normally unwilling to contribute material goods and services. In addition to the fact that the average tenant in Mambabanga has greater socioeconomic security, most of the tenant-farmed lands are owned by absentee landlords and the contracts with their overseers are essentially commercial in character. Many landlords do not even live in Isabela, and the moral, obligatory character of the landlord-tenant tie, i.e., the patron-client relationship, is simply precluded under these conditions. The relative abundance of land with alternate opportunities for tenancy prevents the landlord from getting extra economic and social advantages from this relationship. At the same time, those upper-class landlords who do reside in Isabela, many of whom live in the countryside, cannot demand the goods and services which landlords require of their tenants in Ilocos Norte. Depending upon individual circumstances and inclination (especially toward politics), they will establish wider or narrower sets of obligations with their tenants.

The formal relationship involving the actual division of the crop illustrates the relative difference in socioeconomic security between Ilocos Norte and Isabela. Tenancy laws in the Philippines require that the rice crop be divided on the basis of 70 percent for the tenant and 30 percent for the landlord. In Mambabanga the 70-30 division is practiced in almost every instance.[2] In Buyon, on the other hand, the rice crop is allocated on the basis of a 50-50 division without exception. There is no attempt to conceal the "illegal" 50-50 sharing arrangement. Quite the contrary, it is readily admitted and openly practiced by everyone. Enforcement of the tenancy law is not possible or even considered. The problem of being a tenant in Buyon is further intensified by the fact that landlords of the same or nearly the same social status as the tenant, as well as upper-class landlords, require the extra services. In these cases, the extra services are but a part of the contract bargain with little or no deference shown the barrio landlord. There are still other mitigating factors relating to the kind and number of services involved. The barrio landlord must often acknowledge other obligations and often tenants are the landlord's own neighbors or relatives. In these instances the extra services may be considerably reduced or eliminated. When, however, the tenant is of a different barrio, or is more distantly removed, socially and geographically, in his own barrio, some extra services are expected. In general, the lower-class landlord, unless a close relative, is much less desirable than the upper-class landlord who lives in town, because the landlord without wealth normally requires some services but can provide nothing in return. In Buyon the question was asked, "What good is a poor landlord? What can he do for you?"

The landlord-tenant relationship in Buyon is complicated still further. In Mambabanga the full-time tenant works for two, or occasionally three, landlords, but he seldom performs extra· services for them. In Buyon the full-time tenant works for ten or even more different landlords, most of whom require extra services. In addition, the upper-class townsmen are involved in different political alliances with different partisan loyalties, and they may make conflicting demands for the political support of the tenant. Such problems are not easily resolved, and, in consequence, it is not uncommon for tenant lands to be "reshuffled" following an election. The failure to acquire another plot of land in the "redistribution," or simply the fear of such a situation, is one of the many pressures on the landless tenant to emigrate.

Recent history in Ilocos Norte has provided still another complication of the tenancy situation. As mentioned in chapter 3, many of the large landholdings of the upper class were mortgaged piecemeal, often to barrio people who were receiving funds from relatives newly employed in Hawaii, California, and elsewhere. When the upper-class owners were unable to pay off such mortgages, the lands were often taken over by the tenant moneylender, not uncommonly the same tenant working the land. In other instances the mortgagee was not a tenant, or at least not the tenant farming the particular field concerned, and, no longer "protected" by the patron-client relationship to the former landlord, lost the lands which had been traditionally his to work. Usually the new, lower-class landlord either wanted to work the lands himself or else he permitted a relative or close friend to work them. All of this tended to increase the insecurity of landless tenants and to stimulate further emigration.

Landlord-tenant relationships are essentially the same in Buyon and Mambabanga. In both barrios, they are directly related to both the wider and the specific social differences which exist between people of different classes. Both barrios have contracts where persons are of the same general status position and both have contracts which exist between people of different status and class positions. In each barrio there are examples of the extra exchange, the moral obligation involving the respective exchange of goods and services between patron and client. These relationships are felt rather than defined, and continue over time with no apparent attempt to reach a "balance." Ideally the landlord-tenant relationship involving this extra exchange is one in which both patron and client benefit. It should be an exchange which is essentially based on the prestations of gift and counter-gift giving, and should involve emotionally important obligations. However, as mentioned above, the relationship can be used to serve personal needs and interests both in bargaining initially for the tenancy and subsequently for exploiting an established relationship. The personal or material gain is used and manipulated by both landlord and tenant. Because land is relatively scarce in both areas and because the relationship is, by definition, unequal, the advantage normally rests with the landlord. In Buyon and Mambabanga the relationship is used by both patron and client, depending upon the particular circumstances and upon the wider socioeconomic considerations which tend to favor one or the other. Where it does "work" to the benefit of both parties, it is reinforced and given meaning by the moral principles of Ilocano culture which stress the recognition of a "debt of honor" and the avoidance of personal shame. This, too, is necessarily involved in defining the need for socioeconomic security.

In Mambabanga the interpersonal involvement of landlord and tenant is not of special importance. Much of the land is farmed for absentee landlords, and the social-emotional content of these ties is all but nonexistent. Also, tenants are able to avoid or ignore the material, economic burdens of the asymmetrical dyadic contract.

Because their economic need is not so pressing, they can manipulate these aspects of the relationship.

The tenant in Buyon is caught in a system of conflicting demands and pressures with few corresponding social or economic rewards. Thus, a relationship which should afford social and emotional security as well as economic safeguards instead intensifies social uncertainties and increases the economic burden.

NOTES

1. I was both amused by, and suspicious of, a comment made by an upper-class landlord in Laoag to the effect that tenants "exploited" landlords in Ilocos Norte. Although "exploitation" by the tenants is perhaps a gross exaggeration of what occurs, there was an implied recognition of the fact that tenants attempt to manipulate (often successfully) the relationship with a landlord. Few anthropologists need to be reminded of their own involvement with, and manipulation by, "simple primitive" or "peasant folk." However, local landlords understand the "rules of the game" better than an uninitiated, socially naive anthropologist does.
2. The 70-30 split occurs where the tenant provides the work animals and tools which most tenants ordinarily possess. When these are provided by the landlord other arrangements in the division of the crop are made which, of course, give more to the landlord. However, in some instances a one-third/two-thirds division is made, giving the landlord a small advantage of three-and-one-third percent, this often being the arrangement between kinsmen and friends.

12
IRRIGATION
SOCIETIES:
ZANGJERAS

THE HISTORY OF COOPERATIVE IRRIGATION SOCIETIES
IN ILOCOS NORTE AND ISABELA

Ilocano irrigation societies were reported as early as 1914 by E. B. Christie who provided the first substantial ethnographic reports on the Ilocos area. The *zangjera*,[1] or cooperative irrigation society, is a special development of Ilocanos in Ilocos Norte. Keesing referred to Ilocano irrigation societies and, on the basis of early Spanish reports, dated their origin at about 1630 (1962:145; 305–307). Although they may date even earlier, perhaps predating Spanish contact,[2] they are quite old and their age suggests an early population density of some significance. What relationships and significance the irrigation societies may have had for population density and why they occured in Ilocos Norte and not elsewhere are questions which cannot be answered here. Demography, climate, and topography are undoubtedly important factors and to these one might add the Ilocano personality type ("hardworking, thrifty, industrious"), except that there are no irrigation societies in Ilocos Sur or La Union.

The manifest function of irrigation societies is simply to procure a stable, reliable supply of water, which can increase crop production in some cases by more than half. Given this goal, the zangjeras employ a wide variety of organizational means and methods. It should be stressed, however, that these variations do not reflect different "types" of irrigation societies; they simply reflect various solutions to different technological problems. For instance, some zangjeras are restricted to membership from within a single barrio. Such "restrictions" are incidental, however, and zangjera membership is invariably independent of barrio membership. The point is that zangjeras are not designed to correspond to the members or geographical boundaries of the barrio; they are designed only for obtaining water for particular field areas.

Most zangjeras have members from two, three, and more barrios with some of the largest societies having members from ten or twelve. In some zangjeras the members are all landowners; in

128

some, landowners and tenants; and, in several, all members are tenants. In a few, formal ownership of the land is vested in the zangjera itself with members owning only use-rights to the land. Some societies are dominated by one or more family groups while others have no suggestion of extended family control. In one instance, in a barrio near the poblacion of Piddig, an irrigation society is an independent group which sells or leases water for a percentage of the crop. The members of this "professional" irrigation group farm no land (at least as members) themselves. In the final analysis, membership is "decided" by the hydraulic engineering employed by Ilocanos to get water, and a wide variety of social ties and relationships becomes involved. As Leach has noted for the village of Pul Eliya in Ceylon, the "inflexibility of topography" and the "crude nursery facts . . . that water evaporates and runs down hill" are inescapable conditions for the social organization of zangjeras (1961:9).

Within the municipality of Bacarra there are twenty-six zangjeras ranging in size from less than six hectares to more than one hundred hectares. In the whole of Ilocos Norte there are reported to be 185 societies in all.[3] Among the individual zangjeras there are various "levels" of intersocietal cooperation. The complex of dams, canals, reservoirs, and drain-off systems has resulted in the need for a wide number of verbal and written agreements between zangjeras in any given area. Different zangjeras may share the use of a main canal or even a single diversion dam. In other instances, where there are several *padul,* or diversion dams, located along a desirable section of a river, a number of zangjeras will have agreed to cooperate on the repair of dams damaged or destroyed during the monsoonal flooding. Different societies may have interconnecting canals by which water from one system can be diverted to another system which has become temporarily inoperative. Drain-off water from one system may be used to supplement the basic water supply of a nearby or adjacent society. Usually one irrigation society will be involved with several other societies in various sets of mutually cooperative relationships. As a consequence, the interdependence of various zangjeras tends to moderate any conflicts which might arise among them.

In the Bacarra area, forty zangjeras (including several from the adjacent municipalities of Vintar, Laoag, and Pasuquian) form the *Federation of Communal Irrigation Systems for Bacarra,* an organization which acts to settle disputes between its members and acts on behalf of the membership on matters of political importance, especially those relating to government irrigation developments. The federation operates in situations, internal and external, which threaten one, more than one, or all members, but it exerts no direct control over the "internal affairs" of any single zangjera. Individual societies may join or withdraw as they so choose. Leadership in the federation is elective, and the president of the group is an important and influential man in Bacarra politics. He is a member of two zangjeras and president of still another.

The area of land occupied by all zangjeras in Ilocos Norte is estimated to be in excess of 17,000 hectares. Christie's (1914:99) report from over fifty years ago gives 15,000 hectares, which, as far as figures go, is not inconsistent with current estimates. Unfortunately, however, both figures are probably considerably excessive. Estimates in many instances are confused or exaggerated by the fact that most irrigation societies sell water to nonmembers whose lands border the systems, and such lands are often included in government estimates as being within the zangjera. In several instances the area of nonmember lands actually exceeds those formally within the system. Individual zangjeras also tend to exaggerate the size and importance of their organization, especially when government aid may be involved. In any event, the development of cooperative irrigation in Ilocos Norte is impressive, especially by comparison with other parts of the Philippines.

The above description of zangjeras hardly seems to apply to Isabela where there are so few of these organizations. Although immigrants in central Isabela were quick to obtain the water rights to their lands, few groups followed this up by developing cooperative systems. Most of the water used to irrigate the rice-growing fields of Isabela comes from a single source: the 30,000-hectare government-constructed Magat River Irrigation Project located southwest of the town of San Mateo. Beyond the limits of the Magat system there are a few privately developed irrigation systems, usually the work of one of the large haciendas, or, very occasionally, an Ilocano zangjera. The actual number of cooperative systems outside the Magat River project is difficult to ascertain as records on these are much less complete. Some are but paper organizations, a few have ceased to function, others were absorbed by the Magat River project, and a few were appropriated by individuals. In all, there are probably no more than six effective irrigation societies (four were actually examined) in the whole of Isabela. They exist for the same reason that their "parent" organizations in Ilocos Norte exist: to provide irrigation water. They also exist because the migrants from Ilocos Norte had a history and tradition of irrigation cooperatives and possessed the knowledge and the incentive to construct them—something which the indigenous Ibanags and other immigrant lowland groups did not. The few zangjeras in Cagayan Valley were all constructed by Ilocano immigrants from Ilocos Norte.

Yet, the same ecological conditions which encourage the operation of zangjeras in Ilocos Norte were absent (and, for the most part, still are absent) in Isabela. Zangjeras in Isabela "suffer" as a consequence of the relative prosperity of the people and agriculture in Cagayan Valley. The few zangjeras there function quite differently than do those in Ilocos Norte because there is less need for irrigation and because the social factors relating to irrigation societies are so different. This is especially evident with regard to the derivative functions of zangjeras in the two provinces.

IRRIGATION COOPERATIVES IN AND NEAR BUYON

The Laoag District Engineer's Office lists two zangjeras as being located in Buyon: the Zangjera de Camungao and Zangjera San Antonio. Most members of the Zangjera de Camungao live in Buyon, and a large number of those in the Zangjera San Antonio also live there. The land for both cooperatives is located generally within the formal boundaries of Buyon. Eight other zangjeras also have members living within Buyon, the most distant of these zangjeras being about three kilometers away. The bamboo and rock diversion dams for both Camungao and San Antonio are located on the Bacarra-Vintar River just south and west of the town of Vintar (see map 2). The main canal for Camungao is approximately three kilometers long; the main canal for San Antonio is about one kilometer. About one kilometer northwest of the town of Vintar, and for another one-half kilometer downriver, there are four dams representing five irrigation cooperatives: the first and farthest upstream belongs to the Zangjera Narpayat; farther downstream is the dam belonging to San Antonio; the third dam is used by Camungao and the Zangjera Dibua; the fourth and farthest downstream belongs to the Zangjera Curarig. For specific problems associated with the dams, these five zangjeras will act as a single, essentially cooperative, group. For instance, when any single dam of the four is damaged or when excessive silting has occurred at the entrance to a main canal, all five zangjeras will act together as a cooperative body to undertake repairs.

In addition to the arrangement among these five zangjeras, there are several sets of relationships within this group of five, plus special arrangements by one or more with still other zangjeras affected by their operations. For instance, the main canals from all four dams pass through the lands irrigated by Narpayat, San Antonio, and another zangjera, the Zangjera Bangbangkag. Camungao and Dibua share a single main canal which continues past Camungao's lands and through the lands of Zangjera Curarig. The main canal of Curarig passes through Camungao, and some of the overflow from Camungao is emptied into the Curarig system. Where the main canals of the upstream systems pass over (via stone or brick aqueducts) the canals of the more downstream systems, arrangements have been made for diverting an emergency supply of water from the higher into the lower system. In addition to the primary source of irrigation water supplied by the diversion dams, there are secondary water sources—creeks, springs, secondary diversion dams, water drained off from other systems—which are utilized by one or more of the cooperatives. All of these arrangements involve special agreements between two, and often more, of the zangjeras in any given area, and such agreements may involve either oral or written contracts.[4] The diversion, passage, and drainage of water involves a complexity of arrangements much greater than the simple bamboo dams would seem to suggest.

At the time of the field research, the Zangjera San Antonio was faced with problems of major proportions. A flood in late 1960 altered a main channel of the river and destroyed almost all of the member lands, and many of the nonmember lands, irrigated by the system. Some of the land which was not completely removed or buried under rock and gravel was being reconstructed. An attempt was being made to bring new members into the zangjera and some suggestions were even made that San Antonio should join with Camungao. Despite the seriousness of the situation, which involved the loss (since their lands were washed away) of working members, the Zangjera San Antonio remained a small but viable organization.

Camungao lands have suffered almost as badly as a consequence of a more prolonged process. The main channel of the Bacarra-Vintar River abruptly alters its east-west course below the main highway bridge at Bacarra; at that point it turns directly south to hit and turn again against the main lands of the Zangjera de Camungao (see map 5). The riverbank has become undermined at this point with chunks of land regularly dropping into the river.[5]

Members of the zangjera claim that over three-fourths of the original lands have been washed away. Out of perhaps an original thirty hectares, the member lands of Camungao now number no more than six hectares. More land, thirteen hectares, is irrigated for nonmembers in Buyon than for members.

The organization of San Antonio is structured along more general lines: members own their own lands or are tenants for landowners. Each member contributes work on the repair of the dam and main canals. Individual members have to contribute small amounts of money to buy bamboo and other materials used in dam and canal construction. Nonmembers pay 10 percent of their production as the fee for using water, and, if they so desire, individuals may join as full participating members by contributing one-third the total amount of land to be irrigated (or an agreed upon equivalent) to the zangjera. Given the importance of land in Ilocos Norte, it is obvious that new members are not readily or regularly forthcoming, the 10 percent fee being the more usual agreement.

The Zangjera de Camungao has a unique system of organization which discourages potential members from joining. Instead of a group of individuals, each with his own or his landlord's land, the Camungao cooperative itself owns the land and controls the water rights. Individual members own only the use-rights to that land, rights which are invariably inherited, and, when available, the shares of which can be purchased for 250 pesos, or about one-fourth the local land value. The shares of land are about one *uyon* in size, or, translated into land measure, about one-fifteenth to one-tenth of a hectare (.16 to .25 of an acre). In some instances there are half, and even quarter, shares, these being the result of adjustments made over past years because of the continuous erosion of the land. In addition to individual member shares, there is a communal section of land representing two *uyons* (an area equal to two shares), which is set aside for the use of the zangjera as a whole. This section is cooperatively worked and provides the means for obtaining the necessary supplies used in the maintenance of the irrigation system. An additional half-share is also set aside for the head man, called the *pangulo* or *maestro,* as payment for the extra work he must perform. No one in Buyon knows the original basis for such an organization. The original "constitution" no longer exists but the written agreement, mentioned above, between Camungao and Dibua, dated 1937, states that the Zangjera de Camungao was founded in 1793. The name derives from a local family, and a few people with the same name still belong to the organization. Whatever the historical origins for this kind of organization (and an extended kin group ownership seems the most reasonable guess), it is now virtually impossible to attract new members since the individual must give up formal ownership to his land. This, together with the continuous wearing away of lands by the river, means that the Zangjera de Camungao is faced with the possibility of losing all of its member lands.

The amount of work which an individual must do to maintain and repair a system in any given year is considerable. Damage to the bamboo and rock diversion dams can occur a number of times each year, especially during the monsoon and typhoon seasons.[6] Heavy silting occurs in the main canals, requiring considerable yearly maintenance throughout the system. As a consequence, each member must contribute from forty to sixty full working days a year. Fines are levied for work absences, and, if an absence continues, the loss of land may result. In Zangjera San Antonio, where members own their own land, repeated failure to attend work sessions can result "only" in the loss of water, but considering the importance of water and the thin margin of subsistence, the individual simply cannot afford to neglect his obligations to the zangjera.

In addition to the subsistence and technological demands of cooperation, there are certain social rewards, valuable in an environment where there are few such benefits. Camungao, like most zangjeras (though not San Antonio), has a meeting place, or *kamarin,* where, once each year following the harvest, a feast is held. Usually a religious personage is invited—it may be a Catholic priest, an official of the Aglipayan Church, or a Protestant missionary. Considerable amounts of food and drink are provided. Various kinds of meat (beef, pork, goat, sometimes dog) are eaten with rice, and large quantities of *basi,* or sugarcane wine, are consumed. Sometimes food offerings are made to the local spirits, though care is usually taken not to offend a priest or minister. Local and provincial politicians are often invited to these events. In the absence of barrio fiestas, these yearly feasts constitute the only community-wide celebrations in the area—the "community" being the zangjera, however, not the barrio. Yet, even work projects are occasions for some degree of sociability; food, such as that provided at the annual feast (items not normally eaten at everyday meals), is provided the working group and here, too, the favorite drink is *basi.* Money derived from the fines assessed against absentee members is usually insufficient to cover either the annual feast or the workday expenses since normally very few members are ever absent in a given year. During 1963, a total of fifty pesos (the usual fine being two and one-half pesos for each day's work missed) was collected with no fines outstanding. Funds for covering social expenses largely come from the income derived from selling water to outsiders.

IRRIGATION COOPERATIVES IN AND NEAR MAMBABANGA

There are two zangjeras in the general area of Mambabanga: the Society Mambabanga and the Union Bacarrena.[7] The fact that people from Mambabanga belong to two zangjeras is certainly atypical for Isabela—especially since there are probably no more than six operative systems in the whole province. The zangjeras have not made Mambabanga more cohesive, however. The Society Mambabanga may be used as an example of what has happened to at least some of the early ideas and plans for developing irrigation which were based on the traditions brought by Ilocano immigrants into Cagayan Valley.

Water rights to the original land grant were acquired by the founders at the time the barrio was settled in 1918. However, no action was taken to develop an irrigation system until more than twenty years after this and only then because of the efforts of a single individual, whom we have called Mr. Cruz. During that twenty-year period Mr. Cruz had become the single largest land-owner in Mambabanga, acquiring just over half of the original two-hundred-hectare land-grant purchase. From the very beginning, his holding of over forty-three hectares was the largest in the barrio; in the process of acquiring land from other less fortunate or less successful individuals he created considerable enmity and jealousy. At the same time, whether it was his original design (as some people contend) or not, his lands were strategically located further upstream on Macanao Creek, and consequently, nearest the dam. According to a number of persons in the barrio, he attempted to use this geographic position for his own personal gain. Even more animosity developed against him when, through a legal maneuver, he obtained the formal title to all water rights. A number of families in Mambabanga claimed that he used these rights and his location upstream to create difficult circumstances for the families more removed from the dam by withholding amounts of water at crucial times. By creating a severe hardship, he attempted to buy up the lands of the more hard-pressed, small farmers. If this was his intention he was unsuccessful, for no new lands were added to his total holdings after the construction of the irrigation system.

Along with the development of his irrigation system, Mr. Cruz brought new tenants in to work his land; all of them settled in the western section of the barrio, or what is now Harana (see map 6). Most of Mr. Cruz's tenants were Ilocanos newly arrived from Pangasinan and considerably poorer than the people of Mamba-banga, who considered them rude and aggressive—as the Ibanags had considered the people of Mambabanga a quarter of a century earlier. Partly because of the increasing animosity towards him and partly because of his age, Mr. Cruz sold the land and moved to a town located a considerable distance away.[8]

The sale of land took place in the mid-1950s after Harana had become a separate barrio. The new landowner was a Chinese mestizo who owned a large tract of land in Pangasinan, and many of the more recent tenants were attracted from his holdings there. This individual went out of his way to settle some of the problems created by the former landowner, and water is now distributed equitably to all members of the society. All people within the system, the tenants in Harana as well as a number of families in Mambabanga, are required to contribute work on the dam and on the main canals. The officers of the organization are almost all tenants of the new landowner, the reason being given that their residences are much closer to the dam and they are thus in a position to regularly check and control the flow of water. An annual feast is held each year following the harvest, and the large landholder makes the major contribution of food and drink on these occasions. Dominated as it is by a single, important individ-ual, the Society Mambabanga is much less a communal effort than the other irrigation cooperative, the Union Bacarrena. The mem-bers in Mambabanga are happy with the system as it operates despite the fact that it was used quite differently by the former landholder, Mr. Cruz.

The Union Bacarrena covers about half again as much area as the Society Mambabanga, but not all of its over 300 hectares is regularly irrigated. Named after the Bacarra area, from which many of the original members had come, the Union Bacarrena was originally a group of immigrants who, like the settlers of Mamba-banga, had applied for and purchased a land grant from the Friar Lands Estates. All of the Bacarrena land lies north of Macanao

Creek (see map 3). These settlers first established three different barrios: Puroc, where today almost a third (twenty-seven) of the members reside; the nearby barrio of Luna (now the poblacion of Luna), which has nineteen members; and the barrio of Concepcion, currently with eleven members. Through intermarriage and inheritance, memberships have spread to other barrios as well. The actual barrio sites having members in the Union Bacarrena are located on less fertile or higher spots of ground within or bordering the system of irrigated fields; Mambabanga, however, is located well outside the system. There are eleven members in Mambabanga. As mentioned in chapter 3, several families moved there from Concepcion following a flood in 1937, and it is these people and their offspring who are the members from Mambabanga.

In terms of formal organization, the Union Bacarrena is like the Zangjera San Antonio in Buyon: members own their own land; the society controls the water rights; individuals must contribute work on communal projects; water is sold to nonmembers; a feast is held each year. Both the Society Mambabanga and the Union Bacarrena take their water from Macanao Creek where Bacarrena has a concrete and log dam which backs the stream up to form a reservoir. Although this dam and the one of Society Mambabanga are subject to some damage by flooding, the threat of high water is never as serious as it is on one of the major rivers. Partly because of this, only one-third to one-half the number of workdays are required by Union Bacarrena members as are required of the zangjera members in Ilocos Norte where, as was mentioned, water is diverted from the Bacarra-Vintar River.

Even though members of the Union Bacarrena are less often called upon to work, they are also less willing to work. Some members regularly fail to appear for labor details, and fines assessed against them are often impossible to collect.[9] Many complain that the system itself is inadequate and that it only provides sufficient water for those fields nearest the water sources. Several individual members farthest removed from the dam, those most commonly affected by water shortages, withdrew entirely from the society. New members were solicited from among the outsiders buying water from the Bacarrena, but most prefer to pay the required 10 percent of their crop rather than contribute work on the system. New memberships were opened simply on the basis of participation, but no new members were forthcoming. The national government has twice provided financial assistance and without this the Union Bacarrena would probably have had serious, if not insurmountable, maintenance problems. The stated hope is that the system will be eventually incorporated into the planned extension of the Magat River Irrigation Project which ends only a few kilometers away.

It is not greater motivation which makes zangjeras in Ilocos Norte work more "efficiently" than those in Isabela. Zangjeras (like varieties of rice, the cohesiveness of extended families, or the amount of money saved in banks) differ according to the circumstances. Although the physical environment has a direct effect on the operation of the zangjeras in two areas, there are important social factors as well. One of the most important of these is the relative significance, the variable latent function, which the zangjera has in the municipal and provincial political scene.

IRRIGATION SYSTEMS AND POLITICAL SYSTEMS

Like many other barrios involved in the pioneering development of Isabela, Mambabanga was formed out of common purpose and maintained out of shared needs and fears. A socioeconomic basis for barrio communalism still persists in Mambabanga, through a complex of overlapping and interrelated ego-centered work and landowning groups. Thus, both historical continuity and social interdependency are involved in what constitutes the community of Mambabanga. And, as we shall see in chapter 14, the annual barrio fiestas reflect the importance of the barrio as a socioeconomic unit in most of Isabela; the virtual absence of fiestas reflects the poverty of the barrio as a socioeconomic unit in Ilocos Norte.

In Buyon the historical conditions of barrio communalism are long forgotten. Because shared ammuyo work groups are virtually nonexistent and landownership is invariably a real or potential source of conflict, existing social ties are abbreviated and relatively ineffectual. In Ilocos Norte, only the zangjera forms a meaningful socioeconomic community of any size. Partly because the irrigation societies are effective social units and partly because of the nature of political activity in Ilocos Norte, zangjeras have assumed an importance and function considerably beyond the manifest purpose of providing irrigation water. A brief reexamination of the class and landowning situation is necessary to illustrate these relationships.

A traditional occupation for the Philippine elite has been to manage farm lands, sometimes directly, sometimes as absentee landlords. For what are essentially geographic and demographic reasons, the Ilocano elite (like the Ilocano non-elite) has been much less endowed with land than the upper class of other cultural groups in the Philippines. Because of this the Ilocano upper class has more often turned to politics. Reference has already been made to Hollnsteiner's (1963) and Lynch's (1960) work on the importance of the "alliance system." Beyond the relatively narrow limits of shared interests and individual loyalties, the most important component in maintaining alliance systems is wealth. This becomes especially important in the complex of alliance systems making up the larger alliance system and the following of a political person. Although wealth is so often the limiting factor in Ilocos Norte politics, it is to politics that so many of the elite want or need to turn. Intensification of political activity has developed in recent years with a growing number of non-elite persons turning to politics, individuals just as politically ambitious and just as wealthy—or poor—as the elite. The economic rewards of political life in the Philippines are always an inducement to seek elective office; and, corresponding to the relative impoverishment of all classes in the Ilocos area, political office has become that much more attractive and competitive.

Politically active persons have to involve themselves personally and directly with an ever growing number of associates who, in turn, have limited influence and political ambitions of their own. Thus, the promise of support in this election may be partly based upon supporting others in future elections. The consequent lack of continuity in office adds still more to political instability. Though often owning little land, the landowning elite attempt to make the widest use of their resources in property to influence a large number of people. Consequently, the landowner breaks his two- or three-hectare holdings into fifty to seventy-five tenth-of-an-acre plots to acquire as many tenants and, hopefully, as much support as possible. Other "political landowners" do likewise, so that a single tenant may be subject to the demands of several landowners, not one of whom has an exclusive "right" to his support. In the face of increasing competition and decreasing reserves of wealth and influence, the politically ambitious individual builds what he can on political promises, commitments, and social obligations—a precarious and often hazardous alliance system. Pressures and the potential for conflict continue to mount, competition increases, personnel shift between alliances, promises are made and broken, animosity grows, and the final complication of political life in the Ilocos emerges: political warfare and feuding. In fact, political killings and terrorism have themselves become an important means to the realization of political ends—and not simply when all else has failed!

Within the Ilocos area itself there are significant differences in the intensity and instability of political life. This is most pronounced when comparing Ilocos Norte to the southern Ilocos area, particularly Ilocos Sur. During the election year of 1963 (a non-presidential off-year election) more than 100 "political" killings were reported for Ilocos Sur and twenty-five for Ilocos Norte.[10] The reason often given in Ilocos Norte for the difference is that Ilocos Sur has a particularly large number of *Bagos,* or "new Ilocanos," the new or recently Christianized Tinguians from adjacent Abra Province. The assimilation of Abra people may indeed play some part in this inasmuch as some of the most politically explosive areas border Abra, but just how or in what way is impossible to say here. The significant difference is in the presence of irrigation cooperatives in Ilocos Norte and the particular agricultural economy which exists in Ilocos Sur.

To illustrate, tobacco has been grown as a commercial second crop on the Ilocos coast since Spanish times and, in fact, in the late eighteenth century a revolt was narrowly averted in the Laoag area over the imposition of a tobacco monopoly by the Spanish colonial government. The varieties established early in that period, now called "native tobacco," are used for cigar production. A major change in tobacco production occurred shortly after World War II with the introduction of Virginia leaf tobacco which is better suited for cigarette production. In 1952 the national government established import duties and a local price support program to aid the growing industry and to protect the growers against foreign competition. Partly to keep the Chinese business interests from gaining control of the market and partly to gain political patronage, the program—grading, purchasing, payments, jobs, etc.—was administered by local political officeholders. This resulted in an intensification in the political alliance systems. First, it provided a means by which those in power could not only increase their rewards to the political faithful and attract new support, but could punish the opposition in terms of low gradings, delayed payments, etc. Second, it has made the attainment of political office increasingly more popular and correspondingly more competitive. Finally, it has made the individual farmer more independent and more difficult to reach by the traditional social and economic means. A study of the effects of Virginia tobacco in Ilocos Sur and La Union noted the following:

> The economic prosperity of the farmfolk has somewhat lessened the tenant's subservience to his landlord in the matter of choosing national as well as local officials.
> Political leanings of the Barrio folk are more influenced by material aid. . . . [Garcia, 1962:10]

Except in the southernmost section, relatively little Virginia leaf tobacco is grown in Ilocos Norte. This is apparent by the absence of tobacco-drying sheds north of Batac. The most important second crop in central and northern Ilocos Norte is either garlic or onions or, less commonly, the traditional "native tobacco." The sale and marketing of these are more subject to changes in the marketplace and not directly to changes in the local political system. The highly arid and extended dry season of Ilocos Norte which makes the growing of Virginia leaf unfeasible, probably influenced the early development of communal irrigation societies. Also, because of the longer growing period required for bayag varieties of rice, artificially irrigated lands are much less commonly planted to tobacco than are nonirrigated or naturally irrigated lands.

The irrigation societies constitute the second condition distinguishing the relative political stability of Ilocos Norte. The decline in affluence and influence of the upper class, the increasing isolation of the individual, the various interrelationships of these factors and the resulting weakness of the political alliance systems have already been outlined. Only the communal irrigation systems constitute relatively large and, at the same time, stable social groupings with shared community interests. These groupings generally must protect their water rights and obtain materials (especially cement and other building materials) to improve upon and maintain the irrigation works. The zangjeras, in the absence or incapacity of other social forms, particularly the barrios, are an important political resource. The backing of several irrigation systems can widen and extend the scope and effectiveness of a politician's alliance system. Because of the presence of zangjeras, and because of the corresponding absence of the highly political Virginia tobacco "industry," the political situation in Ilocos Norte is somewhat less intense than is the case further south. Competition for the zangjera vote is intense, and political violence is by no means abrogated; but the influence of the irrigation societies in Ilocos Norte provides at least some block support together with a higher degree of voter predictability. The extremely individualized, intense house-to-house search for votes which is found in the southern Ilocos area is tempered and less frenetic. The difference is only relative, however, not absolute.[11]

POLITICS AND THE BARRIO

Political feuding does occur in Isabela, but it is by no means as pronounced or intense as it is in Ilocos Norte. It is normally the landed, elite class in Isabela, as elsewhere, which occupies itself with politics. The builder of a personal political alliance system there is wealthier, and has a relatively large and stable social group, the barrio, to which he can appeal. Though tenants in Isabela are relatively independent and can usually find other lands to work, nonetheless, landlords do exert considerable influence over the voting of their tenants. It is, after all, the landlords who ultimately control part or all of the tenants' means of livelihood. Yet, as mentioned earlier, this superordinate-subordinate relationship is not without its rewards for both parties, and the tenant does not feel particularly coerced or forced into voting against his will. In fact, except where the charisma or ethnic position of a candidate intervenes, the barrio voter will make his choice according to the immediate and practical considerations relating to his voting—his landlord's wishes, his ties with barrio mates, the promises made by a candidate, an obligation to a friend, relative, or compadre, the need to sell a vote, and so on. Because barrios are effective social units, they can often be influenced to vote for one party or alliance system. The older barrios, such as Mambabanga, vote along traditional lines which have been maintained and nurtured by both voter and politician. Although particular barrios are often described as "Liberal" or "Nationalist," what is meant, in fact, is that these barrios have traditionally supported particular alliance systems in Luna which are associated with one of the national parties.

Mambabanga differs from some barrios in that it is split into Liberal and Nationalist factions; yet the split is along traditional, essentially predictable social lines. The original settlers of Mambabanga have traditionally given support to certain alliance systems which are now identified as Liberal. This is also true of Harana, in large part a result of Harana's having been a sitio of Mambabanga, so that all of Harana and most of Mambabanga identify with Liberal Party candidates. Of the sixty-one houses in the barrio, thirty-six identify with Liberal Party candidates; nineteen claim to have traditionally supported the Nationalists; and two claim to be "nonaligned." These latter two families are very recent arrivals, one having ties established in the town of Cabatuan and the other not having yet established itself. The nineteen supporters of Nationalist candidates are all members of the families which moved to Mambabanga from Concepcion in 1937. The thirty-six families which support Liberal Party candidates are the descendants of the original settlers in Mambabanga plus several "converts" from the later arrivals. Most of these converts from the Nationalist group are second-generation families or families from Concepcion who intermarried with the original Mambabanga families. Although most of the late arrivals from Concepcion still own land and have important economic and social ties in the old area, they have become increasingly involved and interdependent with the original Mambabanga families. Mambabanga now holds a rather special position in the municipal political scene for it can deliver a pivotal block of votes in an election. The barrio people, as a consequence, have profited from both sides.

Irrigation societies in Isabela, on the other hand, are almost nonfunctional with respect to political life. While politicians seldom miss the opportunity to speak at a gathering of either the Society Mambabanga or the Union Bacarrena, it is to the barrios that they direct most of their political efforts. Besides the fact that barrios are socially and economically important, the irrigation societies in Isabela are simply too few and too poorly organized to constitute an important political focus. In Isabela, because of the interdependency of various socioeconomic ties, the barrios are significant politically. In Ilocos Norte, because of real social and economic poverty, the zangjeras partly fill a political vacuum from which they are able to profit. Thus, communal, cooperative efforts to obtain water by the same cultural group have been applied in two environmental settings with strikingly different results. All this points up the fact that the behavior of a given group does not result from social arrangements or cultural tradition or environment alone. The behavior of Ilocanos in both Buyon and Mambabanga is a consequence of the shared social and cultural traditions as those traditions relate to and are interrelated with their respective natural and social environments.

NOTES

1. The name apparently derives from the Spanish word *zanja,* an irrigation ditch or conduit. At first glance the word *zangjera* (sometimes spelled *sanghera* or *sanhera*) might suggest that it was derived from *sangre,* or blood, but I was informed, on good authority, that this is not so. At the time, the suggestion of a link to the word *sangre* seemed pregnant with meaning for the kinship system!

2. Keesing's evidence, from the Blair and Robertson collection (1903–09: vol. 7, p. 174; vol. 12, p. 210) is based upon references by Spanish priests who were developing irrigation systems at "mission-created settlements." There are no comments, unfortunately, as to whether or not such irrigation projects existed elsewhere but there is no reason why the Spanish should have limited such success to the northern Ilocos area. The use of a Spanish-derived word, *zangjera,* is not necessarily solid evidence for origins since there is an Ilocano equivalent, *pasayak.* Also, none of the technical or operational terms associated with zangjeras are of Spanish derivation; all are Ilocano words—*puttot,* a dam for stopping water; *padul,* a diversion dam across a large stream or river; *kali,* a main canal; *aripit,* a small ditch; *sayugan,* a flume; *bingai,* a share or membership; *gunglo,* working sections of land; *kamarin,* a community meeting place; etc. We are not, however, considering etymology here.

3. Some of the more general figures and information on zangjeras outside the Buyon area were graciously provided me by the Bureau of Public Works, Office of the District Engineer in Laoag. Francisco T. Tamayo, the senior civil engineer, was especially helpful. However, neither he nor other members of the District Engineer's Office are in any way responsible for the interpretation given the data here.

4. A written contractual arrangement exists between the Zangjera Camungao and the Zangjera Dibua with regard to sharing the diversion dams and main canal. There are, however, no written agreements between the Zangjera Camungao and the other zangjeras regarding the various other intersocietal arrangements mentioned. Whether such "contracts" are written or simply verbal should not be taken as an indication of the relative importance of one agreement over another. All such contracts have relative and immediate importance with regard to the particular needs and problems solved in any given agreement, and the existence of a written contract can be related to the specific circumstances and the particular individuals concerned at a given time and place.

   The written agreement between Camungao and Dibua was made in 1937 and is written in Spanish. I was somewhat bothered by the fact that Spanish was used because, as far as I could ascertain, none of the members of either zangjera spoke any Spanish. The officers of Zangjera Camungao were good enough to loan me the contract which was duly translated and I subsequently provided the members with the English translation. Two of the officers expressed their thanks for copies which they could read and both agreed that it said, in fact, what everyone thought it said. My question as to why it was written in Spanish instead of Ilocano, or even English, was answered by the older members. They informed me that it was drawn up for them by a local lawyer who felt that Spanish was the appropriate "legal language." The written document was, in effect, a symbolic, essentially decorative, gesture involved in a *real* social contract.

5. This was instrumental in bringing about the sharing of the same canal and dam by Camungao and Dibua. The main canal of Dibua was located along the northern border of Camungao but was lost to erosion by the river. In 1937, the two zangjeras agreed to share both dam and main canal plus all construction and maintenance work. Because Dibua is considerably larger, Camungao was "compensated" for having to widen the canal by acquiring three times the labor force it could normally muster for itself.

6. A comment is perhaps necessary about the dams. One of the first statements made by Christie (1914:99) concerns the "crudely constructed dams" which are "either completely destroyed each year or require considerable repairing." These rock and bamboo dams are not, however, as impractical as Christie suggests. Bamboo is relatively cheap, and rock and cooperative labor involve no formal expense; in addition, the dams are comparatively easy to repair. Without government aid and assistance, a concrete dam would be prohibitively expensive to construct, and, except on the smaller streams, impossible to maintain. Such a dam was constructed for the Zangjera Curarig at the lower end of Tamucalao Creek (see map 5) and, during the flooding of 1960, the dam was broken. After the flood Curarig rebuilt their bamboo diversion dam on the river. The traditional bamboo and rock dams, being so easy to repair and replace, are more "reliable." The danger from flooding comes at the middle of the rice-growing season when there can be no delays such as waiting for the dry season or waiting for government assistance. A concrete dam is practical only in a society which can afford the time, money, and delay involved in construction, maintenance, and repair. The people in Ilocos Norte can afford none of these.

7. Only the older men and more recent immigrants to Isabela refer to irrigation cooperatives by the term zangjera; invariably the Ilocano term *pasayak* is used. I never noted the use of Spanish words, except for *sombra,* or sluice, used with reference to a *pasayak.* The honorific term *don* was used in some instances in Ilocos Norte as a term of address to the zangjera officers, but it was never used in Isabela. Ilocano terms were always used.

8. Shortly after my arrival in Mambabanga a legal case which developed from the sale of this land was completed in Luna. Mr. Cruz was taken to court by his brother, a Hawaiiano and a resident of the United States, who contended that he had financed Mr. Cruz for the initial purchases and the subsequent additions to that land. Mr. Cruz claimed that this was

not true and, since no formal agreement existed between the brothers, the claimant from the United States lost his case. Although quick to state that this was very un-Filipino-like behavior, the people in Mambabanga were not unduly surprised, for the incident corroborated what they already "knew" about the character of Mr. Cruz. My own opinion is that such behavior between close kinsmen, in this case siblings, is not as uncommon as anthropological literature would suggest.

9. During my field research period, the officers of the Bacarrena met to take formal, legal action against recalcitrant members. The amounts due in outstanding fines were totaled up and a list was made of all persons in arrears. This caused some embarrassment since 90 percent of the members, including most officers, had outstanding debts! The list was shortened to include the "really" outstanding debtors, those owing P1,000 or about $250, and even this amounted to over 30 percent of the members. A local attorney in Luna who acts as their legal representative informed the officers that their "constitution" had no formal, legal status so there was no legal way to enforce the fines. The attorney was well aware of the social importance of a zangjera, and informed them that "to be a cooperative you must cooperate!" The concerned members then asked the municipal mayor to speak to the delinquent members. This action was considered by the older members to be especially bad policy. It would have been understandable in dealing with another organization, they said, but it was inappropriate for outsiders to settle an internal problem. The mayor called a special meeting in Luna where he admonished the delinquents to live up to their responsibilities; characteristically, however, most of the very delinquent members were absent and most of the fines remained unpaid.

10. It is difficult to distinguish between "political" and "nonpolitical" killings. Authorities in Ilocos Norte and Ilocos Sur are understandably reluctant to add more publicity to that which they already receive. Consequently exact figures are difficult, if not impossible, to obtain. Though the newspapers perhaps tend to exaggerate the number of shootings, it is also true that not all shootings are reported to the newspapers.

11. In November 1963, just before an election, an ambush occurred outside the poblacion of Bacarra which resulted in the death of four persons, one of whom was the Liberal Party candidate for mayor of that town. The attack was explained as being the result of a long-standing blood feud between the candidate for mayor and the leader of the ambush group. The complex of relationships within each group (the attackers and those attacked), between the two groups, and in the web of sociopolitical systems and subsystems in Bacarra was fantastically involved. It stands as a classic—and very tragic—example of the highly involved and unstable nature of alliance networks in the Ilocos area.

13
SAVINGS,
SAVINGS ASSOCIATIONS,
AND
MARKET EXCHANGE

The importance of savings in land has already been mentioned. Thrift, specifically that of savings, is considered one of the more characteristic and laudable traits of Ilocanos. Laoag banks contain savings of over fifteen million pesos, not inconsiderable for a population with a cash income of probably less than one hundred dollars per family per year.[1] One bank official in Laoag stated that Ilocos Norte has a 15:1 ratio of savings to loan transactions. In fact, Laoag, with a population just over 40,000, is second in total savings deposits only to the combined banks of Manila, a city of over 1,250,000 population. The contrast between Ilocos Norte and Isabela is perhaps nowhere more accentuated than in the respective behavior of the people toward savings. Ilocanos in Isabela save little if anything at all; in contrast to Laoag, the banks of Santiago have a savings-to-loans ratio of 1:8—savings in Isabela being only one-sixtieth that of Ilocos Norte. There are notably few banks in Cagayan Valley and most are loan rather than savings institutions.

The main source of money for savings in Ilocos Norte derives from "dollar imports" from the United States, which amount to four to five million dollars a year, whereas dollar imports into Isabela are insignificant. Much of this money, savings sent by Hawaiianos, goes into the purchase of land or into the banks where it is often only an intermediate step to acquiring land. Many families in Ilocos Norte depend in whole or in part upon these dollar incomes for a living. In fact, as reported by local banking sources, over 40 percent of all dollar imports are in the direct form of United States government warrants covering military service retirements, social security, war pensions, etc. An unknown but significant proportion of this money is saved by means other than commercial banking. Besides land, money is often invested in jewelry or simply hidden away in homes.

In addition to the individual forms of saving, the Ilocanos make use of social, institutional arrangements in the form of savings associations. In Ilocos Norte and Isabela there are two kinds: the *ammong* and the *arayat*.

FINANCIAL SAVINGS ASSOCIATIONS: *AMMONG*

Though specific details of the ammong may differ from one association to another, all share the same essential features of having fixed contributions at given intervals with a rotational assignment of collections from and payments to members. Such "peasant credit institutions" have been receiving increasing attention in anthropological studies (Ardener 1964; Firth and Yamey 1964; Geertz 1962). Unfortunately, few (if any) have been reported for the Philippines, though casual inquiries suggest their existence in perhaps most lowland and some highland communities. With respect to the rest of the Philippines, it is quite likely that savings institutions in Ilocos Norte are characterized by their significantly large numbers plus their importance as economic, rather than social, entities.

Ammongs are usually organized and operated by women, and women generally make up the vast majority of members in any given association. Participation in an ammong is based upon mutual trust among the membership, and the trust and respect of the members for the organizer. The participants agree to a schedule of collections and payments, with some arrangement made for the order of payments, usually a drawing of names. A typical ammong will involve perhaps fifty persons contributing one peso each for fifty weeks, with some individuals subscribing to more than one share. The "luckiest" individuals will be those who receive the first payments. It is this element of luck which acts as a major attraction to the ammong membership. Whereas a bank will provide cumulative interest, such interest is always small and comes only after a long period of waiting. The "interest" from an ammong consists of a lucky individual receiving his savings after only one or more payments. And, though it has the attraction of gambling, the possibility of immediate windfall, it involves none of the risks because the individual never loses.

The amount of money and the number of people involved ultimately decide the degree of formal organization and accounting. The smaller associations are usually made up of a few socially close individuals who invest a few pesos at most; arrangements in these ammongs are quite informal. Formal accounting will be kept where larger contributions are concerned and where a greater number of people participate. In the larger ammongs, the position of the organizer is more formalized and more demanding: individual collections must be made, payments given, an accounting maintained. In addition, the organizer assumes the financial responsibility when any of the members are delinquent in their payments. For this, and for the extra work involved, the organizer will be compensated by receiving a part or total share; a fifty-peso, fifty-member ammong would involve collections of one peso for fifty-one weeks with one payment, usually the first, going to the organizer. In effect, members contribute one extra payment for insurance against loss and for the organizational services involved.[2]

Membership is often contingent, and can be dependent, upon membership in other kinds of associations. For example, the ammong membership may be composed of people from a particular neighborhood, the teachers from a school, the vendors in a section of the market, the members of a social club, and so on. It is their interaction with persons in the first association which provides the social basis for their participation in the savings organization. It does not matter that the original association is based upon residence (e.g., a particular neighborhood), or upon an economic tie (e.g., fish vendors), or an essentially social relationship (e.g., the Lions Club); the first association is important because it provides the basis for confidence and trust among the membership. Yet, it is necessary in the larger associations for the organizer to back this trust with guarantees against delinquencies. The ammong is primarily an economic institution; it is not designed to be a savings "club"; that is, members do not necessarily socialize or get together in the context or operation of the ammong.[3] It is in the second form of savings association that people socialize and get together.

SOCIAL SAVINGS ASSOCIATIONS: *ARAYAT*

In contrast to the ammong, the arayat is essentially a social institution, only secondarily an economic one. The membership in the arayat is exclusively female; men participate through the membership and activities of their wives, who represent the domestic unit. Payments are often in the form of food, usually rice, rather than money, though cash may constitute part of the payment or may sometimes be substituted for food. Unlike the ammong, payments are unscheduled and occur only as individual needs arise—and such needs are necessarily social in context. A number of women form an arayat with one or more keeping a record of collections and payments. When the need arises, a member will approach the organizer to inform her that a social event, such as a baptism, wedding, church confirmation, or funeral, is about to take place in her family and that she needs her arayat payment. The membership of the association will be notified and, at some time on or before this event, they will deliver their payments to the house of the requesting individual. Payments will continue among the membership until each participant has received her share. Some individuals may not need the payment before others request that a new cycle of payments begin and, if agreed upon, they may allow their uncollected payment to continue into the next round and thereby build up a backlog.

Arayat payments are specifically limited to social occasions, or *"galas"*; recipients cannot use their payments for their own purely economic advantage as they may in the ammong. The individuals who contribute are also those who are normally invited to such *gala* affairs. This makes the arayat a form of "social insurance"; a member is assured of participating in the social events put on by all members. Whereas membership in an ammong is often *contingent* upon another association or social tie, membership in the arayat is invariably *dependent* upon other social relationships. The social basis for the arayat derives from the effective and emotionally important ties of kinship, compadre relationships, exchange labor, neighbors, and friendship. The members of the arayat are the people with whom one relates directly or indirectly through various sets of ego-centered systems in day-to-day affairs. The organizer, unlike the organizer in the ammong, does not receive compensation for her work nor does she offer insurance against delinquencies: the former is of little moment and the latter is unnecessary. The arayat is a form of social savings and social investment which uses economic goods to reinforce established social ties. The arayat helps the individual woman meet the costs of important social events, but it is only an economic means to a very specific social goal. The ammong is specifically a "financial savings institution"; the arayat is basically a "social savings association."

AMMONG AND *ARAYAT* IN BUYON AND ILOCOS NORTE

As already indicated, the number of ammongs in Ilocos Norte is significant. However, ammongs are much less commonly found in barrios than in the larger towns; rural farmers simply have very little money, still less which they can regularly call upon as required by fixed collection schedules. There were no ammongs in

Buyon, though a few individuals with small but regular incomes participated in associations in Bacarra and Laoag. Participation in ammongs in Ilocos Norte is primarily restricted to persons with fixed incomes, however small, and to those who receive some money from overseas on a regular basis; most rural families obtain what little money they get on seasonal crop sales—an impossible arrangement for participation in a rotating credit institution. Arayats, on the other hand, do not require a fixed schedule but few, if any, are to be found in the rural barrios; none exist in Buyon. Arayats reflect a social cohesiveness not found in Buyon plus a social-economic cost and involvement which the barrio people of Ilocos Norte simply cannot afford. There are some arayats in Laoag, but those are restricted to families that can maintain the social and economic burden of participation. People who belong to arayats normally relate to one another in a much wider social context, usually on a commercial or a political basis. The arayat membership constitutes a small core of persons who are socially and emotionally important to each other; the ammongs operate from the mutual knowledge and trust of at least some of the people involved, particularly for the organizer. Arayats are not simply *based* upon social knowledge and involvement; arayats *are* social involvement.[4] Thus, arayats are important where there is a socioeconomic basis which involves people, with shared interests, in various sets of interpersonal relationships. In Ilocos Norte such socioeconomic groups are found, though much abbreviated, in the towns and hardly at all in the socially constricted, economically impoverished villages like Buyon. Arayats, perforce, assume the social basis for cooperation and the economic wherewithal; in villages such as Buyon there are neither the social foundations nor the economic means.

AMMONG AND *ARAYAT* IN MAMBABANGA AND ISABELA

Compared with Ilocos Norte there are few ammongs in Isabela; in Mambabanga itself there are none. Though the people in Mambabanga are economically much better off than are those in Buyon, they are, nonetheless, faced with the same kind of operational problem in belonging to an ammong: they do not have a regular income and scheduled payments are difficult to meet. Unlike the people of Buyon there are no persons in Mambabanga who participate in ammongs located in towns. Part of the reason for this is the different stimulus to save. Some ammongs are found in towns like Cauayan and Cabatuan, especially within the business sectors where such funds can be helpful in business activities such as buying stocks of supplies, paying debts, or lending money. Despite the apparent economic advantage, Ilocanos in Isabela are both less pressured and less able to save. Because the people of Mambabanga regularly interrelate with a wide number of persons, they must contend with an extensive network of effective social ties and obligations. Relatively large numbers of kinsmen, compadres, and friends can and do make demands upon one's accumulated wealth. In Buyon, where wealth is relatively more important, social interaction is much more restricted so that fewer persons have correspondingly weaker claims upon the individual. Thus, the economically poor and socially deprived individual in Ilocos Norte is, because of his poverty, better "equipped" to save than his more richly endowed kinsman in Isabela.

Arayats are found in both the towns and barrios of Isabela. They operate on the same principles in the towns there as they do in Laoag in Ilocos Norte, that is, they reflect the socioeconomic unity of the smaller social communities that make up a town. The principles of socioeconomic involvement are essentially the same for the barrios as for the communities within towns; the actual relationships themselves, however, are structured on different socioeconomic arrangements.[5] In Mambabanga the shared interests and interaction systems deriving from landownership, labor exchange, kinship, compadre ties, and neighbor relations are the conditional factors which make an arayat possible. Yet, although these various sets of relationships are generally necessary for the operation of an arayat, membership itself is a matter of choice, not obligation.

Of the sixty households in Mambabanga less than half, twenty-five, are involved in arayats and four of this number belong to an arayat in the adjacent barrio of Harana. The arayat actually located in Mambabanga contains a total of twenty-nine members: twenty-two from Mambabanga, four from the nearby barrio of Concepcion, and three from Harana. Of the twenty-two members from Mambabanga, sixteen are first- or second-generation offspring of the original pioneering families; the remaining five are the immigrants or descendants of those families who came from Concepcion after the flood of 1937—a reflection of the assimilation of this group into the original barrio population.

The seven nonresident members do not contradict the earlier premise that arayats reflect a basic socioeconomic cohesiveness.

Harana, it was noted earlier, was once a part of Mambabanga and several families there are related, consanguineously and affinely, to the original pioneering families; the three arayat member households are of this group. The four members from Concepcion are all related through the 1937 immigrant group. All of the members from Harana and Concepcion have important and active relationships with both kinsmen and nonkinsmen in Mambabanga. The four families in Concepcion exchange work on their fields, located midway between the two barrios and adjacent to those of their relatives in Mambabanga, and they and their kinsmen in Mambabanga have an interest in the ultimate dispositon of familial lands. The three families from Harana have kinsmen in Mambabanga, and they exchange labor on both privately owned and on landlord-owned fields with people from Mambabanga.

As indicated above, less than one-half of the families belong to the arayat. Two families, only recently arrived in Mambabanga, are virtually not part of the social community: they are unrelated to any persons within the barrio, own no land, farm small fields as tenants, have no shared work arrangements because of the smallness of their fields, and engage in none of the social life. They are, therefore, not members of the arayat. Both families reside in Mambabanga as a consequence of their relationship to their landlords and the landlords' connections with people in the barrio. Many of the older people in the barrio do not belong to the arayat because they no longer put on gala events, and consequently, do not have the economic need of the arayat payments—though they do attend such affairs. Some of the very poorest families do not belong because they themselves cannot afford such events as the arayat payments never completely cover the expenses involved. On the other hand, several of the wealthiest families do not participate. It is their claim that they do not need to belong; the arayat, they say, is for those who do require some help and assistance for festive occasions. Also, these people are less concerned about the "social insurance" which the arayat provides; as one affluent widow noted, "We are always invited, anyway." On the other hand, relative age, wealth, and poverty are only mitigating factors in deciding membership; one of the wealthiest and one of the poorest families in Mambabanga are arayat members. The important fact about the arayat in Mambabanga is that it reflects the general cohesiveness of the barrio as a real social entity. The arayat is, in effect, a derivative association to which barrio people may or may not choose to belong. At the same time, though essentially a product of the underlying social interdependency and cohesion, the arayat itself further reinforces barrio cohesiveness.

AN ARAYAT IN THE BARRIO OF HARANA

The social factors relating to an arayat in Harana are perhaps more illuminating than those relating to an arayat in Mambabanga. Harana, it was noted earlier, emerged as a formal, political unit after World War II. This development was partly due to the increasing number of landless tenants coming from central Luzon to work for the largest landowner in Mambabanga, and partly due to antagonisms and animosities which the people in Mambabanga had developed toward this individual, and, by association, his tenants. At that time, most people in Mambabanga worked their own land; the new arrivals came as landless tenants, persons of lower status, strangers not to be trusted—many of them "not even Ilocanos." The first of these tenant families established itself in the western part of Mambabanga, in the half of Harana which is now nearest Mambabanga; later arrivals settled still farther to the west.

The pattern of immigration into Harana has been similar to that of the original settlers of Mambabanga, who worked first as tenants in one of the settled regions along the rivers before moving into the pioneering areas. Many families came to Harana for only a few years, time enough to acquire the necessary farm tools and animals, and then moved into the newer pioneering communities in the foothills of the Sierra Madres. Consequently, the population of Harana has been much less stable than that of Mambabanga. What was the final stage of settlement for the pioneering families of Mambabanga has become the first step for more recent immigrants into Cagayan Valley.

Of course, not all of the original tenants in Harana moved on, just as not all of the earlier pioneers to Isabela left the river margins to move inland. In fact, each year fewer and fewer people leave Harana because of the rapidly dwindling frontier lands. A number of families have resided in Harana for as much as twenty-five years and over one-half of the people have been there for more than ten. Several of the older families have acquired small tracts of land, so that today not all are landless tenants. It is the older tenant families, some of whom have intermarried with families from Mambabanga, who constitute the established, socially intradependent community of Harana: twenty-five of the sixty-three households, or roughly 40 percent, have been there for more than ten years. "Allied" with them are four families from Mambabanga whose lands, and the social relationships deriving from that land, are closer to the "Old Families" of Harana.

In Harana, as in Mambabanga, not all "eligible" persons belong to the arayat. The important thing, however, is that none of the "non-eligible" people are members. These are the most recently arrived tenants, most of them poor by the standards of the older families, with few family ties and no land of their own. Yet, because the majority of persons in Harana work in nearby or even adjacent fields for one or more absentee landlords, most of the people, from both the older and newer families, exchange labor with at least a few of the "other group." These ties alone, however, are an insufficient basis for an arayat. In time, with continued associations in the many and various aspects of agricultural work, they may become the basis for other ties, e.g., marital and compadre relationships. These, along with the ego-centered and interrelated neighbor ties, may ultimately result in the establishment of social bonds necessary for the functioning of an arayat. Such a community developed among the "Old Families" of Harana, and such a community developed between the original settlers in Mambabanga and the later immigrants from Concepcion.

MARKET EXCHANGES IN BUYON AND MAMBABANGA

The involvement of Mambabanga in a commercial, rice-market economy is in marked contrast to the subsistence, home-consumption pattern of rice production found in Buyon. This contrast may be vividly observed when traveling between Ilocos Norte and Isabela. Yet, despite the apparent difference in economic orientation, the particular kinds of market involvement found in Buyon and Mambabanga do not account for variable behavior.[6] Although the contrast and differences are real enough and would necessarily be considered at a provincial or regional level of contrast, they were determined to be unimportant to an explanation of variable behavior at the barrio level or, more specifically, at the level of the two barrios of Buyon and Mambabanga. However, because such differences are so commonly assumed to be significant, and because it is reasonable enough to expect (as this writer did) that different market situations might account for variable behavior, brief mention is made here of the respective conditions. And, as shall be seen, in demonstrating how the market situations are not functionally important for explaining variable behavior, the factors which, in fact, do account for such differences are again stressed and reemphasized.

> A "subsistence economy" is one in which the factors of production are not transacted by the market mechanism. In a subsistence economy, some produce may enter the market—such a situation can be called a "peripheral market." It does not follow that simply because the factors are not transacted in the market that there are no transactions of the factors of production—we have created only a negative, residual category: the absence of market transaction of the factors of production. [Bohannan 1963:241]

> There has in the past been a common error in defining a subsistence economy. That error is to assume that a situation in which a people produces largely what they themselves consume is the same thing as the absence of a market. [Bohannan 1963:240]

Buyon and Mambabanga are peripheral in that the factors of production are not transacted by market mechanisms (i.e., labor is not bought and sold on a commercial basis): they are conducted through the nuclear family and by means of ammuyo exchanges. On the other hand, both Buyon and Mambabanga are engaged in some market activity along with subsistence production. The difference between the two barrios is essentially one of degree: most of what is produced in Mambabanga enters into the market; very little of what is produced in Buyon does. Yet, though average rural families in Ilocos Norte sell and buy relatively little in the markets of nearby towns, they are neither strangers in, nor novices to, commercial exchange. Although they may not understand or appreciate the complexities or extent of the wider economic system, they do understand that small sector of the economy (the market vendor, the tobacco buyer, the moneylender, etc.) which touches village life. The people of Buyon function in their commercial relationships just as effectively (or ineffectively) as the people of Mambabanga.

Productive arrangements in Mambabanga include the use of the nuclear family together with a wide number of socially imperative, dyadic relationships—ammuyo ties—with other villagers. Virtually no such extrafamilial contracts can be found in agricultural production in Buyon. In fact, although market activities outside the barrio are more intense and financially more important in Mambabanga, it is in Buyon where one finds an essentially monetary, impersonal contractual arrangement within the barrio. Market mechanisms of regional and national significance do directly influence the monetary terms of these arrangements,[7] but such contracts are commonly "awarded" on the basis of existing social ties with neighbors, friends, and kinsmen. In Buyon and Mambabanga, both social cohesion and social variability are necessarily understood on the basis of internal socioeconomic relationships and not on the peripheral market situations.[8]

NOTES

1. This estimate is offered only as a general indicator of the relative income level. A comparative estimate for central Isabela would be about five hundred dollars per family above the subsistence level, but the level of subsistence is also higher. The "needs" of a single individual in Buyon are about 1 to 1¼ cavans of **pagay** a year; in Mambabanga about 2 cavans per year.

2. The ammong organizer is often able to reap considerable benefits as a consequence of her position. Since she usually receives the first payment, she can lend the money out at the accepted rate of 5 percent per month. She may make loans to rural farmers or to members of the ammong who have gambled on receiving one of the first payments and have "lost." The organizer is usually a person of relative wealth and status, and, as guarantor of the ammong funds, is able to improve further her financial position.

3. The word "association," as traditionally used in anthropology, may be inappropriate when applied to the ammong because the ammong does not involve people in association. "Institution" may be a better designation, but, because very similar institutions have been called "savings associations" or "rotating credit associations" (Firth and Yamey 1964; Geertz 1962), the two terms are used interchangeably here.

4. It must be noted that the "real" amounts and kinds of social involvement between members of an arayat in Laoag were never observed. Time did not permit an intensive study of any particular arayat in Laoag or of the wider social ties on which the arayats are based. The most that could be ascertained was that the members of arayats were economically important to each other. Additional social significance was assumed from this.

5. A thorough examination of town communities would be necessary to explain adequately the socioeconomic bases of the societal units within a town. Although there are formal barrio political units within each town, these often do not reflect the actual societies in the town. Many such communities are composed of farmers who work the adjacent lands and are, in effect, rural barrios within a town. It would be necessary to examine the underlying systems of social interaction to understand the functioning of the arayat in these circumstances. The marketplace and other socioeconomic communities may reveal similar structures built around different economic arrangements.

6. Both during the prestudy of the area and during the first few months of actual field research, this difference was thought to be one of the most important factors affecting variable behavior. Among the many assump-

tions taken as "theoretical baggage" to the field were certain notions concerning homogenous characteristics of "peasant" or "folk" societies. There are probably few anthropologists in America who have not been influenced, to one degree or another, by the writings of Robert Redfield regarding the socially disruptive influences of market and urban centers. The research alluded to on pages 3–4 of this study described how the people of Ilocos Norte, depicted as being "traditional" and "conservative," subsequently become involved in commercial rice production in Isabela. This suggested to me a "natural" (i.e., socially disruptive) change in line with my preconceptions about the commercialization of peasant society. When I questioned informants in Mambabanga, I solicited comparisons to life in Cagayan Valley, assuming a folk tradition of harmonious barrio life on the Ilocos coast. As most students of the Philippines will probably agree, there are particular dangers in asking Filipinos leading questions; initial responses all seemed to support my "working assumptions." Daily observations and the information gathered in several house-to-house surveys led me to question my initial assumptions, and ultimately, to study comparatively a barrio in Ilocos Norte.

As the data in this work demonstrate, the assumptions of "folk" harmony and disharmony were not confirmed for Ilocanos in either area. For this and other reasons no attempt has been made at using the classifications and assumptions regarding the subject of peasantry. Though the material presented here may add to the arguments surrounding this subject, I felt that the sample communities might be better understood without employing any conceptualizing of peasant society.

7. By "monetary terms," I include those transactions in which a percentage of the crop is paid as well as those transactions conducted with real currency.

8. I do not intend to suggest that existing market conditions or commercial arrangements are not important, or that market conditions will not in the future directly affect intravillage and interpersonal ties. I contend that existing market conditions do not account for variable behavior *now*.

14
COMMUNITY
AND INTEGRATION
IN BUYON
AND MAMBABANGA

The term, barrio, is employed to describe any and all sub-units of the municipalities which lie outside the poblacion (municipal) as well as subdivisions of some of the smaller chartered cities. Physically, the typical rural barrio corresponds to a small village, consisting of one or more clusters of houses, surrounded by the fields in which the barrio people work. [Romani 1956:229]

Buyon and Mambabanga are both subunits of municipalities; from the standpoint of the larger society, they are formal, politically designated units. This recognition from without is, at least in one sense, important to the unity within both barrios since political raison d'être is to a large degree given or imposed. As formal political units, Buyon and Mambabanga are encompassed by larger social environments (i.e., the municipality, the province, the national government) which require small, village subunits. In many, perhaps even most, rural areas in the Philippines, these subunits correspond to functioning socioeconomic units—though the analogy is probably not exact. As a social unit, in terms of effective, socially interdependent and morally obligatory ties, Mambabanga very nearly fits its formal designation as a barrio. Buyon, on the other hand, has both limited and impoverished social ties; it is hardly more than "one or more clusters of houses, surrounded by the fields in which the barrio people work."

Up to this point, the barrios of Buyon and Mambabanga have been examined and compared in terms of the various sets of more or less enduring, interpersonal relationships which are found in the two communities. In both cases, a given set of Philippine cultural themes and a number of social relationships have been considered, each in terms of the respective ecological adjustments made in the different social and physical settings. When considering these adjustments in Mambabanga, the barrio emerges as something more than the total number of crosscutting sets of interpersonal relationships; it is, socially speaking, something more than just the sum of all its parts. In the case of Buyon, however, a social community of individuals is virtually nonexistent.

In a formal sense, Buyon and Mambabanga are "things," their "thingness" most visible in the physically evident facts of houses, rice fields, and people at work. This comparison has emphasized that Buyon and Mambabanga are communities in terms of the relationships empirically found to obtain there. The variable sets of relationships and their differential importance have evolved significantly different kinds of social units.

BUYON AS A SOCIAL ENTITY

Buyon is important as a unit for essentially two reasons: first, it has psychological-associational, emotional importance for the individuals who live there; second, it is a named and numbered unit (Barrio No. 40) of the municipality of Bacarra with a set of formally elected officials. The people's psychological identification with the barrio as "a place" is but one level of several different such "place associations." There are three sitios (informal subbarrios) in Buyon and each of these is important as a place to the people who live there. Romani describes the sitio as being "comprised of from two to fifty houses [with] no formal governmental or legal status" (1956:229). The three sitios of Buyon (see maps 4 and 5) are in large part a consequence of three natural topographical divisions of the barrio.

In addition to the sitios, and geographically within them, there is still another level of places which generally refers to particular spots, and with which people emotionally identify: the "Banyan Tree," the "Creek," the "Hill," the "Ditch," etc. These are not territories in a social-political sense; they do not relate to formal or, in most cases, even informal social systems. These places refer to things which are associated with particular residence areas; they are local places of geographical or social prominence and importance.

The barrio itself represents both a place and a formally designated political unit. On the one hand, the barrio is a place—a place which has psychological and emotional importance for the residents therein. It is the place that people are "from," and, as such, the barrio has significance for individuals which is, at most, only indirectly related to the social significance of the barrio. On the other hand, the barrio is a political subdivision of the municipality of Bacarra.

POLITICAL COHESION IN BUYON

Although Buyon is a subunit of the municipality of Bacarra in a formal, hierarchical sense, it is not an integral, operative part of the larger political system. This functional separation is especially evident in the voting pattern for barrio officials as against that followed for municipal, provincial, and national political offices. The position and duties of barrio teniente, or headman, are, by and large, idealized constructs of the external political order, and, as such, do not always reflect real leadership within local areas.[1] The sitio, too, is not necessarily the focus of local, rural leadership. The fact that a sitio may be the focus of leadership or that the barrio teniente may be the real political power in one particular sitio or barrio only adds to the confusion of understanding other sitios and other barrios. Certain principles of leadership do operate in Buyon, but to type or classify them with relation to some formally delineated and definitive grouping would only result in making Buyon a unique subtype, different in some degree from all barrios in the Philippines. At the same time, the definition of leadership would simply be lost in the subtyping.

The structure of barrio leadership is the same as that for municipality, province, and national government—the alliance system discussed earlier. Within each sitio there are usually one or more individuals, persons who combine relative economic wealth with personal ability, to whom people will go for advice or assistance. These individuals usually have more land than most (and more need for hired labor) and they "know their way around." Having such individuals for kinsmen may, hopefully, make for some "effective" kin ties; having them as neighbors or compadres may permit more "effective" neighbor or compadre relationships. The barrio teniente is normally one of these influential people but, as we shall see, he may not be the most important. The position of barrio teniente is not an especially enviable one for there are no added privileges or powers that go with the office. It is mandatory that the teniente play host to visiting dignitaries, and the economic burden upon him can be considerable. Though the office is a prestigious one (for those who can afford the price), it is essentially a ceremonial position without real political rewards or power. Support for the position (each household has one vote) comes from the candidate's neighbors, kinsmen, and friends, plus other leaders who wish to support him and who, in turn, urge their kinsmen and friends to do likewise. Usually support for a candidate will come from the sitio where most of his friends and kinsmen live, and the candidate with the most kinsmen and friends—especially if they are other *panglakayen*, or leaders, will acquire the office. This "local support" gives the outward appearance of social unity to the sitio, but the superficiality of such cohesion becomes apparent when examining the substance of political life. Barrio officers are not supported and elected in the same way as are candidates for municipal, provincial, and national office. These latter positions are so much more important that the focus of pressures upon the individual voter shifts and increases dramatically.

The barrio teniente in Buyon is more important politically than some tenientes in surrounding barrios. He is, first of all, one of the most important people in the largest sitio of Buyon: the sitio of Buyon proper. Second, he is headman of the Zangjera Camungao and an officer in the Zangjera Curarig. Finally, he has important kinsmen in the town of Bacarra and generally acts as a *lider* (from English "leader" but is better described as "vote getter") for one of the several political alliance systems in Bacarra (Hollnsteiner 1963:41). Yet, although he is an important person, both in his sitio and in his barrio, his effectiveness in municipal elections is limited. He does exert influence as the leader of an irrigation society because the membership will act as a body. In some instances (for reasons that directly affect or benefit the irrigation group), the membership can be moved to vote for one candidate or another.[2] Both the particular and relative political importance of irrigation societies have been mentioned, but, as stated, their influence on the political scene is not of overriding importance. Most people do not belong to irrigation societies and many of those who do belong have only part of their land affected by the irrigation societies.

Municipal, provincial, even national political figures make appeals and promises to the barrio as a unit, but, to be effective, the liders must seek out and solicit support from individuals and individual families. Though candidates make numerous speeches, the most active campaigning is carried out by liders in the politician's own alliance system. These liders make all possible use of friendship, kinship, and other ties which they have managed to establish and maintain in the rural areas. But because all social ties are commonly weak and enfeebled, the reliability of these contacts is always in question. A friendly audience is given the liders of all sides; but the various considerations, most of them economic, which eventually bear upon the actual voting of a single person are too idiosyncratic and individually important to assure a lider that he has gained new support. The position of the lider is not an enviable one. At election time his activity borders on the frenetic, and it is commonly the lider who becomes involved in political violence and killings.

The Ilocano farmer reacts and votes in response to a wide number of pressures such as that exerted by kinship, by "advice" from one or more landlords, by promise or threat of settling a tax problem, by something which affects his irrigation society, by the promise or hope of a job, or by the highest price paid for his vote. He may even avoid voting at all for fear of physical violence! The real political "issue" for him is the way his ballot can favorably or adversely affect him. His vote is important to him and to the politicians. The reasons and pressures for voting one way or another are as numerous and personally imperative as the need for numerous and widely scattered, minuscule rice plots. It may be necessary to split the family vote in a number of ways to fulfill different, often conflicting, obligations.

Thus, the election of barrio teniente in Buyon is not very critical because the post itself, in contrast to regional positions, lacks political importance. As a general rule, the man with the most kinsmen and friends will obtain the position—if he wants it. The point is that the support given or not given means little because the office itself means relatively little or nothing. An individual can afford to be loyal to kinsmen when his right to farm a piece of land is not at stake. Although his vote for barrio teniente may well suggest a unity in the sitio, it is unity without substance or importance—an almost idle social gesture. In municipal and provincial elections, kinship ties are but one factor to consider, and usually such ties are not very important. Voting for a particular candidate is important in regional elections because the offices contested are politically and economically important, and a wide number of political and economic pressures will be brought to bear on the individual voter to make him politically "aware."[3] Appeals to the barrio people's sense of group consciousness or to their collective interests are sure to go unheeded. "Group consciousness" depends upon various sets of reciprocal and effective obligations and these ties, with the exception of those in the irrigation societies, are absent or ineffective in Buyon. The "collective interests" of the people of Buyon rest on or near the margin of subsistence and relate to very specific, very individual, problems and considerations.

RELIGIOUS COHESION IN BUYON

"Socially, the fiesta functions to renew community and kinship ties, to reinforce status and prestige, to bolster existing authority, and to express the system of reciprocal obligations" (Lynch n.d.:26), and perhaps nothing points up the vacuous social character of Buyon and other barrios in Ilocos Norte as much as the absence of a barrio fiesta.

The people of Buyon rationalize the absence of a barrio fiesta by saying that it is a reflection of the Ilocano predilection for being "thrifty." They see it as a cultural virtue, not a social deficiency. Anyway, they say that there are fiestas in town and people can attend those if they wish. The lack of a fiesta, however, cannot be explained simply by economic poverty or the desire to save, though these are factors. It may be explained, instead, by the social narrowness of life in Buyon and the near absence of reciprocal obligations. There is little to celebrate as a barrio. There is no large socioeconomic grouping to warrant and receive ritual recognition and reinforcement; there is no barrio unit which merits the guardianship of a patron saint. The only effective social groupings of any size are the irrigation societies, and, as mentioned in chapter 12, the zangjeras do have a smaller version of a fiesta; they do have social ties which are ritually celebrated and which are annually reinforced. The most effective social tie in Buyon is that of neighbors based and nurtured, as it is in Mambabanga, by reciprocal rights and obligations. But rather than compensating for the paucity of, and conflict in, other social ties, the neighbor relation is itself debilitated and weakened. Whereas conflict between neighbors in Mambabanga can be adjusted by moving to a new location, the shortage of land and house lots in Buyon, often the very bone of contention between kinsmen, seriously limits such a solution. Buyon is in fact very nearly a "place" only.

MAMBABANGA AS A SOCIAL ENTITY

Like Buyon, Mambabanga is a subunit of a municipality and is "a place." Unlike Buyon, there are no sitios, the houses being concentrated in a single, contiguous unit. At one time there were two sitios in Mambabanga: Mambabanga proper and Harana, and the names of the sitios remained the names of the barrios. Mambabanga is broken into the "West Side" and the "East Side," but these are not referred to as sitios nor is the division actually recognized by everyone. As in Buyon, there are various "subplaces": the "Creek," the "Chapel," the "Big Bamboo Cluster," etc.

The most important single social fact about Mambabanga is that it is something much more than just a "place" or just a political subdivision of a municipality. The raison d'être of Mambabanga derives from the network of interrelated and interdependent sets of social ties which effectively relate all but a few families in the barrio. The opening up of Cagayan Valley required the collective, cooperative effort of several families in establishing and developing pioneer communities. Mambabanga was thus founded, developed, and is still maintained, on the basis of interfamily dependence. Unlike Buyon, the inheritance of land is not so desperate that it immolates the effectiveness of kinship ties. Kinsmen are usually important because kinship ties are regularly maintained and reinforced in a meaningful way through daily work and association, and because conflict over the inheritance of land is less critical with solutions to such problems more easily found.

Mambabanga is by no means free of conflict or dissension. There are intra- and inter-family disputes over land. Ill feeling is sometimes generated when an individual fails to obtain a loan or repay a debt. The old families of Mambabanga still have loyalties and connections which pull them towards kinsmen and friends in Harana, while the new families still have important connections and obligations in Concepcion. Two families are in virtual social and economic isolation from the rest of the barrio, and a few others are less socially committed than most. The important thing is not so much that conflict exists as that alternative solutions are possible. People move their houses or build new ones in order to improve neighbor relations. If tension develops between tenant and landlord, there are other lands to be worked for less demanding persons. Most important, the social links and bonds which relate people are the very avenues through which social and individual problems can be mediated and solutions found. Although Mambabanga is by no means a community free of conflict, it is very much a community. It is a community based upon the interrelatedness of operationally effective, egocentric ties stemming from the consanguineal and affinal kinship systems, the various sets of ammuyo work groups, the ties between friends and compadres, and the bond of neighbor to neighbor. These ties find expression and reinforcement both in the political activity and in the religious ceremonialism of the barrio.

POLITICAL COHESION IN MAMBABANGA

Political activity in Mambabanga is much more intense and competitive than in Buyon, where the election of barrio teniente occurs with little, if any, conflict. But the point was made earlier that the position of barrio teniente in Buyon is neither greatly sought after nor is it one of importance. In Mambabanga the opposite is true. Because Mambabanga is a viable social unit with a community consciousness and a variety of shared interests, it is important in the larger political scene. The position of barrio teniente is an important political office because the barrio is an important social unit. Mambabanga has significance as a political unit in the same way (but not for the same reasons) that the irrigation societies have in Ilocos Norte. The barrio teniente is the focus of political activity from within the barrio, and he is in an important focal position for political action from without the barrio. As in Buyon, the position involves considerable expense, there is no formal authority, and little, if any, informal political power is associated with the office. However, it does involve considerable prestige and, for the teniente and his associates, it can afford important economic and social links in the poblacion nearby. For the people who can afford the economic burden of barrio office, there are social and economic advantages to be gained from ties and obligations to important townsmen. Thus, because Mambabanga is a socially effective unit, the position of barrio teniente is an important political position; and because the office is an important position, there is competition and sometimes friction and conflict among the candidates and their followers. This competition gives, at first glance, an appearance of disunity, but, in fact, just the opposite is true. The conflict that exists derives from the very social interdependence which gives the barrio a degree of solidarity, and, ultimately, its importance in the larger political setting. In Buyon, just the opposite applies: the barrio is not a social unit, the position of the barrio teniente is not, therefore, important, and there is seldom competition or friction involved with barrio elections. In Mambabanga it is a case of conflict deriving from cohesion.

People in Mambabanga state that partisan support and factionalism in their barrio results from their support of one or the other of the national political parties, the Liberals or the Nationalists. The Liberal Party faction is associated with the original settlers of Mambabanga and their descendants, while the Nationalists are mostly the families and their offspring from Concepcion. The Old Families, the Liberals, outnumber the others by approximately two to one, but, despite this numerical advantage, the Nationalists have several times won the position of barrio teniente. In the most recent election they lost by only one vote.

Although the two groups tend to identify, in name at least, with a national political party, voting is a matter of alliance ties and obligations. The actual voting revolves around six essentially different, socially important, individuals: four from the Old Families and two from the New Families. Effective social ties and intermarriage have tended to blur the lines somewhat between the followings of particular individuals, as in the case of the even less definitive Old Family, Nationalist—New Family Liberal "split." However, when friction does occur, it is normally allayed and ameliorated by the very social fabric which makes that competition possible, the social interdependency linking nearly all barrio families in Mambabanga.[4]

Prior to the arrival of the New Families from Concepcion in 1937, Mambabanga tended to affiliate with one poblacion alliance only, that which is now (more or less) the Liberal Party faction in Luna. As already mentioned, the families from Concepcion traditionally supported the Nationalist faction in Luna. Since 1937 the support of candidates for municipal office along "party lines" has been of some importance for Mambabanga. Each faction has kinsmen involved in municipal elections, and the names of party candidates are often the same as the names of important people in the barrio.

The political situation in Luna is somewhat different than in nearby municipalities such as Cauayan or Cabatuan. Luna is little more than a large barrio with municipal offices, and the social stratification system is not so marked or pronounced as it is in Cauayan or Cabatuan. The real social distance and distinction between the upper-class townsmen and the lower-class barrio people in Luna are not great, and many barrio people have socio-economic ties with higher-status kinsmen and other individuals in the poblacion. On the other hand, the upper-class politicians of Cauayan and Cabatuan are relatively wealthier, and, correspondingly, are less frequently and less emotionally involved with the lower-class people from the surrounding barrios. Between Luna and its barrios the social distance is relatively small and the effective social bonds more personal and intense.[5]

The result of Luna's "small town politics" is to make the "party" factionalism within Mambabanga more pronounced than would be the case if the barrio were linked to a larger town. Mambabangans' socially intense, emotionally important ties to Luna tend to perpetuate and maintain the distinctions between the Old Families and New Families. In towns such as Cauayan, Ilagan, and Santiago, with socioeconomic differentiation and class distinctions much more pronounced and important, the close, interpersonal character of town and barrio ties is less significant. In effect, the ties between Mambabanga and Luna are more nearly those of kinship and friendship, much less those of lower class to upper class. To a considerable degree, the support which is given party politics in Luna still depends on personalities and the individual voter's social and emotional ties to the particular candidate. Depending upon the candidate running for municipal office, and considering the highly egocentric principle of alliance system organization, Mambabanga's voters can shift considerably one way or the other, towards the Liberals or the Nationalists.[6] Though this factional split has caused some political "problems" for Mambabanga, it has also given the barrio a position of special importance, a consequence of its being a pivotal block of votes during an election. The other barrios tend to vote for one or another alliance system, as traditionally did Mambabanga. The split in Mambabanga has made the campaigning for municipal office somewhat more intense than in most barrios, and has caused promises of political favor to escalate.

Politically, the people of Mambabanga are influenced by two different loyalties: the first revolves around the support of candidates for barrio office; the second, on the voting and support given municipal candidates. For barrio election the support is given to the candidate on the basis of his "position" within the barrio alliance systems in respect to any given voter; for municipal office the barrio pattern is often crosscut by wider loyalties and obligations outside the barrio (where they are still socially effective) which link people to the "small town politics" of Luna. But, as already mentioned, intermarriage and interrelatedness have broken down and blurred the distinctions and loyalties separating the Old and New Families. As might be expected, because the New Families were both fewer in number and because they were the ones to

move and socially and economically dislocate themselves, theirs
has been a steady and gradual absorption into the social and economic fabric of the Old Families of Mambabanga. Over half of
the descendants of the New Families now consider themselves
Liberals or else "independents." As one young man informed this
writer, "My father votes for his friends and relatives from Concepcion (i.e., the New Families), but my friends and most of my
relatives are here in Mambabanga, and I vote for the Liberals."
Political loyalties could not be better defined.

RELIGIOUS COHESION IN MAMBABANGA

The people of Mambabanga make no claims of thrift or frugality
with regard to fiestas. They recognize that money could be saved
by not having a fiesta, but "thriftiness" gives way to two annual
fiestas in Mambabanga: one in May and another in November. The
most important of the two fiestas follows the harvest of the main
crop in early May. Although the May celebration is ostensibly held
to honor the Virgin Mary, the people's knowledge of Catholicism
in general and their patroness in particular is somewhat limited
and imprecise. The second and smaller fiesta is held in November
and follows the harvest of the second crop. The November fiesta
was begun by the Old Families shortly after settling the area,
whereas the one in May was established after the movement of the
New Families to Mambabanga from Concepcion. The importance
of the fiesta in May over that in November relates to an essentially
practical consideration: more money is available at that time of
year. Prior to the emergence of rice as an important commercial
crop, the end of one season was as good (or bad) as the other. The
fact that more effort and time goes into the May fiesta does not
reflect a view as to the religious preeminence of the Virgin Mary
nor does it in any way reflect a social preeminence of New Families. Participation and activity in both fiestas is based upon the
various shared interests and associations of individual families. The
social focus in both fiestas is on the barrio as a whole.

The main activity for both fiestas is held near the school at the
west end of the barrio where booths, most of them operated by
town merchants, are erected. Here, games of chance are played
and drinks and special foods are sold. Nearby are a paved court and
a small covered stage which were constructed through the cooperative efforts of the barrio people. A fiesta committee and mayor
(the man in charge of the fiesta) arrange for collecting funds, and

though the assessments are equal, the more affluent families expect, and are expected, to contribute more. A number of money-raising events are scheduled which include dancing and "voting" for Fiesta Queen, a ten- or eleven-year-old girl who symbolically presides over the fiesta. The number of "votes" is equivalent to the number of tickets sold by and for a candidate, so that the girl with the greatest number of friends and kinsmen becomes the Fiesta Queen. The barrio chapel is refurbished and the attendance at the special fiesta mass, which is said by a priest from Cabatuan, is greater than it is at regular times of the year when only a handful of women attend. A number of infants may be baptized at this time establishing or reinforcing social ties and obligations through compadre ties. Hospitality is of special importance and considerable time and expense go into the preparation of food. There is much visiting among families within the barrio as well as with friends and relatives from outside—especially from Harana and Concepcion. A number of important people from one or more of the nearby towns attend, and politicians and nonpoliticians alike give long and florid speeches. The speeches, partying, dancing, and drinking continue unabated throughout the night. A few vendors' booths remain open through the following day.

The people of Mambabanga are proud of the fact that they have two fiestas; most barrios have one. Entertainment, gambling, eating and drinking, seeing relatives, hearing a special mass, displaying and competing with one's wealth all enter into the fiesta activity. The fiestas are a ritual statement of the fact that Mambabanga is a social community and, at the same time, they reinforce the unity of the barrio. The fiestas are shared, cooperative undertakings which, like any cooperative undertaking, reflect the fact that the people have shared aims and interests which derive from and are based upon effective, interrelated, and interdependent social ties. They are a statement to the effect that there is substance to the social ties which involve reciprocal obligations and prestations. The fiesta is probably the most characteristic ritual feature of Philippine lowland life, and it is found in a variety of socioeconomic settings. The socioeconomic arrangements in Mambabanga make the fiesta possible; in Buyon they do not. In Ilocos Norte fiestas are, by and large, restricted to towns and marketplaces where, it can be argued (though it remains to be demonstrated), they reflect political patronage and the quest for prestige by the politicians together with the shared activities and interests of the market community. In the rural barrios of Ilocos Norte there are few fiestas and, to judge from Buyon, there is little to celebrate—economically or socially.

As a social unit, the barrio manifests itself in two ways: ceremonially and politically. In Buyon the former manifestation is non-existent and the latter is maintained primarily by the exigencies of the larger society. The political and ceremonial activities found in Mambabanga have no functional place in the sociocultural situation extant in Buyon. In Mambabanga political and ceremonial activities reinforce and reintegrate barrio unity. Whereas the fiesta is a locally valued, widely practiced activity in most of the Philippines, in the Ilocos it is not. Instead, deprived of both the reasons and the means for fiestas, the Ilocano there makes an economic rationalization of his social poverty and stresses thrift and frugality. In much of Isabela, while still extolling Ilocano virtues, the people express and stress the ties that make theirs a society in fact as well as in name.

NOTES

1. For instance, Republic Act #2370, *An Act Granting Autonomy to Barrios of the Philippines,* June 20, 1959, suggests by name alone the externally structured importance of the barrio. This act established elective officials in all barrios and outlined responsibilities and procedures. Although it may roughly delineate ideal barrio leadership, it is only the approximation of this which is imposed. Since the period of field work, tenientes have been "promoted" to the title of capitan.
2. Seldom would the irrigation group back all of the candidates on a party "ticket" because the zangjera votes for the individual and the individual's promises and not for the political party.
3. It should be mentioned that the number of votes a particular candidate will receive can usually be calculated with fair precision. The effective obligations and loyalties are well known and the various methods used to check "secret" ballots will assure that the voters meet their obligations. A last minute boost in the price of votes might give an eleventh-hour victory to a particular candidate but not to an entire slate of party candidates.
4. The case of Mr. Cruz, mentioned in chapters 3 and 12, is an example of the failure of socioeconomic ties to assuage such conflict. Mr. Cruz was a person of socioeconomic importance and it was his tenants, plus some older families who were loyal to him, who formed the population basis for Harana. As Mr. Cruz became increasingly prosperous, he became less dependent upon his barrio mates and increasingly divorced from the reciprocal ties of barrio life. Eventually his influence caused the community to split into two barrios.

5. This difference is especially pronounced in a comparison of the behavior of barrio people in Luna and Cauayan towards upper-class townsmen. Since socioeconomic differences are more pronounced in Cauayan, the behavior there of the *kabarrioan* (the man from the barrio) toward the elite is reserved and formal. The same person is much more relaxed in relating to the elite of Luna. As a town, Luna resembles several other smaller, economically less important poblacions in Isabela which, like Luna, are geographically isolated within the valley or have only recently emerged as towns in newly pioneered areas. It is in the economically important centers like Ilagan, Santiago, and Cauayan that socioeconomic differences are greatest and class lines most pronounced.

6. As an example of this, the landlord who replaced Mr. Cruz in Harana ran for municipal office in Luna on the Liberal "ticket" and he received a solid block of votes from Mambabanga. The Nationalists in Mambabanga explained that they voted for him because they know him and he is close to them.

PART 4
CONCLUSIONS

15
INTERPRETATIONS
AND
NEW PROBLEMS

FACTORS OF VARIABILITY

As outlined in chapter 7, the same normative social systems and traditional cultural themes are shared by the people of Buyon and Mambabanga. At a higher, more general level of contrast, these are cultural themes and social principles which Ilocanos share with other lowland cultural groups. I have made an effort in this study to delineate the major factors affecting variable behavior and to demonstrate their significance with specific reference to the different socioeconomic environments which confront and involve the two barrios. Thus, Buyon and Mambabanga represent the differential responses of two Ilocano rice-growing communities to the demands, impingements, and opportunities of the wider socioeconomic orders within the context and under the influence of particular historical developments.

The characterization of the Ilocanos as being "hardworking," "thrifty," and "industrious" is interpreted as having been developed and maintained by the limitations of the penurious social and natural environment in Ilocos Norte. A set of folk images and patterns of behavior have developed there which are, in the context of that regional setting, very nearly "virtues of necessity." At the same time, given the different historical factors and less demanding social and environmental circumstances, behavioral patterns in Isabela have deviated considerably from the more traditional, "conservative" Ilocano stereotype. And, despite the fact that the folk view of traditional Ilocano "virtues" is still employed in the set of social norms, the actual behavior of Mambabangans is much more characteristic of the general, less intense Philippine lowland cultural stereotype. The virtues of thrift, frugality, and industriousness which characterize (or at least rationalize) life in Ilocos Norte are not especially necessary or important in Isabela.

It is perhaps impossible to delineate and define the exact importance of environmental, demographic, social, political, and economic variables—those factors which have affected and influenced the patterns of behavior in Buyon and Mambabanga. However,

175

without attempting to measure or quantify these variables, a summary of their significance is pertinent here. For instance, the relative demographic facts, although they cannot be said to explain any particular pattern of behavior, have indirect consequences for a very wide range of activities. Also, the extrasocial environment which confronted Mambabanga in the early stages of pioneering in Isabela, when inland settlements were faced with the threat of "headhunting savages," had significance for the social-historical development of interfamily and intrabarrio ties. Overseas Ilocanos, who have provided a continuous source of wealth and savings, have directly contributed to the social and economic conditions regarding landownership and inheritance in Ilocos Norte. They have directly and indirectly influenced the class structure and the pattern of municipal and provincial political activity.

Climatic and topographical conditions have influenced, and continue to influence, behavior in both areas. The specific geographical correlates related to the emergence of cooperative irrigation in Ilocos Norte (and, by implication, not elsewhere) can at best be only suggested, however. The fact that such irrigation societies are hardly viable in Isabela is, in part, related to the different geographical factors which confront Ilocanos in the upper Cagayan Valley. And, together with the presence of "headhunting savages" (but with a more direct and immediate impact upon community life), the endemic malarial conditions of Isabela were important to the development and cohesion of communities like Mambabanga.

The differential size and relative importance of large landholdings have been significant for Ilocos Norte and Isabela. As indicated in chapters 3 and 12, and again in chapter 14, the relative "poverty" of the upper class in Ilocos Norte, as well as the new sources of wealth made available to the lower class, resulted in the unusual situation by which Ilocano tenants acquired ownership of the land. The subsequent "impoverishment" of the upper class and their virtual alienation from the land have, in part, led to the intensive involvement of the Ilocano elite in political activity. In Isabela, on the other hand, the large, often absentee-owned estate holdings followed successful small-farm pioneering; after profitable (and sometimes legally dubious) land speculation, these essentially economic enterprises became the foci of the emergence and development of commercial rice production.

Differential political conditions have been both cause and effect in the historical development of Ilocos Norte and Isabela. In Ilocos

Norte the political climate which emerged was itself an important factor in the intensification of social pressures which came to bear upon family life and which further debilitated social ties. Partly because effective communal relationships exist in Isabela, political life there has tended to encourage and intensify rather than constrict wider social ties.

Economic relationships affect the behavioral characteristics of each community. The elaboration and maintenance of work-exchange arrangements and the relative effectiveness of land-kin-based ties are especially important to the more inclusive community ties in Mambabanga. Ammuyo work exchanges in Isabela constitute important sets of social ties which are interwoven with other social relationships, specifically those of neighbor, friend, and kinsman. In Buyon, however, circumstances associated with the inheritance of land are especially conflict-laden, and, except within the irrigation societies, work exchange relationships are virtually nonexistent. At the same time, although problems of inheritance exist in Mambabanga, such problems are not so critical, and social and economic solutions to such problems are possible. The ties binding landlord to tenant developed into a unique pattern in Ilocos Norte which ultimately involved the tenant in a complex of politically intense, but socially vacuous, relationships. In Mambabanga, the landlord-tenant relationship neither added to nor detracted from barrio cohesion, despite the essentially commercial character of such ties. It was also demonstrated that the involvement of Mambabangans in the commercial marketing of rice does not result in the impersonalization of barrio life nor the attenuation of social ties.

Finally, it was argued that the social and natural environments of Isabela foster and sustain social cohesion and have direct consequences on the internal structure and integration of communities such as Mambabanga. The social patterns which developed and were enlarged upon in this environment have tended to intensify communal ties and social integration. More precisely, the "social climate" deriving from the relationship of social and cultural components on the one hand, and the environment on the other, has helped to produce the religious and political patterns found in Mambabanga. These patterns are part of the setting and they continue to contribute to further social cohesion. In contrast, the environment of Buyon does not functionally add to the extension or maintenance of social ties and there are no equivalent religious or political "dividends"; social ties are only weakly elaborated and may, in fact, themselves be sources of social conflict.

Behavioral patterns in both areas relate to a complex of variables none of which specifically or individually accounts for the particular circumstances that exist today in Buyon and Mambabanga. An adequate study of variable behavior involves a consideration of the wider environmental circumstances, in terms of historical and immediate importance and as they relate to the normative social systems and cultural themes. An effective explanation of the particular or exact importance of such variables is perhaps impossible because such variables constitute a *system* of variables and are not simply the total number of factors with which behavior patterns are functionally structured and arranged.

Philippine culture and social organization perhaps may be best characterized as being flexible and adaptable. However, it would be wrong to assume that social diversity and cultural regionalism in northern Luzon are exclusively matters of economic or even ecological circumstances. Throughout the history of Ilocos Norte institutions (e.g., irrigation societies, the arayat, the sabong) and attitudes (e.g., thriftiness, hard work) have developed which collectively constitute patterns of behavior and attitudes which are distinctly Ilocano. These attitudes have helped to produce the kind of individual who is successful in pioneering wilderness areas, expanding into already occupied regions, competing with other lowland people, and providing the vast majority of Filipino workers and emigrants for overseas.

Yet, the situation in Isabela suggests that the special characteristics of the Ilocano, once he is established in a less demanding situation, become moderated by the more general imperatives of Philippine culture. In a sense, the differences between the Ilocanos in Ilocos Norte and the Ilocanos in Isabela can be reduced to the rational considerations behind, and the resultant choices in, behavior. In Ilocos Norte the range of behavior is very often limited to economic matters and, in a large proportion of families, involves a relatively low level of subsistence. In Isabela, life is much less directly proscribed and, although no less rational, remains less confined by strictly economic considerations. The Ilocano in Isabela is able to meet the economic demands of life and still make behavioral choices on the basis of his sense of personal pride, his loyalty to friend and kinsman, his quest for status and prestige, and the emphasis he puts upon the symbols of success. The relative affluence of life in Isabela permits more than a continuous, nagging concern with mere survival. In very many instances, the Ilocano in Isabela is able to regard economic matters as the means to an end, not simply or exclusively as an end in itself as is commonly the case in Ilocos Norte. Consequently, some of the Ilocano "virtues of necessity" have not been maintained or have been less enthusiastically pursued in Isabela.

A specific Ilocano cultural development was the establishment of irrigation societies, but, despite the fact that such societies would have been an "obvious advantage" in the development of the region, very few irrigation cooperatives were organized and those that were, operate much less effectively, given the goals of obtaining and maintaining a supply of water, than do the parent organizations in Ilocos Norte. The "obvious advantage" to having irrigation societies is based upon economic needs and rationale; in Isabela such needs and rationale are not now so vital or crucial. In the same way, thrift and savings are not major preoccupations of Ilocanos in Isabela; the traditional cottage industries are no longer practiced; and land is neither so dear nor so emotionally super-charged. The people in Isabela recognize that there are more important things in Ilocano life than decisions based simply or exclusively on economic considerations. They do make decisions which involve important economic factors but which are basically and preeminently social considerations.

The principles of social organization are the same for both Buyon and Mambabanga. They are a combination of several ego-centered systems: the bilateral kin "group," affines, age-mates and friends, neighbors, work-mates, ritual or fictive kinsmen, and certain interclass ties. As a result, the whole barrio is a complex of interrelated and interdependent, egocentric social relationships. Mambabanga is not organized on a single principle such as kinship; it is organized on a set of principles which find expression through each individual and each individual family. And, whereas the barrio of Mambabanga is not neatly bounded or independent of other families in other barrios, it does, nonetheless, constitute a viable, ongoing society.

Buyon has the same normative social and cultural principles as Mambabanga, but the total social fabric there is but weakly developed and maintained. This has resulted in a very fragile, tenuous barrio system existing in little more than name alone. The situation may be summed up by saying that, whereas the social and physical environment of Mambabanga encourages the use and extension of social ties, the equivalent environmental factors in Buyon act as virtual deterrents to the same social and cultural principles. Thus, although Buyon and Mambabanga are both formally designated barrios, they differ considerably in terms of their social "substance." To understand the differences between Buyon and Mambabanga, and among other barrios as well, it is necessary to examine the efficacy of existing social ties in terms of the wider socioeconomic arrangements. The Ilocanos have an aphorism to the effect that "there are kinsmen, and there are kinsmen." It is an expression no less applicable to barrios.

GENERALIZATIONS AND NEW PROBLEMS

This study has been concerned with what Eggan has called a comparison of "very small scale" (1954:758). Yet, by comparing the functioning of cultural themes and principles of social organization in two different situations, some of the more dynamic factors of general importance in Philippine society and culture are highlighted. In order to make a really definitive statement regarding the importance or effectiveness of a given culture theme or pattern of social organization, however, it would obviously be necessary to study situations other than those which focus only on wet-rice economics or Ilocano barrios. The comparison made here suggests that there is considerable flexibility and adaptability to be found in the normative systems of Philippine culture and social organization. The essential elasticity of social ties and the stress on the situational logic of cultural themes imply that the fundamental features of Philippine life are extremely flexible, an adaptability which permits considerable re-formation with little or no change in the underlying arrangements. In terms of cultural continuity and the persistence of existing social patterns, there appear to be a wide range of situational adjustments which do not require formal changes in the basic social principles or thematic patterns.

The strict genealogical importance of Philippine kinship has virtually no significance in Buyon and Mambabanga in the absence of real social obligations. The Ilocano kinship system actually functions in different social and physical environments with an almost "accordionlike" facility to adjust to a variety of demands and opportunities. Yet, this is a structural feature applicable to probably most if not all bilaterally organized systems and is certainly not uniquely Filipino. Of more basic and significant importance is the combination and unity of the normative social systems and cultural themes which together, and only together, constitute the essential fundamental character of Philippine life. In this study, the social and cultural dimensions have been analytically distinguished when, in fact, they are but abstractions or models derived from behavior, the phenomenon observed. The problem with such abstractions is that their heuristic worth is taken to represent some degree of efficacy which analytical concepts do not and cannot possess. Thus, the important factor is in the conjunction and unity of normative social systems and cultural themes which we derive from the real data, behavior. To consider the two separately and independently in the study of socioeconomic variability would be to construct a methodologically unsound and unnecessary dichotomy.

This characterization and conceptualization of the flexibility and adaptability of normative systems can perhaps lend itself to the understanding of certain conditions and features of Philippine life. The underlying connaturality of Philippine life is often commented upon but, in the explanation of particular cultural situations, commonly becomes subsumed or lost in the description of situational and subcultural uniqueness. The Islands present a variegation of cultural distinctions in ritual, artistic, and material expression. Yet, the feeling is never lost that the differences are but nuances—cultural veneers that merely overlay the basic social substance that makes up all Philippine groups. Keesing noted the same thing in examining the multiplicity of groups in northern Luzon: "One of the striking features of the northern Luzon record . . . is the repetitive nature of certain phenomena of persistence and change," which he characterized as the "indigenous stamp" of the "cultural milieu" (1962:343).

Eggan's work (1941, 1963) has also been concerned with certain "internal factors" which help to explain the direction of change in northern Luzon. In the first of these two studies, he examined both the social variability and the regularity which are characteristic of different ethnolinguistic groups (from the Ifugao in the eastern Cordillera Central Mountains to Ilocano populations on the west coast), and in the later study he examined a similar pattern of differences and regularities found within a single group (the Kalingas).

Without taking up the concept of cultural drift, the central issue of Eggan's studies, I believe that essentially the same social and cultural focus appears to be important for understanding the direction of change among mountain populations as is required for understanding the respective patterns of behavior that characterize and distinguish Buyon and Mambabanga. "The factors responsible for certain of these variations [in northern Luzon] are both external and internal ... *the variations in social organizations which we have noted seem to represent a series of correlated phenomena which has an internal consistency* and which is related to factors such as population density, relative wealth per capita, and the like, rather than to external contacts" (Eggan 1941:16; italics mine).

In further describing the nature of culture change in the light of new evidence, Eggan later noted with respect to kinship systems and kinship behavior that, "where theory and practice differ, we can suspect directional change. . . . One might ask: 'Where is the norm?' Here there seems to be only a series of sliding scales. . . ." (1963:354).

Eggan is especially concerned with demonstrating the importance of the "inner dynamics and adaptive processes" in the study of social and cultural change. The suggestion made here is that the combination and unity of the normative social systems and cultural themes constitute an essential, fundamental feature of Philippine life. No attempt has been made to demonstrate the specific form and content of such a pattern or theme; it is suggested, rather, that such a feature can be of importance and significance in the study and restudy of other Philippine groups and perhaps other Malaysian peoples as well. Employed as a working hypothesis for future research, it can perhaps be more rigorously demonstrated and defined to add to the understanding of Philippine populations. Though many students of Malaysian cultures still look for, and consequently still find, social and cultural differences within and between the Philippines, Indonesia, and Malaya, it is perhaps time that social scientists, particularly anthropologists, concentrated more on the dynamics of cultural persistence and regularity in Malaysia and less on cultural uniqueness and particularism.

EPILOGUE

In June 1970 I had the opportunity to revisit Buyon and Mamba-banga. From my interests as an anthropologist I was eager to see the changes seven years had brought about, particularly those changes which had followed the introduction of miracle rice—hybrid varieties developed at the International Rice Research Institute in Los Baños south of Manila. On a more personal level, I was interested in seeing the people and places that I had known in Isabela and Ilocos Norte.

In both Mambabanga and Buyon a number of older people had died, among them two of the most important informants on the early pioneering history of central Isabela. A few people in both barrios had moved away, some as individuals and some with families. Most of the teenagers I had known in 1963 had since married and now have children of their own. All of the four young people who had worked with me on interviews and surveys had moved away. One of them had moved from Mambabanga only as far as Cauayan; another had moved from Buyon to within a few miles of my own residence here in Honolulu! In a few short days it was impossible, of course, to see these individual events as part of larger social patterns, and they were not noted for that purpose.

Broad patterns of change, patterns directly relevant to what has been written here, were most evident in terms of agricultural developments. Admittedly, any interpretation of these changes is impressionistic but, because my "analysis" is based upon a more comprehensive study of an earlier state of affairs, the generalizations which follow are perhaps not without merit.

Because I had begun my original fieldwork in Mambabanga, I visited there first. I had heard and read that Isabela was a "priority province" for the development of miracle rice production and, given my own interpretations of earlier events, I assumed that the changes there would be more pronounced and dramatic than those in Ilocos Norte. In Mambabanga the most significant change has not come directly from the introduction of new rice varieties but, rather, from the extension of the Magat Irrigation System. This irrigated area now includes the higher land on the secondary flood plain, land south and east of Mambabanga which was single cropped to early maturing varieties seven years ago. This now means that very nearly all rice fields in Mambabanga are bayag and, more important, two crops of rice are now grown.

The pattern of double-cropping rice is possible because of the much shorter growing periods, 120 to 130 days, required of the miracle rice series. Now, with added lands under controlled irrigation and with the increased productivity possible with miracle rice, overall grain production is said to have increased by roughly three times that of 1963. At the same time, however, corn is no longer grown as a cash crop. This, together with increased expenses of production and the rising costs of goods and services, has meant that people are not three times wealthier today than they were in 1963. Yet, whatever the actual degree of difference, people are much better off today. Despite some difficulties in obtaining the desired kinds and amounts of new seed, coupled with some problems of marketing, they are successfully growing the miracle rice.

For the people in Mambabanga, taste remains an important consideration when choosing what varieties of rice to plant. The few farmers with whom I talked indicated that they and others still grow some of the older commercial varieties of pagay tagalog, but most of these crops are kept for home consumption. These farmers are also growing small plots of glutinous pagay iloko—and still harvesting this variety with the rakem. Both irrigation societies, the Union Baccarina and the Society Mambabanga, are functioning, and there have been no moves to incorporate them into the newly extended government system. I was told that the two zangjeras now operate with less internal friction. This may be a consequence of the added premium which is placed upon irrigated land.

The more visible material changes within the residential area of Mambabanga include several new, relatively expensive houses, a new school, a new chapel, and much improved barrio roads. (The latter development may be a consequence of the fact that the mayor of Luna, who is from the adjacent barrio of Harana, is the landlord for most of the tenants of Harana and for many of the part-time tenants in Mambabanga.) I was told that transistor radios are now found in every home. Two hand tractor-cultivators are now being used in the fields. Perhaps of more direct social significance is the reported change in the tenancy relationship. Whereas the 70–30 arrangement was the normal pattern in 1963, "many" landlords, it was said, now require a 2/3–1/3 division of the crop, a slight increase in profit for the landlord. This undoubtedly reflects the increasing numbers of people on the land and may affect social patterns within the barrio. These changes in the material well-being and the economic relationships of Mambabanga have undoubtedly altered social relationships in some way. In such a short visit one sees only the outward signs and symptoms of such change.

Perhaps because I expected Buyon to have changed the least, and perhaps because any change there is relatively more pronounced, I was especially surprised at the magnitude of change brought about by the introduction of miracle rice. Like their counterparts in Mambabanga, the farmers of Buyon now grow two crops of rice. In addition to these they continue to grow a cash crop, usually garlic. This triple cropping has been made possible with the shorter growing period required by the new miracle varieties. And, while Ilocos Norte is still a rice-import area, the rice grown there now feeds more than just the families of the farmers who raise it. The fact that rice has now become a cash crop is evident by the number of rice mills that have developed.

The changes in Ilocos Norte are more complex, more convoluted than they are in Isabela. It would be much more difficult today to generalize about the system of rice production than it was in 1963. In a very loose sense there are two systems: that associated with growing the traditional pagay iloko and that of the miracle rice. But because there is a great deal of experimentation going on by the individual farmers involved, a generalization about the two systems would be much too simplified. The farmers themselves talk about this experimentation: the reports of new varieties, improved tastes, shorter growing periods, greater disease resistance, better marketing possibilities, the requirements for weeding, the costs and uses of pesticides and fertilizers, and so on.

Having studied in 1963 the methods by which rice was being grown, I was especially impressed with the new and changing patterns of cropping. In adjacent fields farmers can be seen harvesting one of the miracle rice series with a sickle and, next to that, farmers harvesting a field of pagay iloko with a rakem. Nearby, a family can be seen collecting the seedlings for transplanting to still another field. Between the fields will be several rows of corn grown for very short periods and used only as fodder for the draft animals.

The price of land has continued to rise: 12,500 to 15,000 pesos per hectare for irrigated rice land in 1963; 16,000 to 20,000 pesos for the same land today. One bank manager in Laoag stated that more dollars are coming into Ilocos Norte than ever before and that savings have more than doubled in seven years. The fact that there are now twelve banks instead of three would seem to substantiate this. In general the economy seems much improved but how this relates to the economies of individual families is impossible to say here.

The most interesting aspect of the changes taking place in Buyon is not that the system of agriculture has changed. The system (as I saw it, at least) changed when Ilocano rice farmers made the decision to grow miracle rice. More interesting is the question of what was involved for the individual farmer in changing from a long established pattern of farming to one where the risks are relatively so great. At what point and on what bases were the risks worth taking? As it was with pioneering and overseas employment, this new change has involved decisions, involving considerable risks, that have had to be made on the bases of individual judgments. The individual adaptations and decision making are perhaps the real "miracle" of what has happened in Ilocos Norte.

However, there is in all of this bountiful change an ominous specter of starvation, a situation perhaps not unlike the Irish potato famine of the last century. While there has been no fundamental change in the Ilocano's reliance upon rice as the main staple—quite the contrary, of course, since production has dramatically increased—the character of this dependence has been drastically altered. Two, perhaps by now four, varieties of highly productive miracle rice have largely replaced the ten to twenty types grown in any one barrio and the unknown hundreds of types found in the whole of northern Luzon. The characteristic features of pagay iloco are its dependability and resistence to disease, pests, and extremes of climatic fluctuation. Agricultural advances like that of miracle rice have all involved changes to more productive, more simplified, and, consequently, more unstable environments. Thus, the security derived from a large number of subspecies which are adapted to a variety of situations and local environments has been largely substituted for a very few, highly productive subspecies which require great amounts of care and protection. In a bad year the loss of one, two, or even more traditional types would involve serious problems for the individual families in the areas affected. The loss of a single miracle rice variety could be a regional disaster of major proportions.

There may not be such a "natural" disaster. I simply cannot speak knowledgeably about the ecology of miracle rice agriculture nor, least of all, can I predict events. However, based upon what I know of Ilocano rice farming, this concern is perhaps not without foundation. Like farmers of miracle rice elsewhere in Asia, the Ilocano farmer has made significant changes in his environment, and they are changes which may involve harsh punishments as well as rewards.

I am concerned about the changes in social life in both Buyon and Mambabanga. Beyond my interests as a professional anthropologist are personal questions and concerns about the quality of life for the people there. The book has made the point several times that social ties in Mambabanga are both more extensive and more important than they are in Buyon. The reader may have assumed, as I have, that life was better because of this. I would guess (or "predict," if you prefer) that the character of life has not greatly changed in either of the two barrios. People may be happier in both barrios because they now have more material things than they did before. The quality of social life itself, however, does not seem to have been significantly altered, but this is only surmise. Whatever the changes that lie ahead and however great the pressures that arise to proscribe the lives of these people, I feel quite confident that they will meet such challenges largely on their terms; and what has been essentially Ilocano and fundamentally Filipino will remain.

APPENDIX 1
ILOCANO
KINSHIP
TERMINOLOGY

There is some variability in kinship terminology but the variation is among the members of one family, or between one individual and another in the same barrio. There are no collective differences distinguishing Buyon from Mambabanga. Consequently, the set of terms listed here is generally acceptable in both Buyon and Mambabanga. For comparative material, see Bello (1956), Cole (1945), Nydegger (1960), Orr (1956), Scheans (1963), Vanoverbergh (1956), and Widdoes (1950).

Relationship	Term of Reference*	Term of Address
CONSANGUINEAL SYSTEM		
father	amang, tatang	ama, tata
mother	inang, nanag	ina, nana
older brother	manong	manong
older sister	manang	manang
younger sister	ading	ading, name
younger brother	ading	ading, name
grandfather	lolo, apo	lolo, apo
grandmother	lola, apo	lola, apo
great uncle	lolo, apo	lolo, apo
great aunt	lola, apo	lola, apo
parent's siblings	uliteg, ikit, unkol, anti	uliteg, ikit, unkol, anti
parent's cousins	uliteg, ikit, unkol, anti	uliteg, ikit, unkol, anti
first cousins	kasinsin	name, manong, etc.
second cousins	kapidua	name, manong, etc.
third cousins	kapitlo	name, manong, etc.
one's own child, male	anak	name
one's own child, female	anak	name
sibling's children	kaanakan	name
cousin's children	kaanakan	name
grandchild	apokko	name
sibling or cousin's grandchild	apokka	name

*The possessive suffix -*ko* or -*k* (my) is omitted except where it is basic to work usage and understanding.

Relationship	Term of Reference*	Term of Address
	AFFINAL SYSTEM	
spouse	asawa	name or term of endearment
sister's husband	kayong	manong, ading, name or (if same age) kayong
brother's wife	ipag	manang, ading, name or (if same sex) kayong
spouse's sister's husband	abirat	manong, etc.
spouse's brother's wife	abirat	manang, etc.
mother-in-law	katugangan	inang, nana
father-in-law	katugangan	amang, tata
son-in-law	manugang	anakko, name
daughter-in-law	manugang	anakko, name
	FICTIVE KINSHIP	
godfather	amak ti buniag	tata, ama
godmother	nanang (or) inang ti buniag	nana, ina
child of godparent	kabagis ti buniag, kabsat ti buniag	manong, manang, etc.
neighbor	kaaroba	any term (including name) applicable to age, sex, and social distance
friend	gayyem	name, nickname and any kinship term indicative of social distance

APPENDIX 2
EXAMPLE
OF A
SABONG

This particular sabong was offered by a woman whose husband was residing and working in Hawaii. Being from one of the "wealthiest" families in Buyon, she purchased the land partly from her own inheritance and partly from lands bought with savings acquired by her husband in Hawaii. She, her other children, and later her husband, continued to make a living from the lands provided by her husband's family as a sabong at the time of her own marriage. The family of her prospective daughter-in-law was about equally well endowed in land.

Names of individuals and tax certificate numbers have been omitted. The total amount of land, not including the house lot, is approximately .36 hectares, or about .9 acres of rice land. The crucial factor is, of course, production, and the figure of three uyons is sufficient for a family of two adults and one, or perhaps even two, small children. Also, as noted in the contract, an additional six hundred pesos will be paid at a later time. Real currency can constitute a part of or all of the sabong, but land is preferred.

"Know All Ye Present:

I,   , married to   (who resides in Hawaii), born and resident of Bacarra, Ilocos Norte, Philippines, depose and say:

That in behalf of my son   , single, 24 years of age, who desires to be married to become a complete man and Christian. He loves and desires to marry   , 18 years of age, single, daughter of   and   residents of Barrio Buyon, Bacarra, Ilocos Norte. I have gone with members of my family to convey the love and desire of my son and to give the things necessary for the marriage proposal.

That the dowry of my son is land yielding three uyones of pagay yearly, more or less, with the following description:

1. Irrigated rice lands—Located at Barrio No. 40, Bacarra, Ilocos Norte. Bounded in the north by   [name of field owner]   , on the east by   , on the south by   , and on the west by   ; measuring 328 square meters more or less

under Tax Certificate No.   with an assessed value of 20.00 pesos on tax receipts in the name of my grandmother, A.

2. Irrigated rice lands—Located at San Antonio [i.e., within the lands irrigated by the Zangjera San Antonio], Bacarra, Ilocos Norte, bounded on the north by the Zangjera San Antonio [canal], on the east by   , on the south by   , and on the west by   ; measuring 348 square meters, more or less, under Tax Certificate No.   in my name   , with an assessed value of 20.00 pesos. Only half of this property will be given as dowry by my son

3. Half of a piece of irrigated rice lands—Located at Barrio No. 40, Bacarra, Ilocos Norte, with the following boundaries: bounded on the north by   , on the east by   , on the south by zangjera [i.e., lands owned by the Zangjera de Camungao], on the west by   ; measuring 380 square meters, more or less, under Tax Certificate No.   with an assessed value of 50.00 pesos in the name of my uncle, C.

4. Half of a piece of irrigated rice land—Located at Barrio San Antonio, Bacarra, Ilocos Norte under Tax Certificate No.   with the following boundaries: bounded on the north by   , on the east by   , on the south by zangjera, and on the west by   ; measuring 837 square meters, more or less, with an assessed value of 100.00 pesos in the name of my uncle, C.

5. Half of a piece of irrigated rice land—Located at Barrio San Antonio, Bacarra, Ilocos Norte with the following boundaries: bounded on the north by   , on the east by   , on the south by zangjera [i.e., lands owned by the Zangjera de Camungao], and on the west by   ; measuring 600 square meters, more or less, under Tax Certificate No.   in the name of   [uncle C]   with an assessed value of 40.00 pesos.

6. Irrigated rice lands—Located at Barrio No. 29 (Curarig), Bacarra, Ilocos Norte with the following boundaries: bounded on the north by   , on the east by   , on the south by zangjera, and on the west by   ; measuring 1420 square meters, more or less, under Tax Certificate No.   in the name of   [B]   with an assessed value of 90.00 pesos.

7. Irrigated rice lands—Located at Barrio No. 29 (Curarig) Bacarra, Ilocos Norte, with the following boundaries: bounded on the north by zangjera, on the east by   , on the south by   , and on the west by   , under Tax Certificate No.   in the name of   [B]   ; measuring 100 square meters, more or less, with an assessed value of 20.00 pesos.

8. Parcel of irrigated rice lands—Located at Curarig, Bacarra, Ilocos Norte with the following boundaries: bounded on the north by   , on the east by   , on the south by

zangjera [Zangjera de Camungao] , and on the west by   ;
measuring 432 square meters, more or less, under Tax Certificate No.
in the name of   [B]   with an assessed value of 30.00 pesos.

9. Irrigated rice land—Located at Curarig, Bacarra, Ilocos Norte with the following boundaries: bounded on the north by   , on the east by   , on the south by   , and on the west by   ; under Tax Certificate No.
in the name of   [B]   with an assessed value of 30.00 pesos.

10. Residential Lot—Located at Barrio No. 16 [Dibua] Bacarra, Ilocos Norte with the following boundaries: bounded on the north by a street, on the east by a street, on the south by   , and on the west by   ; measuring 478 square meters, more or less, under Tax Certificate No.   in the name of   with an assessed value of 190.00 pesos.

I further testify that these properties given as a dowry by my son   to his beloved and prospective bride are further described as follows:

That the parcels of land in the name of my grandmother   [A]   was inherited by my mother   as share from her brother and sister which I also inherited. Also, No. 2, under my name, No. 3 under the name of my uncle   [D]   and Nos. 4 and 5 under my uncle   [C]   are the share of my late mother.

That, it has been an understanding with my prospective abelayan, [parents of my daughter-in-law] ,   and   , that only one half of these properties described above are to be given as dowry by my son and are also to be worked on the ditch called San Antonio [i.e., ditch of Zangjera San Antonio] .

In the parcels of land described in Nos. 6, 7, 8, and 9 in the name of my grandmother   [B]   half of it was held in common by my mother and her brothers who are already dead. Half of it was also purchased by me from my grandmother   [B]   . But this half will be given also to my daughter as additional dowry and security pending my payment of 600.00 pesos in cash additional dowry.

I also give one residential lot as described in No. 10 of this document. I purchased this lot from my late uncle   [C]   which I also give to my son and his prospective wife, so that they have also their own residential lot.

Therefore, as of this date, I am giving these parcels of agricultural lands and residential lot to my said daughter-in-law and surrender or pass my ownership to them so that they will work on them and reap its harvest. Should there be any liens or incumberances which will disturb their peaceful possession of the land I shall answer for it without molesting said couples and should I be deprived of these parcels of land by the courts of justice I shall change these lands herein described with lands of the same yields and measurements.

In affirmation of my statements I sign my name on this document this 25th day of January, 1950, in Bacarra, Ilocos Norte, Philippines.

Witness   [Mother's Signature]

Acceptance:

I,   , accept with all humility and with my free will and consent the parcels of agricultural lands and residential lot given as dowry by my mother-in-law in behalf of my marriage to her son   in the presence of both parties. I also express my gratitude for their love to us.

In witness hereof I sign my name this 25th day of January, 1950, in Bacarra, Ilocos Norte.

Witness   [Daughter-in-law's Signature]
                 [Her Parents' Signatures]

MAPS

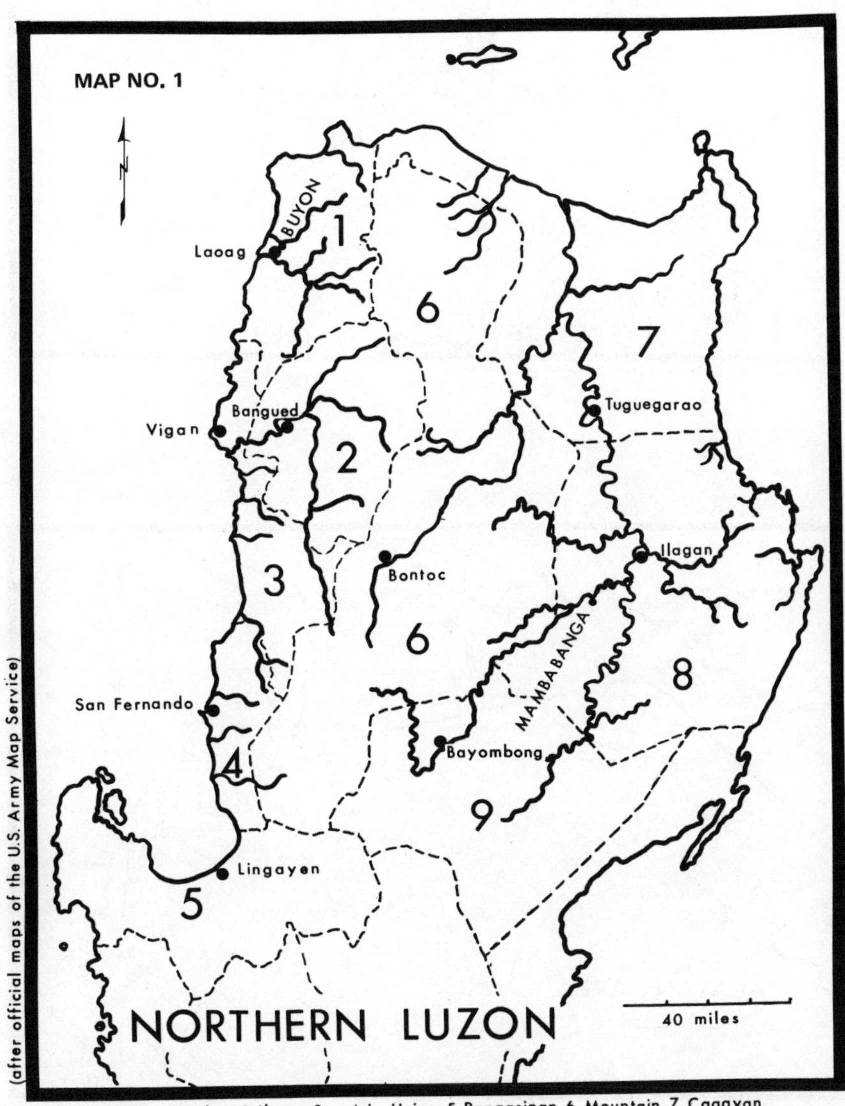

1. Ilocos Norte, 2. Abra, 3. Ilocos Sur, 4. La Union, 5. Pangasinan, 6. Mountain, 7. Cagayan, 8. Isabela, 9. Nueva Vizcaya

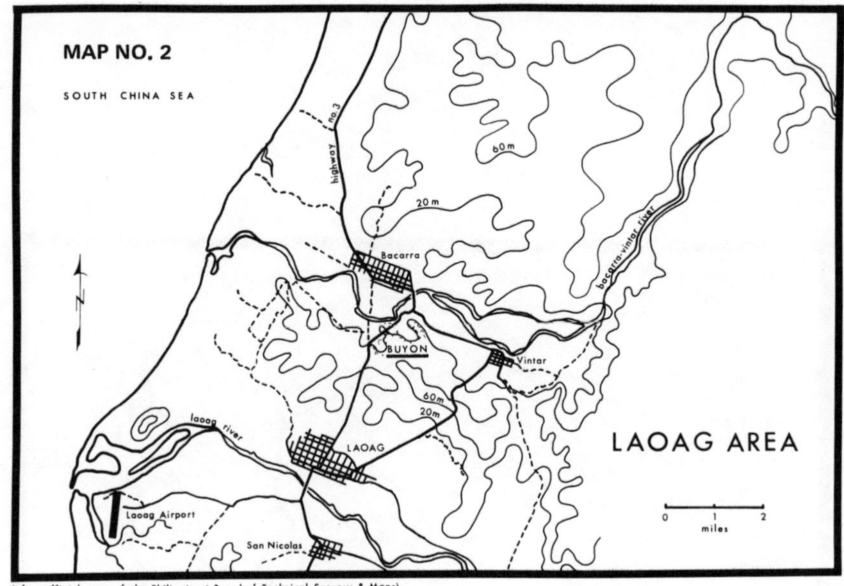

(after official maps of the Philippines' Board of Technical Surveys & Maps)

(after official maps of the Philippines' Board of Technical Surveys & Maps)

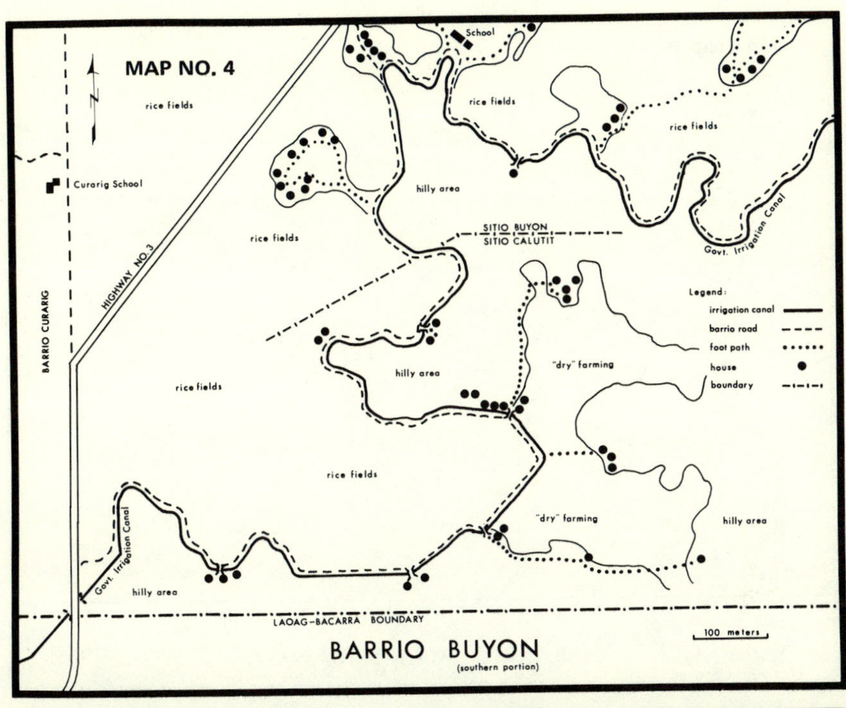

MAP NO. 4
N
rice fields
School
rice fields
rice fields
Curarig School
hilly area
SITIO BUYON
SITIO CALUTIT
Govt. Irrigation Canal
rice fields
BARRIO CURARIG
HIGHWAY NO. 3
Legend:
irrigation canal
barrio road
foot path
house
boundary
"dry" farming
hilly area
rice fields
hilly area
rice fields
Govt. Irrigation Canal
"dry" farming
hilly area
hilly area
LAOAG–BACARRA BOUNDARY
100 meters
BARRIO BUYON
(southern portion)

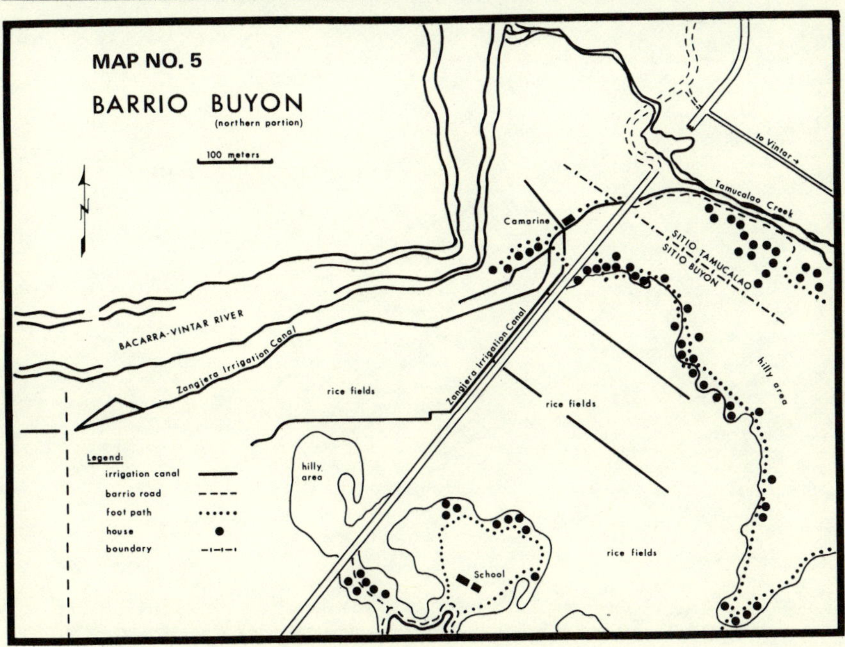

MAP NO. 5
BARRIO BUYON
(northern portion)
100 meters
N
to Vintar
Tamucalao Creek
Camarine
SITIO TAMUCALAO
SITIO BUYON
BACARRA–VINTAR RIVER
Zangiera Irrigation Canal
Zangiera Irrigation Canal
rice fields
hilly area
hilly
area
rice fields
Legend:
irrigation canal
barrio road
foot path
house
boundary
School
rice fields

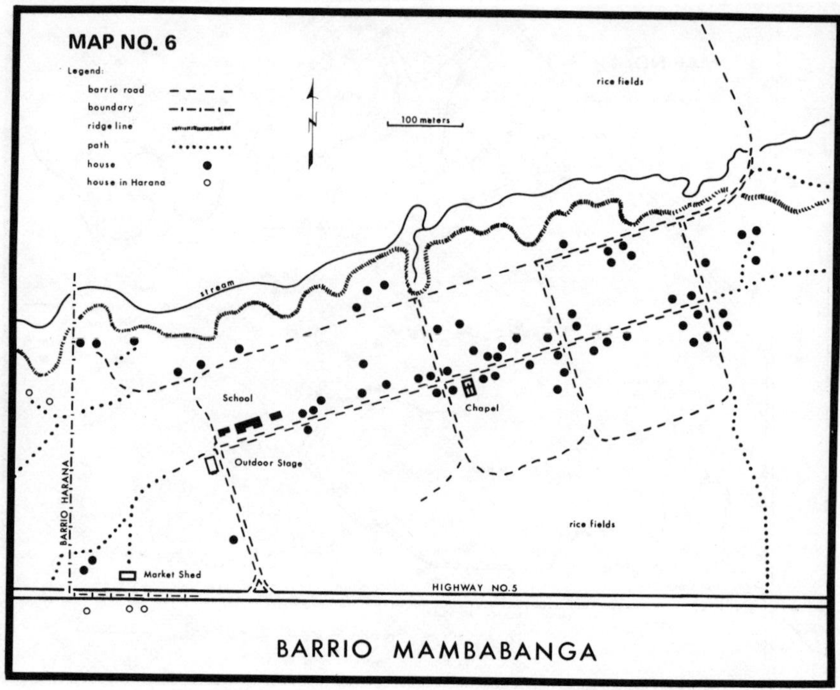

BARRIO MAMBABANGA

GLOSSARY

ABIRAT. Special term of reference for the sister or brother of one's spouse who is, in turn, married to one's own brother or sister. Also used as a term of address applied to many other affinal kin.

ADING. Younger sibling.

AGLIPAYAN. Members of the Philippine Independent Church, a schismatic group founded by Gregorio Aglipay in the late nineteenth century.

AMMONG. Financial savings association.

AMMUYO. Reciprocal exchange of labor associated with agriculture.

ANITO. Local spirit.

APAYAO. Alternate term for Isneg, a mountain people living east of the province of Ilocos Norte.

ARAYAT. Social savings association.

BAAR. Measure of unthreshed rice, the tenth part of an *uyon*. The actual amount varies throughout the Ilocos coast.

BAGO. Ilocano word for "new." When capitalized it refers to various mountain groups, e.g., Isneg, Tinguian, Kangkanai, which have become "new Ilocanos" by affecting lowland, Ilocano life styles and by becoming Christians.

BAIN. Individual, personal shame.

BAKNANG. A member of the elite.

BANTAY. Hill or mountain. With respect to agriculture it refers to a field regularly farmed on a steep slope.

BARRIO (Sp.). Village. Smallest designated political units within the formal organization of Philippine society. Barrios may or may not be effective social units as well.

BARRIO TENIENTE (Sp.). Village lieutenant or headman; an elected position.

BASI. Wine made from fermented sugarcane juice.

BATARIS. Special help given in times of emergency. Within the context of agriculture, it is the emergency help given an *ammuyo* partner.

BAYAG. Refers to both type of field and the varieties of rice grown therein when man-made irrigation is involved.

BENGKAG. Dry-farmed fields less steeply sloped than bantay fields.

BETTEK. Measure of unthreshed rice. A bundle about the size of a wrist or forearm, six of which make up a *pungo*.

BOGOONG. A salted and fermented fish sauce used to season food.

BONTOC. A mountain people of the central interior region of the Cordillera Central.

CAGAYANES. Indigenous groups in Cagayan Valley, e.g., Gaddang, Yogad.
CAMOTE (Sp.), KAMOTIT. Sweet potato, *Ipomoea batatas*.
CENTRALES (Sp.). Sugar mills.
COMPADRE (Sp.). Ritual kinsmen.

DANAO. Wet-rice fields bordering a pond or lake and irrigated by the existing water table. Differs from *lubo* fields in that danao can be plowed by water buffalo.
DIKET. Generic term for glutinous rice, varieties of which are used for making sweets.

GADDANG. Indigenous people of Cagayan Valley, both Christian and pagan. They are particularly concentrated in Isabela and Nueva Vizcaya provinces.

HAWAIIANO. An Ilocano who has lived or is living in Hawaii, though also applied to Ilocanos on the mainland United States as well.
HUKBALAHAP. Often shortened to Huk. Originally anti-Japanese, later anti-government, agrarian, guerrilla movement in central Luzon and southern Cagayan Valley.

IBANAG. Indigenous Christian population living in Cagayan Valley.
IFUGAO. Mountain peoples of the southeastern part of Cordillera Central, most famous of the rice terrace builders.
IPAG. Sister-in-law.
ISNEG. Mountain people east of Ilocos Norte, sometimes called Apayao.

JEEPNEY. Jeep bus.

KAAROBA. Neighbor.
KALINGA. Mountain people in the central and eastern portion of Cordillera Central.
"KALINGA." Ilocano usage applied to all pagan groups in Cagayan Valley. Literally, "savage."
KAMARIN. Meeting place for irrigation society members.
KAYONG. Brother-in-law.
KOMPAY. Sickle.

LIDER. From English "leader." Better described as "vote-getter."
LUBO. Literally, "mudhole." Wet-rice fields in lowest drainage areas in which water buffalo cannot be used for working the land.

MAESTRO (Sp.). Head man. Term used for leaders of zangjeras; also school teachers.
MAGUPRAK. Generic term for nonglutinous rice.
MANANG. Older sister.
MANDALA. Stack of unthreshed rice commonly seen in Isabela.
MANONG. Older brother.
MARONGGAY. The horseradish tree, *Moringa oleifera*. Edible leaves, fruit, and blossoms.

MASAYOD. Refers both to a type of field and the kinds of rice grown therein where natural irrigation, i.e., rainfall, is used.

MAYOR (Sp.). Person in charge of fiesta.

MESTIZO (Sp.). Persons of mixed racial background. In addition to persons with Spanish "blood," it is used to designate "Chinese-mestizo," "American mestizo," and other possible admixtures.

MONGO. The mung bean, *Phaseolus aureus*.

NANA. Mother.

NIPA. The nipa palm, *Nipa fruticans*. Leaves are used for thatching.

PADIGO. "Extra" foodstuffs given to one's neighbors.

PADUL. Diversion dam.

PAGAY. Unthreshed rice.

PAGAY ILOKO. Traditional awned or "bearded" varieties of Ilocano rice.

PAGAY TAGALOG. Awnless varieties of rice.

PAKIAWEN. Hired labor.

PANGLAKAYEN. Leaders.

PANGULO. Head man.

POBLACION (Sp.). Town.

PUNGO. Measure of unthreshed Ilocano rice. Six *bettek* tied together form a *pungo*; two *pungo* make a *baar*.

RAKEM. Hand knife used for harvesting *pagay iloko*.

RICE BLAST. Various fungal diseases that attack stems and foliage of the rice plant.

SABONG. Male land dowry.

SALDA. Form of mortgage.

SALDA GATANG. Mortgage with option to buy by the mortgagee.

SALUYOT. Semiwild, leafy vegetable. *Corchorus olitorius*.

SARI-SARI STORE. Small shacklike stores with a very limited stock of goods. They operate primarily on credit.

SITIO (Sp.). An informal geographic or social subdivision or "site" within a barrio.

SWIDDEN AGRICULTURE. Shifting or slash-and-burn agriculture.

TABUNGAO. Traditional Ilocano hat made from a bottle gourd *Lagenaria leucantha*.

TAGNAWA. Communal assistance provided by close kinsmen, friends, and neighbors.

TALON. General term for a field of wet-rice.

TINGUIAN. Mountain people nearest Ilocos Sur, especially concentrated in Abra Province.

UMA. Ilocano system of shifting agriculture.

UYON. Largest measure of unthreshed rice. Composed of ten *baar* but the actual amount varies from one area to another. Within the Bacarra-Vintar

River Valley it is equal to approximately eleven fifty-pound sacks of un-threshed rice.

YOGAD. A very localized, lowland Christian population in Isabela, most of whom live in the municipality of Echague.

ZAMBALS. Native peoples of Zambales Province. Usually refers to Negritos.
ZANGJERAS. Irrigation societies characteristic of Ilocos Norte.

BIBLIOGRAPHY

Ardener, Shirley
1964   "The comparative study of rotating credit associations." *Journal of the Royal Anthropological Institute* 94:102–229.
Barton, Roy F.
1949   *The Kalingas*. Chicago: University of Chicago Press.
Befu, H.
1965   "Contrastive acculturation of California Japanese: comparative approach to the study of immigrants." *Human Organization* 24:209–216.
Bello, M. C.
1956   "The Ilokano." In *The Philippines*. New Haven, Connecticut: Human Relations Area Files.
Blair, E. H., and Robertson, J. A., eds.
1903–1909 *The Philippine Islands, 1493–1803*. Cleveland: A. H. Clark Co.
Bohannan, P.
1963   *Social Anthropology*. New York: Holt, Rinehart & Winston.
Christie, Emerson B.
1914   "Notes on irrigation and cooperative irrigation societies in Ilocos Norte." *The Philippine Journal of Science* 9:99–113.
Cole, Fay-Cooper
1945   *The Peoples of Malaysia*. Princeton: D. Van Nostrand Co.
Copeland, E. B.
1924   *Rice*. London: Macmillan Co.
Dobby, E. H. G.
1960   *Southeast Asia*. London: University of London Press.
Eggan, F.
1941   "Some aspects of culture change in the northern Philippines." *American Anthropologist* 43:11–18.
1954   "Social anthropology and the method of controlled comparison." *American Anthropologist* 56:743–763.
1963   "Cultural drift and social change." *Current Anthropology* 4:347–355.
Erasmus, C. J.
1956   "Culture, structure and process: the occurrence and disappearance of reciprocal farm labor." *Southwestern Journal of Anthropology* 12:444–469.
Firth, R., and Yamey, B. S., eds.
1964   *Capital, Savings and Credit in Peasant Societies*. Chicago: Aldine Publishing Co.

Foster, George M.
  1961   "The dyadic contract: a model for the social structure of a Mex-
          ican peasant village." *American Anthropologist* 63:1173–1192.
  1963   "The dyadic contract in Tzintzuntzan, II: patron-client relation-
          ship." *American Anthropologist* 65:1280–1294.
Garcia, Natividad V.
  1962   "A study of the socio-economic adjustments of two Ilocano vil-
          lages to Virginia tobacco production." University of the Philip-
          pines Community Development Research Council, Abstract
          Series, no. 15.
Geertz, Clifford
  1962   "The rotating credit association: a 'middle rung' in devel-
          opment." *Economic Development and Cultural Change* 10:241–
          263.
  1963   *Agricultural Involution.* Berkeley: University of California Press.
Grist, D. H.
  1959   *Rice.* 3d ed. New York: John Wiley & Sons.
Hollnsteiner, Mary R.
  1963   *The Dynamics of Power in a Philippine Municipality.* University
          of the Philippines Community Development Research Council,
          Study Series, no. 7.
Huke, R. E., and others
  1963   *Shadows on the Land.* Manila: Bookmark.
Keesing, Felix M.
  1962   *The Ethnohistory of Northern Luzon.* Stanford: Stanford Univer-
          sity Press.
Lambrecht, Godfrey
  1959   "The Gadang of Isabela and Nueva Vizcaya: survey of a primitive
          animalistic religion." *Philippine Studies* 7(2):194–218.
Lava, Horacio
  1938   *Levels of Living in the Ilocos Region.* University of the Philip-
          pines, College of Business Administration, Studies, no. 1.
Leach, E. R.
  1961   *Pul Eliya: A Village in Ceylon.* Cambridge: Cambridge University
          Press.
Lynch, Frank S. J.
  1959   *Social Class in a Bikol Town.* Chicago: University of Chicago
          Press.
  1961   "Lowland Philippine values: social acceptance." In *Proceedings of
          the Fourth Annual Baguio Religious Acculturation Conference,
          Baguio City,* pp. 100–120. Manila.
  n.d.   "Town fiesta: an anthropologist's view." *Philippines International*
          6:4–11; 26–27.
Mauss, Marcel
  1954   *The Gift: Forms and Functions of Exchange in Archaic Societies.*
          Glencoe, Illinois: Free Press.

Nydegger, William Frank
    1960   *Tarong: A Philippine Barrio* Ph. D. dissertation. Ann Arbor, Michigan: University Microfilms.
Nydegger, William Frank, and Nydegger, Corinne
    1963   "Tarong: an Ilocos barrio in the Philippines." In *Six Cultures: Studies of Child Rearing*, edited by Beatrice B. Whiting, pp. 693–867. Ithaca: Cornell University Press.
Orr, Kenneth G.
    1956   *The Christianized Ilocanos and the Pagan Tinguian: A Study of Acculturation in the Philippine Islands*. Falls Church, Virginia.
Pelzer, K. J.
    1945   *Pioneer Settlement in the Asiatic Tropics*. Special Publication of the American Geographical Society, no. 29. New York: American Geographical Society.
Phelan, John L.
    1959   *The Hispanization of the Philippines: Spanish Aims and Filipino Responses 1500–1700*. Madison: University of Wisconsin Press.
Philippines, Department of Commerce and Industry, Bureau of the Census and Statistics
    1962*a*   "Report by Province, Ilocos Norte." In *Census of the Philippines: 1960 Population and Housing*, vol. 1.
    1962*b*   "Report by Province, Isabela." In *Census of the Philippines: 1960 Population and Housing*, vol. 1.
Reed, R. R.
    1963   "The Tobacco Industry." In *Shadows on the Land*, by R. E. Huke and others, pp. 347–367. Manila: Bookmark.
Reynolds, Harriet R.
    1959   "Background and distribution of Chinese families in the Ilocos Province, Philippines." Thesis submitted in partial fulfillment for the degree of Master of Arts, Kennedy School of Missions of the Hartford Seminary Foundation, Hartford, Connecticut.
Reynolds, Ira H.
    1959   "Economic acculturation of the Chinese in Ilocos." Master's thesis, Hartford Seminary Foundation, Hartford, Connecticut.
Romani, John H.
    1956   "The Philippine barrio." *The Far Eastern Quarterly* 15:229–237.
Sawyer, F. H.
    1900   *The Inhabitants of the Philippines*. London: S. Low, Marston & Co.
Scheans, D. J.
    1962   "The Suban Ilocano kinship configuration: an application of innovation theory to the study of kinship." Ph. D. dissertation, University of Oregon.
    1963   "Suban society." *Philippine Sociological Review* 11:216–235.
    1964   "Kith-centered action groups in an Ilokano barrio." *Ethnology* 3:364–368.

1965   "The Ilocano: marriage and the land." *Philippine Sociological Review* 13:57–62.

Steward, J. H.
1955   *Theory of Culture Change*. Urbana: University of Illinois Press.

Vanoverbergh, M.
1956   *Iloko-English Dictionary*. Baguio, Philippines: Catholic School Press.

Wernstedt, F. L., and Spencer, J. E.
1967   *The Philippine Island World: A Physical, Cultural, and Regional Geography*. Berkeley: University of California Press.

Widdoes, H. W.
1950   *A Brief Introduction to the Grammar of the Ilocano Language*. Manila: G. Rangel & Sons.

INDEX